Julie Lynn Evans is one of the UK's foremost psychotherapists helping young people and their families in times of stress. She works with consultants from many hospitals, and helps troubled children in schools around the country. She has appeared on television programmes in Australia and the UK, and has written numerous articles on troubled childhood and adolescence. She is divorced and the mother of three children.

What about the Children?

How to help children survive separation and divorce

Julie Lynn Evans

BANTAM PRESS

LONDON · TORONTO · SYDNEY · AUCKLAND · JOHANNESBURG

TRANSWORLD PUBLISHERS
61–63 Uxbridge Road, London W5 5SA
A Random House Group Company
www.rbooks.co.uk

First published in Great Britain
in 2009 by Bantam Press
an imprint of Transworld Publishers

This book is a work of non-fiction based on the experiences and recollections of the
author. In some cases names of people have been changed solely to protect the privacy
of others. The author has stated to the publishers that, except in such minor respects
not affecting the substantial accuracy of the work, the contents of this book are true.

A CIP catalogue record for this book
is available from the British Library.

ISBN 9780593060704

Addresses for Random House Group Ltd companies outside the UK
can be found at: www.randomhouse.co.uk
The Random House Group Ltd Reg. No. 954009

The Random House Group Limited supports The Forest Stewardship
Council (FSC), the leading international forest-certification organization. All our
titles that are printed on Greenpeace-approved FSC-certified paper carry the FSC logo.
Our paper procurement policy can be found at
www.rbooks.co.uk/environment

Typeset in 10.25/16pt Palatino by
Falcon Oast Graphic Art Ltd.
Printed and bound in Great Britain by
CPI Mackays, Chatham, ME5 8TD

2 4 6 8 10 9 7 5 3 1

Every effort has been made to obtain the necessary permissions with
reference to copyright material, both illustrative and quoted. We apologize
for any omissions in this respect and will be pleased to make the
appropriate acknowledgements in any future edition.

Mixed Sources
Product group from well-managed
forests and other controlled sources
www.fsc.org Cert no. TT-COC-2139
© 1996 Forest Stewardship Council
FSC

for Lucy, who beat the odds

Contents

Foreword

Some forty years ago, general population studies made it clear that, in instances of 'broken homes', divorce was a greater threat to children's mental health than the death of a parent. Looking back now, it seems surprising that sophisticated epidemiology was needed to reveal this. Divorce is part of a process rather than an event in its own right and usually follows months or years of strained marital relationships, often with open rowing between partners. Children overhear this, know what is happening and are frightened by it. Or there is the sudden shock when deception is revealed or confirmed and one parent is knocked sideways emotionally, leading to months of strained family relationships.

As a trainee in paediatrics and psychiatry at the time, I remember that these findings led some authorities to teach that we should look positively upon divorce as a way of terminating discord or distrust. Yet we now know that it is not automatically the case that it is less distressing for the children if warring or deceived parents separate. Relationships between parents are likely to worsen after divorce, and children are so often drawn into this. The divorce process, however civilized it may be when it begins, nearly always becomes antagonistic, because of legal issues and practice. An angry, bemused, exhausted, betrayed or depressed parent is an alarming figure for a child. For children, there may also be unwanted changes of house, school and therefore friends. Everyone becomes poorer. There is a nagging fear in a child's mind that they will be the next to have to leave the home or that they will imminently be deserted by the second parent. And then there are the visiting arrangements, which can be artificial and strained or a source of broken trust. The list of ways in which divorce can cause distress to children goes on. There are so many reasons for children to be fearful, upset, angry or brokenhearted, feelings which underlie behaviours that, at first sight, may be hard to understand.

It is easy to trivialize or even overlook distress in a child. A common adult assumption is that small people have small emotions and that they will 'get over it', in any case, given time. Certainly, the young mind is ready to find ways of adapting to adversity, yet some of these attempts to adjust may be dismissed as attention-seeking, playing up or simply wilful opposition and disobedience. It has been said that a child causing a problem is trying to solve one, and this is a useful reminder that children's behaviour is not random. But children often cannot explain the reasons for what they do, unless listened to carefully by someone who knows that children are likely to understand a situation differently from an adult, or that they may have information and beliefs which the adults around them do not. The examples in this book show vividly that much of what children do during or after a parental divorce can be understood, given an adult's preparedness to listen. The children described here demonstrate the power and intensity of children's emotions and the underlying causes for what may seem on an initial glance to be inexplicable or unreasonable behaviours.

Indeed, this is a remarkable book. It draws upon the author's years of experience to illuminate just how these various stressors change the emotional lives of children and teenagers. It describes real people in painful situations. The predicaments of children in these vignettes are vividly described from their point of view. Yet the book does not lack hope and illustrates how inspired therapy can heal without recourse to abstruse theories of the mind and its development.

Julie Lynn Evans is an original therapist. She is an active listener and, by using the creative arts, can discover a will to communicate in the most unforthcoming young person. She is creative herself, energetic, proactive and resourceful. Her work is not simply to offer a sympathetic ear and generate understanding; she is an active champion for her clients, confronting feckless parents, going into schools, accompanying children on missions. She is alive and passionate on their behalf, and it is stirring stuff. This is what true child therapy should be about. Children usually express their state of mind primarily in behaviour rather than words, so it is not surprising that it is adult behaviour rather than words that they trust. I so often hear the following complaints about a parent: 'He says ... but then he doesn't ...'; 'She goes on about it but nothing happens.' For so many disturbed and disturbing children, the seated, non-judgemental therapist who merely comments in words is powerless. I hear and know this from those I see.

Julie Lynn Evans goes further than this and actually does things. It is her vigour in championing her clients' causes, ensuring their safety when they are putting themselves in danger or talking with them in real-world places as well as in her consulting room (or shed), that makes the difference. Blending the skills of individual and family therapy, she recognizes that the power to induce change lies with parents and therefore she works actively with them. This recognition forms the basis of a wise, productive, modern therapy carried out with true and inspiring mastery. Although I suspect her primary mission in this book is to show us how children caught up in divorce may be more distressed than we think, she also gives us an insight into how they can be reached and helped – and into how so many of us professionals might do it better.

Professor Peter Hill, Consultant Child Psychiatrist,
Great Ormond Street Hospital for Children

Acknowledgements

I love my job, and I love the children who come for help. They have taught me to take nothing for granted and to listen and watch with an open mind and an open heart so that I can hear what it is that they have to tell me. One of the most frequent topics of conversation is how much they suffer from the breakdown of the relationship of their parents. As parents separate and divorce, something dies; children lose what is familiar, and they need to mourn. This book is about how to help them face up to their loss and to enable them to move on to enjoy a different life as free of care and damage as possible. I have been able to write it because of the honesty of the hundreds of bright, wonderful, confused and wounded children who have talked and played with me for hours and hours as, together, we have worked out the best way forward to help with their particular journey. I want to thank these children, and I also want to thank their parents, who have trusted me with the most precious people in their world.

I also thank my friends and family, who understood that my own three children and I needed the kind of help that I talk about in this book. The kindness and generosity received by my shattered family was quite extraordinary. I especially want to thank Charlie and Melissa Alexander, Lucy and Quentin Baer, Sally Brampton, Robbie Campbell, Sabrina and Douglas Campbell, Matthew and Ann Carr,

Ros and Mark Collins, Sebastian Conran, Tim and Lizzie Drake, Al Fraser, Mark and Emma Freeman, Maria Gardener, Annabel Giles, Charlie Glass, Tess Graydon, Dom and Sharon Guard, Peter and Emma Letley, Caroline Logsdail, Alex and Leslie Moors-Jennings, Quentin and Annabel Portsmouth, John and Norah Ricciardi, Sarah and Robbie Richardson, Sarah Rafael (who died so sadly in 2003), Sophie and Piers Simpkin, Flora and Peter Soros, Julian Wadham and Fleur and John Walbeoffe-Wilson. Without you all we would have felt a great deal more lost for a great deal longer.

Professionally, I have been lucky to have been taught by and worked with inspirational people. Ian Gordon-Brown acted as my 'guide' for ten wonderful years until his untimely death in 1997, Nan Beecher-More encouraged me to take risks and taught me to believe in myself as a therapist, while Claire Chappell stood by as my supervisor with clarity and kindness and has become a true friend over the thirteen years that we have worked together. Psychiatrists Dr Mark Collins and Professor Peter Hill have supported my work with their sensitivity, intelligence and experience, and I cannot thank them enough for their help as I struggled with tricky children and teenagers in trouble. Head teachers such as Maria Gardener and Ben Thomas have shown me what a difference can be made at school to the life of a child in distress. It has been a joy to work with them over the years. Two lawyers and a mediator/counsellor have helped me check the information in this book, and I have also enjoyed working with them on a professional basis. Nicole Hackett and Ruth Smallacombe from Family Law in Partnership and Henry Hood from Hunters Solicitors have demonstrated a careful and impressive 'family and children first' philosophy when working out the intricacies of the legal aspects of divorce.

When I decided that I wanted to write I was told that I needed Maggie Hanbury to be my agent. She agreed to take me on and, within a short space of time, had found Sally Gaminara at Bantam Books to publish *What about the Children?* Without Maggie, I would not have known where to start and, of course, without Sally there would have been no book. Stephen Gomersall helped me to edit the book and encouraged me to write it. Thank you for believing in me and giving me your time and encouragement.

Two men deserve my special thanks. Julian, my ex-husband, has been a good and available father who has never wavered in his love for his children. In many ways our children's successes are his successes and I hope that he is aware of how his elegant behaviour as a non-resident parent and an involved father has helped their development. And now there is Stephen, who has given me so much; without him I doubt that I would have had the courage to write. It is good to have him in my life and I thank him for being there.

Most importantly, I thank my three children: Lucy, Sam and Harry. They meander in and out of the book under their own names, at their own request. They are proud of what they have achieved and aware of what they have gone through. I am proud of them and I love them.

In order to protect the identity of the many families in this book, I have changed names and places, numbers of siblings and genders of individuals. When a case study is specific to a child and its family, I have obtained permission to use it so that I do not feel that I am stealing from the bank of stories with which I have been entrusted. In many cases I have woven together the tapestry of a narrative that I have been listening to for more than twenty years and produced a composite study. I hope that, in this way, I have been able to reveal just how difficult it is for a child to deal with such powerful topics as sex, money and split loyalty, while maintaining the anonymity of those who placed their trust in me. I have alternated the use of 'he' and 'she' throughout the book, though I have generally used 'she' when discussing a problem that tends to be more prevalent in girls, such as self-harming and eating disorders, and 'he' when the problem is more particular to boys, for instance refusal to accept any discipline at all. However, they are, of course, interchangeable.

Introduction

DIVORCE AND SEPARATION ARE DIFFICULT. I have watched closely in my consulting room and seen the damage and despair that family breakdown inflicts on the lives of all that it touches.

Approximately one in three marriages in Britain are failing, while one in two couples who live together will not do so for ever. There are more single parents out there than ever before. Fathers are fighting for their rights to see their children. Courts are being asked to use the law to deal with affairs of the heart. Teachers are being asked to be counsellors, and the social services to interview children whom they hardly know to decide where they should live. The newspapers are full of information and statistics suggesting that children from broken homes will do less well than other children and are more likely to follow the same sad pattern of family breakdown in their own lives.

What was rare thirty years ago is now commonplace. Our western world is full of children of divorce and separation, and we do not serve them well. The churches stand empty, the social services are out of their depth and the idea of family means less than at any time in our history. We live in a difficult world, a world in which the pace of life is becoming faster and faster and where people are charging around almost unable to catch up with themselves. We no longer seem to be good at understanding that life is tough – and when it gets too tough, people tend to cut and run. Nowhere is this more obvious than in the thousands of marriages that bite the dust. Day in, day out, another decree absolute makes its way to court, another family home is sold and more single parents make their way on to the 'available' market to try their luck for a second time.

Silently but surely a social revolution is taking place. The Office for National Statistics tells us that in the first decade of the twenty-first century, over 28 per cent of children in the UK will be coping with the dramatic effects of the separation of their parents, and often they will be coping alone. Children will be eating and sleeping, playing and learning, and attempting to go about the important business of growing up while full of difficult feelings and unanswered questions. Recent research from the NSPCC revealed the appalling statistic that only 10 per cent of children will find someone to talk to when their family is breaking apart. In the meantime, some adults will reassure themselves with the all too familiar cliché that 'children are resilient' and continue on the painful path of undoing the promises made in happier days. Other couples will watch brokenhearted, knowing that they are hurting the people they love the most but finding themselves powerless to stop the process.

Twenty years of working as a therapist and my own experience of guiding three children through adolescence as a single mother have taught me that children are not so resilient. Although ill equipped and unable to use adult words, children show me that they hate the fact that their parents are separating. They want their family to stay together so that they can keep what is familiar; they feel abandoned when one parent walks out of the door and do not understand why he or she has to go. They think that maybe there is something wrong with them if a parent has to walk away, or fear that the other one may leave as well. They hate to be caught in the crossfire.

As a therapist, it is my job to listen, understand and translate the language of childhood so that I can guide children through the maze of their unhappiness. If I can untangle the knots of a child who is suffering from the break-up of his home and give some comfort and something to hold on to when confusion is the order of the day, then I am doing my job.

But one does not have to be a professional in order to hold out a hand and provide comfort. A kind heart, common sense, a little time and an open mind will make a huge difference to the life of a child in distress. And if that difference is made quickly enough and early enough by people around them, then children will suffer less. They will be helped to make sense of what is happening so that they can be free to enjoy their childhoods and not have to bear too many psychological scars which could badly affect their future.

What about the Children? aims to guide the reader towards a greater understanding of how children might feel or behave when families fall apart and during the aftermath of divorce and separation. The important role that all grown-ups can play is stressed, with an emphasis on just how much mothers and fathers suffer, how much support they need and how important it is that as many adults as possible respond sensitively and carefully to all members of the breaking family.

In order to help adults understand what children need at various points in their lives, there is an explanation of the different ages and stages of child development, with practical advice, tips and case stories to demonstrate what to expect from babies, pre-school children, five- to ten-year-olds, ten- to thirteen-year-olds and teenagers.

Children can find it hard to verbalize their sadness and confusion, especially as, very often, the people to whom they would normally turn are the very people who have caused their problems. In the two 'Difficult Times' chapters, there are descriptions and examples of some of the physical and behavioural symptoms which children may exhibit because of the stress of family break-up. Case studies will show that, although children cannot always give words to their sorrow, they certainly feel it, and feel it deeply. If adults listen to these symptoms as if they were spoken, they will be able to hear what needs to be heard and therefore be able to help. And, sometimes, adults need to step in more energetically and use their courage and commitment really to help a child in trouble.

Often family break-up happens because of a difficult underlying problem such as addiction or depression. Once the centre of the family fails to hold, this problem can become more obvious and more dangerous to the children who have to deal with it without the presence of the other parent. In the chapter 'Double Trouble', there are descriptions of some of the difficulties children may have to face on top of coping with the disintegration of their family life. These cases, while distressing, illustrate how, with the right help, children need not be too hurt by some of the damage they, unfortunately, have to witness.

And finally, *What about the Children?* will offer a practical guide as to what to do and how to do it, with a list of the things which work for children and a list of things which definitely don't. If parents and other adults are able to follow some of these basic rules, children will suffer less and grown-ups will do a better job in looking after more than a quarter of the children from the next generation who come from broken homes.

The purpose of this book is not to state that people should stay together for the sake of the children. Divorce is often unavoidable and is no longer unacceptable in our society. The purpose of the book is to help all involved in a family breakdown to do the right things so that, eventually, the children, together with their parents, can emerge from the turbulence. If children are heard, respected and made to feel safe, they will feel better about the world and better about themselves. If they feel better, they will not be so challenged. If they are less challenged, they will be more able to have a childhood and, if they have a proper childhood, they are more likely, together with their parents, to emerge from the difficult process of divorce as healthy individuals who are ready to live a new and different life.

1 • • • • •

Facing up to divorce and separation

IT IS A MISTAKE TO UNDERESTIMATE the effects of divorce on children. Broken relationships hurt children, and clumsy divorces can create serious and lasting damage. Mary Lobascher, for many years the head clinical psychologist of Great Ormond Street Hospital, wrote in a paper recently that 'there is evidence to indicate that children of divorced parents have higher rates of disturbance than when there is bereavement in a family.' We need to take the problems of children living through the process of a breaking home as seriously as if one of their parents had just died.

There is no single recipe for children when their parents separate. Every family is unique, and no two break-ups are identical. To add to the complexity, the children within each family will often behave completely differently from each other. Every tale is different, every perspective is personal and true to he or she who holds it. Probably everyone is a little bit right and a little bit wrong, and that applies to children as well as to adults.

But children as victims deserve special attention. They do not ask to find themselves caught between parents who no longer love each

21

other, and they do not ask to find themselves part of the sad and frightening national and international statistics showing that children from single-family homes will do far less well than their two-parent contemporaries.* From my own experience of working with children, I feel that their situation, as revealed by these negative statistics, is not fair, and that something needs to be done about it.

One way of approaching the problem is to ask how best to provide support, given that it is hard to prevent the separation of parents and the disintegration of family life. And why it is that parental separation can have such a devastating effect. How can concerned adults undo these appallingly negative statistics and move towards a more positive solution which will give children a ray of hope when their hearts are aching and their homes are breaking and nothing around them makes any sense? What do we do to stop young innocents becoming part of a database of negative statistics?

The real-life stories in this book, told often by the children themselves, convey consistent messages. The first is that, if adults can listen to and read the multifarious signs of distress and behavioural disorders, they can do a lot to help. A second is that there are rules, disciplines and simple diversions which can be of immense help in limiting the damage and even bringing fun and life back into young lives that have been caught up in the misery of parental break-up. A third is that it is not only parents but also all the other important adults in the life of a child – grandparents, other relatives, school-teachers, doctors and professionals – who can and should be involved in the helping process.

We need to listen

The NSPCC knew what was needed a few years ago, when it led a poster campaign with the caption 'This child needs a jolly good

* See Appendix 1

listening to'; and Dr Sebastian Kraemer knew when he told a *Panorama* television programme that 'there is a conspiracy of silence about the painful effects of divorce'. We need to hear our children, we need to give them the right to start a conversation and we need to let them return adult problems to adult shoulders in order to leave children free to enjoy their childhood.

Children need to be able to find someone to talk to who will listen, accept and understand what they are thinking or feeling. Children experience hurt in lots of different ways. They will tell us what they need. They might not do it with words, but they will talk through their behaviour, the expression in their eyes, their eating habits, their sleeping patterns and what they don't say as much as by what they do say. They may not be conscious of what they want to tell us but, if we are open to hearing them speak and watch them with understanding, we will be able to help them.

Parents need to behave so that their children feel as safe as possible

Parents need to realize that, while their decision to separate can have negative consequences on the lives of the people they have created, they can still do a lot that is right to help their children. It is vital to understand that divorce and separation are not an excuse to neglect good parenting. Indeed, the break-up of a family home requires the best parenting practice possible, even though it is not easy to be a good parent when one's own world is in pieces. Structures must be re-created so that boundaries and the limits of acceptable behaviour are clear; unconditional love must be a given; and domestic arrangements should be in place which will make children feel less frightened and more secure.

The loss of the family structure that cradles the child is fundamental. Unless a workable alternative replaces the familiar system, children and adolescents are likely to feel emotionally, physically and even mentally insecure. If one parent goes, then another may leave as well. If one parent obviously dislikes the other, then how is a child able to love both? Who is a child to trust? Who is he to talk to? Who can she believe? Who can be respected, loved, relied upon, listened to and turned to? Where will a child live? Will she still go to the same school? How often will he see the absent parent? What is happening and who can she trust to tell her the truth? Is Mum OK? Is Dad OK? And if there has been violence, alcoholism, poverty, or even simply the bleak, cold atmosphere of the toxic ending of a relationship, what model will a child have for future happiness?

If we want our children to grow up as well as possible, we need to provide them with emotional, mental and physical security so that they have a safe foundation from which to explore their worlds and develop their personalities. We need to replace what has been lost with something as good as or even better. Children must know deep inside that they are safe within the love that is available to them, safe in the care that is given to them, safe within the boundaries that are provided for them and safe to go out into the world and experiment with being alive.

Wider society can help

Adults from all walks of life need to be encouraged to watch out for children whose mother and father are in the process of separating.

Grandparents, friends and godparents have an important part to play in providing comfort, support, boundaries and security at a time when small worlds are shattering. These people need encouragement to help and intervene rather than feeling that they should look the other way in the belief that collapsing relationships are a private affair.

It will be a great help to teachers and doctors, who are now on the front line in dealing with this new generation of children, if they understand what children are likely to be feeling when they say one thing and mean another, stop performing well at school or arrive in surgeries when there is nothing physically wrong with them.

All involved adults can help more if they understand why and how a child living through the process of family collapse may be experiencing hurt, and all grown-ups will be able to help if they are prepared to listen to the conversation of a child who might not be able to use words to tell us how they feel.

2 • • • • •
The role of grown-ups

OUR CHILDREN TODAY GROW UP in the tough, competitive world that we have created. In Britain, the phrase 'broken society' has entered the vocabulary, and the high incidence of divorce and single parenting is only one aspect of this. Perhaps we have made some kind of collective mistake in creating a world with too much freedom, too ready a pursuit of happiness and not enough boundaries. Combine that with the technological, computer-based revolution of the end of the twentieth century, and we are spinning in a new age of infinite possibility and non-stop activity. Progress is exciting and, on one level, it suits our children. They instinctively understand our machines better than we do, pick up the new language and run with the swift speed of our communication; in many respects, they are well equipped to inherit this world. But they do it at some cost. As we have concentrated on our outside, we seem to have forgotten about our inside. As we have speeded up, we have neglected the important process of slowing down. Our emotional lives are still calling, our hearts are still yearning, we still need to find meaning but, somehow, somewhere along the line, many of us have forgotten how to look after ourselves and, as we have done so, we have sadly also forgotten how to look after our children.

All families going through a separation and all children who come from broken homes need support from a wider world. This will involve a surprisingly broad range of adults who can play an important role in providing help and comfort.

Mothers and fathers suffer when their long-term relationships fall apart and will benefit from help from their family and friends while they find their feet in a new world which may not be of their choosing. Parents should be encouraged to look after themselves so that they are in a strong enough state to look after their children. Some categories of grown-ups are in particularly key positions to make a difference. Grandparents and other close relatives, friends and neighbours will know when there is suffering that needs to be alleviated. Teachers will be spending huge amounts of time with the children who are feeling hurt. Lawyers, doctors and therapists may be called to assist and, when things really go wrong, the social services and the police will become involved.

I will describe how the key players can help children in distress. It is important that we attempt to do our best, for, if we as adults do not help the children, we will not give them the tools to help us. We will find our old age hard if we turn to a younger generation that has been moulded by lack of care. Concern for others, responsibility, kindness, respect, warmth and important life skills will be in short supply if we have not taught by our own example. It will be difficult to grow old in a world in which we have failed our children.

Mothers

Women can leave marriages and long-term relationships. There is no social taboo on walking away from the vows made at the altar, and the chances of a woman re-establishing financial independence are increasing. The divorce laws are arguably skewed to the woman's advantage, in that the courts favour children living with their mothers and being supported by their fathers. So, although it is hard for a woman to leave her spouse, it is no longer impossible. Of the women I see going through the process of separating in my consulting room, about half are actually seeking to leave marriages or long-term relationships. The other 50 per cent are women who have been left. The latter arrive less composed and infinitely more broken than the women who have made the choice themselves, but the questions are always the same. Mothers do not want to damage their children.

As with childbirth, it is impossible to explain what divorce and the dissolution of a family home entail unless one has experienced them oneself. One can describe the sleepless nights, the inability to eat, the crazy midnight phone calls, the loss of plot and self-control, the re-uptake of cigarettes and too much wine. It is harder to explain why the idea of breaking the bedroom window and rubbing one's wrists against the glass should be a tempting way of making the internal pain external and more visible and then maybe more easy to treat. The break-up of the family is indeed difficult to bear.

While the emotional impact is painful enough, there are hard practical issues falling on the shoulders of the custodial parent, such as changing financial circumstances, maybe a house to be sold and often a fight to be fought through the divorce courts. The stress on women is huge. Just look at their faces in the supermarket and in the school playground as they go about their duties; at work, holding down a job, finding time to make it to the school play and get home to an ill child; in the gym as they attempt to run away from their problems; and in the bars, attempting to drown their sorrows. The haggard appearance of a woman going through a family break-up tells its own story. I have never seen a face that escapes its temporary ravages, but I have seen many that recover.

It does not matter how a family home breaks or who breaks it. If a woman has children she needs to care for, she will, almost inevitably, sometimes feel guilty, afraid, lost, overwhelmed, lonely and sad. Few women who have been in long-term relationships and had children will escape the raft of negative emotions that come with the end of a marriage or be able to navigate the waters of single motherhood without feeling bereft and exhausted. When a new baby is born, friends, relatives and neighbours gather to celebrate the birth and support the tired mother. Would that the same kind of support automatically fell into place when it becomes obvious that a family is falling apart.

Mothers who lose long-lasting marriages and relationships are likely to behave a little oddly while they find their way. Loneliness, sleeplessness and worry do not make for serenity or relaxed good humour, and women who are suffering need huge dollops of patience and understanding. They do not need to be made to feel in the wrong when they attempt to escape from acute unhappiness while bringing up their children on their own, and it does not help anyone if the friends they need appear to sit on the sidelines watching with disapproval.

Alison discovered that her husband of sixteen years had had two mistresses for six of them and that he was getting ready to buy a flat to share with a woman she actually knew. When he left, not surprisingly she found herself questioning her attractiveness and her ability to be a functioning, sexual woman. At forty-five, and feeling as if she had been slapped across the face, Alison unconsciously went man-hunting, in an understandable effort to heal the wound her husband's behaviour had inflicted. Sometimes, Alison went out too much, sometimes she looked for text messages and emails when she should have been checking homework, sometimes she seemed a little over-eager to bundle her children off to stay the weekend with their friends.

Alison was attempting to recover from her shock and, though she was not wholly aware of what she was doing, in her own way she was trying to find her feet. She was also looking after two children. She got them up in the morning, made sure they went to school, had their friends to tea and continued to encourage them in their clubs and extracurricular activities. She drove them where they needed to go and was always there to pick them up when it was time to go home. When her son cried at night with tummy ache she got into his bed and held him, stroking his hair and promising him that she would never leave and that it would all work out in the end. Alison was a good mother. But she needed someone to put their arms around her and tell her that she would be OK. Because she was used to the comforting arms of her husband, and because she had been brought up to believe that she needed a man in her life, Alison looked for those comforting arms elsewhere. In another time, in different circumstances, she probably would not have chosen the company of the men she linked up with during the first three years of her separation but, at the time, she gained companionship, comfort, sex and a feeling of some kind of safety.

It did not help her to be told by one of her best friends that what she was doing was wrong, that she needed to go home and spend more time with her children. This apparently helpful but ultimately judgemental intervention left Alison feeling bereft and ashamed. She had indeed lost her bearings, but now she felt that she was losing her friends and that she had made a complete fool of herself. Looking at it long term, the friend who told Alison to fly away home was probably right; the men she was hanging out with were not good for her and her attention was not all devoted to her children. However, to be told off when one is suffering and barely making it through the day can very much feel like the final straw. As compassionate adults, we need to keep our negative opinions to ourselves. It is better to trust that mothers will find a way through the difficult parts of their journey and let them know that, during this time, they will find us waiting or walking beside them. Even if we don't like their behaviour while they find their feet, it might be better to scoop up their children rather than risk bruising and losing a friend who really needs us. If a mother looks as if she is really going to damage herself or her children, then she will be much more able to turn to us for help if she can trust us not to disapprove but genuinely to care for her and her children's welfare.

It can be difficult to be compassionate when we see a woman break a home apart because she has fallen in love with someone else. When such mothers first come to me, I can find myself working hard not to pass the very judgement that Alison's friend made. It is hard to understand how a woman with a small child or children at home can put herself first and walk away, knowing that she is causing damage to those she is meant to love most in the world. But one of life's wisest lessons is never to judge a man until one has walked a mile in his moccasins. Instant judgement is best avoided, and then one may learn about a childhood, a marriage and a life, and will be able to make sense of why this woman had to break her vows and break her children's hearts.

Rachel came to see me, ostensibly for help in dealing with her husband's fury. I opened the door to a woman who was angry, nervous and unhappy in equal quantities. She had been having an affair with a man who made her feel loved and wanted. Her husband made her feel bullied, unworthy and plain. She felt that nothing that she did for him was right, and that everything she did for her lover was appreciated. Rachel lived for the times that she could be in her lover's arms and dreaded the cold evening meals with her husband. And yet she had two children, a beautiful house and a happily integrated life that worked well in the close community in which she lived. An intelligent woman who excelled in everything she did, Rachel could not make her marriage work, and she felt as if it was drawing her down into a depression from which there was no escape.

Rachel had attempted suicide when she was eighteen and had received no treatment after the attempt. Perhaps she was told to pull her socks up and never to be so silly again, or perhaps she was punished for frightening her family. Her father was a perfectionist who wanted the very best for her, and her husband was made from the same mould. When she met him in her early twenties, she believed that she would be free of the corrosive paternal criticism that had nearly killed her. What she did not know, and what most of us are unaware of, is that we tend to choose what is familiar to us. Rachel married a better-looking, better-educated and richer version of her father. She thought that she was lucky. She did not know that, within fifteen years, she would want to be dead again.

As her marriage faltered, as sex became nothing but a memory, as her misery increased and as she tried harder and harder to become a more and more perfect wife, Rachel found that she could not go on. She went to a restaurant with a girl-friend and unexpectedly met the man who was to become her lover. Very quickly, she was in his bed and, before three months were out, she declared herself to be in love. No wonder her husband was angry.

The months that followed were pure agony for the entire family. I saw the decent, loyal and likeable husband who could neither understand nor forgive; I saw the children who displayed pretty much every symptom of a breaking family; and I saw the mother who desperately wanted to return home and mend the unmendable but who could not give up the comfort of a man who loved her. She attempted to leave her lover, but her life at home was, naturally, colder and she was more subject to criticism than before. Her behaviour had, unfortunately, become public, and good friends chose to side with her husband. She found herself ostracized in the school play-ground, and her children and husband were offered invitations which did not include her.

How Rachel wished that she could turn back the clock, how she wished that she had never met the man who had made her feel alive again. She had given him up, but it was too late, and she found that her marriage was irreparably broken. The house had to be sold, she was prescribed anti-depressants, a man who had done nothing wrong found himself unhappily living alone, and the children were miserable. Rachel made a mistake but, given her life story, one that could have been forgiven and worked through. She lost everything she had ever wanted, and a part of her will suffer for the rest of her life. It would have been kinder if she had not lost her friends; if the parents at the school gate had not taken sides and left her isolated; if people had understood what she had been suffering, that she had had to leave in order to live and had not taken her decisions lightly. Her parents took her husband's side, too. Her brother and sister continued to contact him and ignore her phone calls, and she was left in charge of two children, with no one to approach to bring some joy into a family home which she was blamed for breaking. Inadvertently, Rachel's friends and family turned away from her children when they turned away from her, and it did not help two small people to have no one to talk to when they saw their mother crying every night when she put them to bed. It would have been better for the children if judgement had been suspended and a helping hand given to a woman who had become lost and found herself with nowhere to turn.

I have rarely met a mother who was not doing her best for her children, given her circumstances. In twenty years of practice, there have been only two incidents when I wanted to shake the mothers in my consulting room by the shoulders and tell them to wake up.

In each instance, the woman had a caring, thoughtful husband who carried the majority of the burden of the childcare. The women earned the family money and made the important decisions. Both of these women had met and fallen in love with other men and, with unseemly haste, left the marital home to set up house with their new partners. One can accept that women leave men and men leave women, but it is difficult to understand when parents of either sex attempt to steamroller their family into an acceptance of a replacement status quo that is suited entirely to their immediate needs. The mothers I am thinking of wanted half the family money, to keep the children and to set up home with their new love, all within the space of a year. There was no thought for the finer feelings of the partner who was being left behind or the fact that the children needed time to come to terms with what, for them, was dreadful and confusing news. These women behaved like bulldozers. When I tried to tell them to slow down, for the sake of everybody around them, they did not like the message and did not book another appointment. When faced with behaviour which so disregards the remaining family, there is little that can be done, as the often adolescent-like love experienced by the woman for her new partner is impossible to challenge. The best way to help in this situation in the short term is to offer support to the parent who is left home alone and to the children, who often feel that a thief has stolen their mother. As time passes and the dust settles, friends can start to reintegrate the bolting mother back into their lives so that the children can see that others accept the changed situation and that it is possible that they can do the same.

How to help mothers

A compassionate availability to mothers who are spinning from the drama of the process of family break-up is the best response. We need to look after ourselves, have some boundaries and be able to say when our own lives are simply too busy to encompass their misery. But if we are there when we can be, then mothers will have a secure base from which to talk about, understand and come to terms with their situation. It is a difficult job to watch one's friends and relations suffer, but the suffering need not go on for ever, and small shoots of optimism often lie not too far beneath the surface. While it is heartrending to listen to the desperate outpourings of mothers who feel as if they are at the end of their tether, it is wonderful to watch them begin to find their feet again and start to make a whole new life.

Mothers often need to talk. And talk and talk and talk. From the loneliness of their empty homes and the muddle of their sleepless heads, women who are sorting out how to take the next steps need a sounding board. To be this sounding board can be exhausting, as the phone can ring at all times of day and night and the weeping woman on the other end may be drunk, exhausted or distraught. The phone is a separating woman's lifeline and is probably used too much. Children listen, and the phone takes attention away from them. However, it is better that their lonely mother feels connected to the outside world than that she sit alone in a desperate heap. If possible, the separating mother should be encouraged to delay her phone calls until after the children's bedtime and to extend her network of friends so that she has a selection of people to call. In that way, she will not risk the chance of causing compassion fatigue to one poor person on the end of a phone at midnight, and she will ensure that her vital safety net remains as large and intact as possible.

It is hard to give advice to a woman who is mourning the end of a long relationship and coping with children on top of finding the necessary paperwork to fight for money and establish contact arrangements. These women are consumed with trying to do their best and so exhausted that they will take almost any advice as criticism. Of course, the outsider will see the problems in her behaviour: that perhaps she is leaning on alcohol, that drink-driving has become a part of life, that the children have too much information, that toys are being bought in an attempt to make young hearts lighter or that boundaries have been abandoned simply because they are too hard to keep in place. Mothers at the end of their tether simply cannot keep it all together. But if we point out where they are falling down, they are likely to retreat and fall down more dangerously and more significantly in private. I had a client once whose parents told her that it was a pity that she had stopped cooking and seemed to be relying on ready-meals. Too battered and too weak to defend herself, my client simply ducked from seeing her parents again until she was ready to produce a Christmas dinner, several years later. What seemed like a simple pointer from one generation to another pierced her heart and was experienced by her as an implication that she could no longer do her job. It is best to be careful with what we say; it is best to offer unconditional love and trust while broken friends and relations heal.

Invitations are a useful and important way of giving mothers in the process of a separation a well-needed boost. When one's diary is empty, when one looks ahead to a future that feels lonely and desperate, a dinner date, a ticket to the theatre or cinema, a walk by the river, a girls' night out or a phone call about the possibility of a weekend visit can be a huge tonic. When these invitations come, the lonely mother has something to look forward to, a reason to wash her hair, something nice to tell her children, and she will remember why she has good clothes in her wardrobe which deserve the occasional outing. If one is friends with both members of the separating couple, tact is needed when issuing such important tickets to the beginnings of a new life. It may be natural to favour the party who seems the more abandoned, or easier to spend time with the friend who is more fun, but it is better to be open and even-handed. By informing both members of the couple that one of them has been invited with or without the children, there is no implication that the other is being cut off.

An important exception to not giving advice is gently to see if it is at all possible to stop the mother demonizing the father of their children. This is a golden rule when considering how best to look

37

after children who are experiencing the disintegration of their parents' relationship. It is the most natural thing in the world for a mother to belittle and criticize the man who is causing so much heartache. But doing this within the family home does nothing but harm to the children. Fathers have contributed 50 per cent of a child's genetic make-up; if he is made bad, then they are likely to pick up the corrosive and negative idea that they are half-bad too. On a more positive note, they need a male role model to love and respect. Just as importantly, a mother will need the father's support when things settle down in order to co-parent their children effectively. It helps no one if the emotional toxicity within the hearts of the couple splitting up spills over on to the wider family. The more bitterness displayed in the relationship between the separating parents, the more sadness, confusion and damage to the children. The message that a mother will be shooting herself in the foot and hurting her children if she teaches them to mistrust and dislike their father may take a friend or family member courage to broach, but it will ultimately help the entire family.

In addition, mothers need to help themselves in order to stay sane and available for their children. They need to forgive themselves in their suffering, stay off the phone when their children are around, keep away from sharp and critical tongues, find a trustworthy and careful lawyer, resist the temptation to talk badly of their ex-partner and arrange treats for themselves or find nice things to do with friends and people whom they trust. If they feel as if they cannot cope, they need to seek out help either from friends, family, support groups or trained professionals. If depression begins to bite, a visit to the doctor is essential. Although it can feel impossible, as months pass a tiny speck of light will begin to shine at the end of a very dark tunnel. With the help of a good support network mothers can walk towards it, although they will often need to lie down and weep when they find themselves too tired, too upset or too flattened to take another step.

Fathers

Fathers need as much help as mothers when they are going through the difficult process of a family break-up, but it is a different kind of help. Men tend to be more practical and want to fix things, while women like discussing options and discovering how they feel before they decide what to do next. If a woman needs a listening ear and a compassionate heart, then men tend to need people with whom to undertake activities, practical help with how to look after the children and someone with whom there is an unspoken kind of agreement that they are there for them in their darkest hours.

Fathers have a tough time with divorce and separation, and statistics reveal just how badly they can suffer. According to CIVITAS, divorced men aged between twenty and sixty have a 70–100 per cent higher rate of death than married men and are twice as likely to increase their drinking compared to those who remain married, and are significantly more likely to use drugs, drink-drive and indulge in unsafe sex. With the no-fault divorce arrangement of today, the wife can walk away with custody of the children and half of the assets. I have seen male friends and clients shattered to learn that they have to move out of the family home and that they can only see their children every other weekend. Not only do they often have to find somewhere to live, and earn the money to keep themselves and their family, they also need to provide an appealing atmosphere in which to entertain their children, who are already unhappy and appalled at what has happened. On top of living through the stress of the upheaval of the broken family home, fathers are automatically meant to understand a language which mothers have had the whole of their children's lives to learn. Fathers suddenly need to know who their children's best friends are, where they keep their favourite things, what they like to eat, where they like to go and what time the judo and tennis classes are at the weekend. Of course, some fathers will already know but, on the whole, just as, statistically, it has been

39

proved that most women still do most of the household chores, so it is that most women deal with most of the important minutiae of childcare. Many male brains are not good at handling different tasks at the same time and, when fathers are handed their children with no back-up, they can often feel very lost, practically as well as emotionally.

Richard was one of the sweetest men I have ever met and he is a good example of a man who had successfully challenged depression and the seductive call of suicide while remaining a wonderfully competent and hands-on father who ensured that his three girls did not suffer too much from the consequences of the failure of his marriage. His family of origin had not been entirely functional, and he carried quite a bit of baggage from his past, but the life that he had carved for himself had seemed happy. Undoubtedly he could have black moods and get angry with his girls, and he probably wanted sex with his wife more than she wanted it with him, but his were not big crimes and did not in my view call for the break-up of a family with three children. However, his wife wanted out and, after a half-hearted attempt at marriage-guidance counselling, Richard moved to the basement of a friend's house.

I got to know Richard well over the next three years and came to respect and admire him for his courage and to laugh with him at some of his understandable attempts to overcome his loneliness. Richard went girl-hunting in order to assuage his unhappiness. He had quite a few successes, which he enjoyed telling me about in interesting detail but was never able to give his heart fully. Richard was not really made to go out with women twenty years his junior and, anyway, whenever the relationship passed a certain point, the women started to talk about babies and he abruptly found himself running back to his empty bed and an early morning cup of tea. Dating can be a minefield for divorcing men who already have children; the woman to whom they turn for understandable and necessary comfort can often have her own understandable and necessary agenda but, while a newly single father is finding his feet and learning to look after his own children, the last thing he needs is to have to think about taking on or starting a new family. It is not surprising that we may have to guide some of our newly divorcing male friends through a series of relationships. We need to hold their hands as they ricochet around looking for somewhere to lay their heads in order not to have to think about what they have lost.

When Richard was not busy looking for a young beauty to ease his aching heart or looking after his children, he found himself depressed and bored. He had his work as a successful artist, but it was a solitary life and gave him time to brood. Basically, he just wanted to go home and could not understand why he was not allowed to try. His wife wanted nothing more to do with him and would and could give no other reason than that she no longer loved him. And so Richard had to hand over half of his savings, sell the family home and take only a third of the proceeds, as his ex-wife needed to house the three girls. Richard was angry and distraught, and he hid himself away, not wanting to burden his friends with his white face and his black thoughts. Sometimes, in the small hours of the morning, I suspect that he was a danger to himself, but he never rang me to tell me quite how bad it was until the darkest eye of the storm had passed. Sometimes he drank too much in an attempt to dull the pain, but he realized that the alcohol which was meant to take away his despair made him feel much worse.

Luckily, Richard had the courage and wisdom to go to a therapist, who gave him a space in which to talk and think and feel and work out his next move. I was his friend, and we walked in the park and joined each other as families to eat on Sunday

41

afternoons. Gradually, I saw Richard's misery diminish and a sense of possibility return. He had suffered a near-mortal blow but, with the help of friendship, therapy and the love of his children, he managed to crawl out of the pit into which his divorce had sent him. He returned to life a stronger and more interesting man and one who turned into the kind of father whom any child would be proud to have.

Men who choose to leave the family home do not have an easy time. They often leave because they have fallen in love with someone else and cannot work their way through the maze of complications that this entails. Perhaps they have been discovered and confronted, or perhaps they know that they simply have to go. It is not a small step to leave children, a house and half of life's financial packaging.

Andrew fell in love after a twenty-year marriage which had produced three children. He did not mean to fall in love, but it was there waiting for him in his office. Perhaps if he had not worked so hard, perhaps if he had taken opportunities to enjoy himself more with his family and have more fun with his wife, then the hurtful passion would not have taken such a hold. Andrew did not take the decision lightly and, when he did, it nearly cost him his health. Sleepless nights, depression, an inability to think, a loss of enjoyment and a perplexed misery haunted him, and he sought answers wherever he could find them. He tried leaving his new love, he tried going on holiday with his wife and without the children, he tried therapy, he read books, he tried drugs and he tried exercise in an attempt to run away from his demons, but all to no avail. When his mistress issued an ultimatum, he could not resist. He told his wife that he loved another woman and was gone within a day.

The following three years were to prove miserable. Although Andrew had the freedom to love again, he lost so much that sometimes, looking at his face and tired eyes, one had to wonder whether it had been worth it. He felt guilty, he felt broken and broke, he felt badly for his children and he did not know how to begin to find the words to say sorry or how to make things better for his nine-year-old son when he asked him to come home. Andrew had made his bed and had to lie in it, but he was also fortunate. Friends made their homes available so that he and his children could meet and have the type of fun that was familiar to them and not become yet one more family sitting mournfully in McDonald's. His ex-wife encouraged him to see his children and told him their plans so that he could take an interest and not lose touch. His mother and family stood close by and chose to support him, although they did not condone his behaviour. And the medical profession, with the help of self-support groups, came to his rescue. Andrew for a while was very lost, but as he came out of his despair he found that, with this help, his children had not turned their backs and were still there.

How to help fathers

One of the best ways to support fathers is gently to encourage them to see the vital importance of keeping in contact with their children. It will make it easier if there are invitations and offers to spend time with fathers and their families. Activities such as football, tennis and swimming tend to give an overwhelmed man something to do and will keep children busy and start them on a learning curve so they know that it is all right and even fun to be out with Dad alone. Weekend lunches and holiday suppers are a good idea, too, because, very often, men in the early stage of a separation have nowhere to offer their children to stay, and their cooking skills can be a little rusty. Children will see that life has not ended and that, even though their mother and father can no longer live together, other people still accept their dad and want him to be around.

Practical help with childcare can also have a positive effect on a father who is finding it difficult to cope and might help ensure that he stays around for his children in the future. The younger the children, the more likely it will be that a man will initially be all at sea when dealing with his offspring on his own. Without years of training and the day-to-day experience of sorting out what goes where and who does what, there will probably be a fair degree of chaos in the early days. The more focused thinking of the male brain will mean that doing more than two unfamiliar things at once may cause problems. Changing a nappy while keeping an eye on a five-year-old while wondering how to pick up an eight-year-old from a birthday party is enough to make the sanest person feel completely lost. A newly single father may find that he and his children have a really awful time until he gets used to and understands the practicalities of child-rearing. A helping hand from an experienced friend can go a long way to diminish the unfamiliarity and confusion of the early days and go some way towards making the children want to keep seeing their father and making the father feel that it is not too difficult to see them.

A further means of support is to offer to spend time with men whose families have broken apart. Men are not nearly as good as women at telling the world how bad things are and are much worse at finding help. They seem to prefer to bottle up the bad stuff and keep it away from the world while they brood in misery in their lonely homes. This is not necessarily the best way forward: while more women are reported to be depressed after a divorce, more men commit suicide. If they reached out for help, maybe the number of men taking their own lives would decrease.

Grandparents

We have an increasingly mobile population and an older generation who are fitter and richer than they have been in the past. The archetypal granny living not so far away baking cakes and cooking Sunday lunch is mostly an anachronism, and we are more likely to find grandparents jumping on easyJet flights and taking computer courses than making traditional apple pie and custard. Members of the older generation are busy and spread about the country and may not be easily available when their children get into trouble. Yet all the grandparents I know hate family breakdown, worry terribly for their grandchildren and wonder what on earth to do and how to help.

Physical presence, non-judgemental emotional support and time with the grandchildren seem to be the most valued gifts. Grandparents might feel they do not want to intrude on a time of turbulence and private grief, but it is better to offer help and be refused than not to offer it at all. I have often heard of grandparents who do not know how to comfort their children when their relationships fall apart. I would encourage them to put aside their emotional reserve and pull out all the stops to help steer their family through this difficult process.

Elizabeth had a grandmother who had a positive influence on her while her mother and father were going through a difficult and protracted separation which included financial hardship and paternal depression. Elizabeth had to leave her private school and her house and ended up in a rented flat in a different part of town. She lost her father, her school, her schoolfriends and the place where she grew up. The one constant in her life was her grandmother, who had her to tea every Thursday, lunch every Sunday and took her on jaunts during the school holidays. Sometimes Elizabeth's mother would join them. Sometimes she would take a well earned rest or go out and about in an attempt to put her life back together. Elizabeth loved her grandmother. When talking about her, her eyes would shine, and she would smile and laughingly tell me about their antics and latest plots. They went shopping together and to the movies and, when Elizabeth stayed the night, she slept in Grandma's bed and they both read Harry Potter and pretended that Elizabeth could help with the crossword. Elizabeth had someone to turn to and somewhere to go when her world crashed around her ears. She has turned into a beautiful and wonderful young woman, and her grandmother can take much of the credit.

Practical help can be a life-saver.

Patricia was abandoned by her partner two days before Christmas. He 'forgot' to come home and left a young mother with a new baby and a two-year-old in a daze of confusion. He celebrated his new life in the pub with a child-free woman who did not need him to make a bottle of warm milk at midnight. The mother of his children was at home on her own, unable even to make it to the shops to buy food for the holiday. Patricia's mother stepped in. She bundled the entire family into the car and took them to her house, shopped and cooked and cared for all three of them. She got them through the first terrible month, when nobody even knew where the children's father had gone, and then she settled down to a consistent plan of helping her daughter. She changed her work schedule to have two days a week free in order to look after the children. This meant that she had to work at the weekends, but it was worth it to her to enable her daughter to begin to build a life for herself. Patricia's mother moved heaven and earth for her family. She had no money, but endless energy and compassion.

Intelligent sensitivity is important when considering how grandparents should help. It is easy for them to take sides, say harsh things and offer unsolicited judgements. For the sake of the grandchildren, it is best not to say anything too negative. Just as one parent should not demonize the other, grandparents should not demonize one or other parent. Children want to continue to respect and love both parents as they grow up and will not want to believe that either parent is in any way bad or unworthy. There is a danger that if a parent is talked about in a negative fashion, a child will believe that they too have something wrong with them, and their self-worth will be doubly knocked. Eventually, too, when things have calmed down a little, both parties in the broken relationship will want to be able to look back and remember that it was precious once. It is a pity if some of the most important years in one's life are made to seem as if they were one big mistake.

It is best for grandparents to hold their own counsel, even though they may be angry. They can let off steam when they are with their own close and trusted friends. When Susan was told by her parents that it was probably a good thing that her husband had left her because they had never liked him, she did not feel comforted. She felt she was being criticized for her choice of partner and as if she had somehow brought her problems on herself by choosing the wrong man.

There is so much that grandparents can do, if they have the time and the inclination and are allowed access to their grandchildren. Favourite food, board games, movies, dog-walking, cooking lessons, help with homework and night-time cuddles with special books read aloud all give a huge amount to children whose worlds have been temporarily shattered. Grandfathers can act as important male role models and give valuable time in a male world. Childcare was never meant to be left only to women, and children who have little contact with their father need male company. Hobbies can be shared and encouraged, and new opportunities offered to a child to become involved in something he or she would not otherwise have considered.

Christopher's grandfather made a big difference to the life of a child when he spent every weekday evening with his grandson during the first two years of his son's divorce. When the homework had been put away, they spent the time carefully constructing and painting toy Warhammer models. When it was time for Christopher to leave, his grandfather would buy him an ice cream to eat on the way home. Christopher's grandfather saved his struggling son the cost and necessity of finding after-school childcare; he also found that he himself was happy and busy in the early evenings of a long retirement and was glad that his son had turned to him for help.

Issues of discipline can be difficult for grandparents to adjudicate. Children of today play on the computer, read less, eat faster food, swear more and wear strange clothes. They have a whole new world, which is not necessarily wrong or right but is certainly different. If a grandparent tries to impose a boundary system based on personal beliefs and values from fifty years ago, then they will probably come up against an understandable resistance. Family rules are just as important as they ever were, but they are probably best left to the parents of the children, who will better understand what is suitable for the age of their child. Grandparents can help by giving their sons or daughters a support system while they recuperate. As parents recover their energy, they will – or should – work out and put in place a new system of boundaries that works for the new configuration.

Just as I have seen some grandparents playing a vital role in easing children and grandchildren through the various stages of family disintegration, I have seen others who sadly become sidelined and left out. When a daughter- or son-in-law is brittle with anger and exhaustion, they can be liable to reject any help, but it is important for grandparents to try to offer comfort and stay in touch. It can be heartbreaking for grandparents to lose contact with their grandchildren, and it is usually destructive and unnecessary. Often it is the parents of the husband who become estranged from the children as the bitterness of the separation spills over to the wider family. When the mother has to take control of the childcare and finds that she is unable to have any kind of relationship with her ex-husband, she will often turn her back on his entire family. This is a pity. Her ex-husband's parents and relatives may appear to have taken sides, things may have been said in the heat of the moment or the relationship may never have worked in the first place, but these are issues between adults. Children deserve to have as wide a network of family as possible, and they need to grow up knowing who they are and where they come from. To remove them from their history and their connections and to take away their inheritance is unhelpful and emotionally damaging for all concerned. If at all possible, adults should behave like adults and keep their differences separate from the care of their children. Children will then have access to the vital support that grandparents have to offer, and grandparents will be allowed to maintain contact with their family and its future generations.

Family, friends and neighbours

Trusted friends and siblings can make all the difference to whether children will be all right during the process of parental separation and its aftermath. They need to step in pretty much as soon as it becomes clear that a family is breaking apart. Male or female, our friends will need someone to talk to. It is lonely to lose one's mate, and confusing to be unable to talk to the person who used to share one's life. Talking to a trusted friend will greatly relieve the suffering.

This early stage is a good time to invite the family out in various combinations. Godparents can take individual children for treats, to talk and listen to them so that they feel heard and less alone. Brothers, sisters and friends can offer to look after the children for the weekend to give the parents a chance to collect their thoughts or catch up on some sleep. It is good for children to spend time in happy homes away from stress and to know that not all marriages have to end.

In the early days, neighbours and friends can offer practical support, such as offering to do the shopping, the school run or a pick-up after a club or party. Parents juggling emotional exhaustion with learning to live a new life will be grateful and probably pleased to accept, as most people whom I see initially want to keep away from the scrutiny of the school playground and other public places. Friends can bring food and flowers or, even better, arrive with a meal to share so as to provide company and evidence to the children that life is not over and that they still live within a framework that is safe for them and has not entirely collapsed.

Fathers may need a friend to guide them through the complicated unwritten programmes of their children's lives. If the children are of school age, a father may not know nor want to ask about homework, school bags, school uniforms, clubs and activities, or his children's friends. If the mother of his children attempts to teach him through gritted teeth or unshed tears, she will probably seem controlling and difficult. It is better if an objective friend can give a little help so that overnight stays and weekends with Dad are not a nightmare of too little sleep, unfinished homework, wrong kit for school and forgotten diary dates. The children will enjoy it more and the father will be more in control if he knows what they are supposed to be doing and what is expected of them.

Friends can also help defuse the drama. When couples ask how to tell their children that they are separating, I usually suggest they have someone whom the children know well close by. One can never tell how a child will react immediately on hearing the news, and it is better to be ready for any eventuality. Many children simply cannot take in the enormity of what they have heard; they go into shock and do not want to talk. At this point friends can take a child for a walk, a meal or an outing and say very little but just be with them while they process the ghastly information. Other children want to run away from home; a friend who is on standby can run with them and bring them back when they are ready to face the news. A friend is useful when there are more than two children, so that each child has an adult to turn to. The parents will probably be reeling, and it is good for there to be a steady person in the background who can at least make a cup of tea or stay to comfort those who are left behind.

If there is a problem with alcohol or drugs, or if there is open aggression or violence within the family, reactions all round can be more dramatic. Friends can provide a lifeline to children by simply giving them their telephone number and telling them to call day or night if life gets too frightening or if they feel as if they have nowhere to turn. That telephone number will often live under a pillow and never be used, but it will give great comfort and is one of the best gifts one can give to a child with an unstable and difficult home life.

Divorcing and separating parents can be very demanding. Because of the enormity of what is happening, they probably have very little space for those around them. What can look like self-obsession and an inability to be interested in the lives of others can in fact be a survival mechanism. A parent who is spending hours alone or looking after children while coping with anger, grief and loss will need to lean on the outside world while not always having room for the people within it. It can be tiring and sometimes dull for those of us who have offered help, and we might need to flag up that we are not endlessly available. It is also possible to end up stuck in the quagmire of raw feelings and animosity between two fighting friends who misinterpret one's good intentions. When this happens, it is best to hold one's counsel, leave advice on divorce issues to the lawyers and remain steadfast while understanding that our friends are having such a difficult time that it is easy for them to lose perspective. It is not always possible to be totally even-handed. One parent may need more support than the other, especially if he or she is struggling with childcare. The behaviour of one of our friends might become so unacceptable that we find ourselves having to choose which side of the fence we are on. But it is better, if possible, for friends to avoid openly taking sides.

Divorce and family breakdown is something our friends will get through, but it is important to remember that there is no time limit for the recovery process. Some books suggest a two-year period for mourning a lost marriage or long-term relationship but, in my experience, each individual has their own time frame, and it can take a long time to really recover. When Alison was told 'that it was time to pull herself together and to get on with her life', she felt bemused and ashamed and shut the doors on the world in order to weep alone. If the friend had known of the courage it took for Alison to attempt 'to get on with her life' on an empty, endless Sunday, she might have kept her advice to herself and invited Alison to lunch.

Divorce and the shattering of a family unit is a nightmare, and those going through it have to live with it every waking minute of every waking day. Children have to watch parents in their misery and are themselves miserable because they never ever wanted their mother and father to split up. If we can give an hour or two of relief to a breaking family, even if it means challenging our busy schedules, we will make the process of separation easier for all to bear and help the children see that it is not all over and that there is a possibility of light at the end of the tunnel.

Teachers

Teachers are on the front line. With 28 per cent of our children living with single parents, class teachers will learn all too often that one of their pupils is experiencing the break-up of the family home. They will be asked to mop up the tears and provide extra care and a careful eye, while still being expected to keep to targets, impose discipline, respect the children and teach their subject. Most advice given to separating parents is to tell the teacher and keep the school informed as soon as they know that a break-up is looming. I often wonder what teachers are supposed to do with this sensitive information and how they are meant to help individual children on top of their teaching tasks. As far as I know, there are no training days put aside for teachers to study the subject of divorce and family breakdown and its impact on children in education. Yet this new social reality finds itself right in the middle of their work, and it might be a good idea for teachers to have some support in learning how to deal with it.

A child from a breaking home will be full of unasked and un-answered questions and difficult emotions. They might be afraid, sad, lonely, overwhelmed, confused, angry or all of the above. In the worst cases, they may hold too much information about matters that have nothing to do with childhood and be silenced into a mute despair or even terror. Whatever the circumstances of the dissolution of their parents' relationship, children will not be happy or free of care, and they will show their distress in any number of different ways. Perhaps they will not want to go to school because they feel they have to stay at home to look after an unhappy parent. Maybe they will be unable to concentrate during lessons. Some children could become isolated and fail to join in with the rough and tumble of the school playground. Others will be so frustrated and bottled up that they might lash out at an unsuspecting friend. Homework will probably slip or be left undone entirely, and there could be a marked deterioration in the standard of work. As friend-ships suffer, work begins to slide, play holds less appeal and behaviour becomes unacceptable, there is a danger that children who are full to the brim with difficult thoughts and feelings have their problems made worse by their not being understood. Teachers can play a vital role in helping a child through the tough times; they can make a real difference.

An example of how to help a child came from an inspirational headmistress who took care of Max. He was a bright and funny eight-year-old with a serious smile, a mop of unruly brown curls and a huge pair of brown eyes which filled quickly with tears. His mother and father divorced because of one fling too many on the part of the father and a depressive illness on the part of the mother. Poor Max arrived at school without his homework, with clothes unwashed, with only one gym shoe and usually without signatures for permission for school trips. Rather than punish him for his lack of organization and lost homework, his head of school quickly understood what was happening and stepped in to help. She kept spare uniforms in the school and dressed Max quickly when he needed to tidy up, she found some shoes that he could wear so that he was not left out of the games that he loved, invited him to stay for home-work club so that work could be done at school, took him out for pizza and talked to him about what was going on in his head and in his home. The teachers in this school were wonderful. They understood that neither the father nor the mother could do any better at that moment and that Max needed support. They did not punish him for slipping a little bit with his work, or burden him by asking him to remember too many things. His school kept him on an even keel when everything else around him was falling apart and he managed to get through the difficult process of his parents' divorce without too many problems.

Alexander went to a different school with a different head-master and suffered from their lack of understanding. His father left home without a word of explanation, and two brothers of nine and seven had to make sense of a new world while their mother wept and talked on the phone and looked for a way to pay the bills. Alexander had been at the top of his class in his studies and had been a popular boy in the playground. Five months after his father left, Alexander had lost most of his friends and his grades for effort had fallen. He knew that he was slipping to the bottom of the class and hated it.

Instead of realizing that this child needed help, his teacher hammered him with criticism and called the mother in to say that there was a problem with her son and he must pull his socks up. This poor small boy, who could see very little point in education when he just wanted to be at home with his mother, began to refuse to get into the car in the morning. He started to hit and kick on the school run and to sit pale-faced and un-communicative in the classroom. What he did not express at school he gave to his mother in spades in the evening, and she found him hard to manage. Not only was she suffering from the collapse of a marriage but she had a son who was so angry that she found him hard to recognize. By the time an exhausted Alexander appeared in my consulting room, he was a boy who refused to go to school and was sliding into depression. He needed the help which the school had failed to provide.

It is good practice in schools to discuss the sensitive subject of a breaking home in the confidential weekly staff meeting so that all teachers are in the loop as to why a pupil might be off colour. This makes it much easier for a hand of comfort to be offered on the sports pitch or during a chemistry lesson when a white-faced child can suddenly not take one more moment of pressure. The opposite, very public, system of pinning a note on the board in the staff room is a bad idea. I have had a client whose family tragedy was spread throughout the school by a sharp-eyed pupil. My client found it difficult to face other children because they had information that she had wanted to keep to herself. Children, especially teenagers, can be private about their business and don't want anyone specifically to watch out for them or treat them differently. However, they are usually very pleased if they know that a trusted someone is in the background. This trusted someone could be a school counsellor, but children should be asked whom they would like to talk to if times get tough. They will usually pick a favourite friend or teacher and will appreciate the fact that there is a vaguely formal arrangement should they need to talk.

It is probably best simply to expect that the standard of work of a child will drop a grade or two for a while. It is obviously a great pity if a pupil is in the middle of important exams when a family crashes but, if at all possible, teachers should understand and try to guide without punishing if the child cannot concentrate or fails to hand in their homework. A school will do well if it can contain the pupil and provide support so that the child continues to turn up and join in with other classmates. If problems with homework, discipline and concentration get too bad, however, then it would be wise to work sensitively with the parents and perhaps suggest family counselling or child therapy.

Emotional instability and real insecurity can account for troublesome behaviour within the classroom, but they can also mask organic problems within the child. Learning disabilities are far more common than they used to be, and up to one in five boys and one in seven girls are now estimated to suffer degrees of dyslexia, dyspraxia, ADD (attention defecit disorder), ADHD (attention deficit hyperactivity disorder), non-specific learning disabilities or Asperger's syndrome. A difficult home life can contribute to these but should not be assumed to be the cause. If a learning disability is suspected, professional help should be called in so that the problem can be identified and all the needs of a struggling child can be catered for.

Separating parents can be difficult for a school to deal with. Anger between a mother and a father may unexpectedly spill out during a parents' evening or in a meeting with a member of staff. Sadness and suffering can be visible to all and can make some uncomfortable with its very rawness. Children may refuse to see a particular parent. I have watched teachers having to negotiate the departure of a father from the grounds because the emotional intensity of the child's reaction to him was having a negative impact on the whole school. I have had to remove a weeping mother from a classroom while the children stared on in amazement. Mothers and fathers may need help from the school and to be encouraged to understand the importance of routine, homework, physical exercise, structure and social life.

Fathers may need special instruction about the routine of the school week and should be mailed separately with reports and news of school activities. Sometimes matters can get so out of hand that the interests of the child require an intervention that a school would not choose to make. In serious cases, when parents are recognized not to be coping, they have to be faced with unwelcome suggestions that professional help be engaged or social services called. Schools are well trained in matters of child protection but, on the whole, my experience is that they would like to see a family and a child sort themselves out before they have to call in outside help.

Doctors and therapists

You don't have to be a professional to help. Violet Oaklander, in her book *Windows to Our Children*, asks that anyone interested in helping children should have the courage to do so: it is not necessary to be expertly trained in order to listen, offer a guiding hand and make simple suggestions that can make a difference. Given the NSPCC's statistic that only 10 per cent of children will find someone to listen to their fears and worries, it is important to take this advice and hold out a hand to a suffering child.

Children who are living through the process of family break-up do not all need to go to a rigorously trained and experienced child therapist. Such experts are hard to find and have long waiting lists, which do not sit easily with a child in trouble who needs immediate help. The child of separating parents is not ill, or mad, or bad. He or she is having a tough time because a collapsing family is ghastly to live in. But there is a place for professionals; they have specialist skills should they be needed, and it is useful to know how they work and when to involve them.

Children have other ways of speaking than with words. Inexplicable tummy pains, frequent headaches and general fatigue can fill a doctor's waiting room on a Monday morning. Children can suddenly stop wanting to go on play dates or become disinterested in activities which once meant the world to them. Friends can disappear and bedrooms can become havens of lonely isolation. Too much food or too little food may become an issue, money may be stolen, sleep can become disrupted, small bodies may appear in beds at two o'clock in the morning, verbal and physical violence between siblings can become the norm. Once, I had a nine-year-old client who started to climb every tree he could find and refuse to come down in order to exert complete power over all the adults around. If difficult behaviour and deep sadness continue and cannot be helped by the available adults in the life of a child, then it might be time to look for professional help.

Counsellors and therapists are well placed to make an informed guess at what a child might be thinking and feeling, but it can be hard to find the right one. Schools, the church, the GP, word of mouth and training institutions are the best places to start. National Health Service medical practices often offer brief counselling periods and usually refer on to family therapy, which deals with the entire family, or cognitive behavioural therapy, which is helpful for cases of depression and obsessive compulsive disorders. In the private sector there is more choice. One should check that a counsellor belongs to the British Association of Counselling (BAC) and that a therapist belongs either to the British Association of Counselling and Psychotherapy (BACP) or the United Kingdom Council for Psychotherapy (UKCP). Counsellors have less rigorous training than therapists and tend to concentrate on guiding clients through the difficult issues of daily living. Therapists will have trained for an absolute minimum of three years and tend to concentrate on how issues from the past are impacting on the present. A GP's surgery will typically only be able to offer six sessions of counselling; if therapy is recommended, there might be a long waiting list within the National Health system, and it will be offered within a mental-health facility.

Some charitable institutions offer free or low-cost counselling. An increasing number of counsellors are beginning to work in schools, and many training institutions have well-supervised trainees who are able to provide low-cost therapy. If funds permit and one has the ability to choose to pay for help, it is important to remember that there are many different disciplines. The world of therapy can be difficult to understand. There are many schools of thought and different ideas about what is right and what is wrong, added to which therapists tend to cluster in certain geographical locations, so in London a parent will have a confusing spectrum of choice while in the countryside there might be little available beyond an NHS-based family therapist with a long waiting list. The United Kingdom Council for Psychotherapy, the British Association for Counselling and the British Association for Counselling and Psychotherapy all have good websites which can answer questions, clarify confusion and guide people towards finding well-trained, accredited therapists in their geographical area.

With no legal requirement (as yet) to belong to a regulating body, it is vital for anyone seeking help to ensure that a therapist or counsellor is well trained and rigorously professional. Having made contact, it is a good idea to ask what kind of therapy is being offered and research the discipline further via the organizations already mentioned. It is worth thinking about what suits a family before embarking on a significant and sometimes time-consuming commitment. It is also important to ask questions about cost, likely duration of therapy, the protocol for payment for missed sessions and how much other family members might be involved. Probably the most important factor when looking for a therapist or counsellor for either an adult, family or child is a sense of warmth and empathy from the professional and a feeling that there is a natural 'fit'.

However, one does not need to sweat too much about getting it wrong when sending children to therapy. Children are so bright and intuitive that if they are bored, if the therapist does not find a way to engage or simply does not get it right, they will usually vote with their feet and let a parent know pretty quickly that it is a silly waste of time. Parents, too, can keep an eye on what is going on; if there is little improvement after an acceptable period, or a child is still showing the same symptoms, it is reasonable to ask the professional if the process is working and discuss if it might not be better to call a halt.

I especially like the tools of the art therapist, which offer an effective means of finding out what is going on in a child's mind. Children do not much like to talk about difficult subjects while sitting still and looking at a grown-up. They are much happier to avoid eye contact and concentrate on something else while they tell you what is up. They are also more likely to tell you their truth rather than attempt to protect a mother or a father if they are engrossed in an activity that feels safe and fun. Painting by numbers, spray-painting, role play with dolls and puppets, made-up stories, board games, sand-therapy, clay modelling and physical activity are all useful in finding out how a child feels. Once brought into the open, negative feelings can be dealt with and difficult behaviour is likely to improve.

A good therapist will work first of all to bring the child's feelings and thoughts to the surface. He or she will be bound by a relationship of confidence with the child, although a child might want the support of this therapist or third party to speak to his parents and look for answers to unasked questions. The therapist or counsellor can suggest ideas to make the broken family function better and can remove unnecessary fear and anxiety so that a child can develop more normally. The therapist will have the child as his or her focus of interest and will be able to give undivided attention in an attempt to sort out problems and understand a child's negative behaviour. It is difficult to suggest a time frame, as children and their situations are so very different. Sometimes only one session can unlock a child and send him home relieved and much happier, other children may need a year or two of regular help, while others will be reassured with the knowledge that they can check in and out if things are bothering them. If the therapy is a success, the child will feel heard and understood, have some fun, feel as if she has found a new friend and learn to take some responsibility for her actions. Instead of being lonely and scared and exhibiting difficult behaviours, children will find answers to unspoken questions, be given tools with which to meet the challenges of their lives and be able to make choices so that they do not find themselves behaving in a way that gets them into more and more trouble.

Family therapy can be very valuable for children and families who are going through the process of separation and divorce. A GP can refer a family to facilities on the NHS where the whole family will be asked to look at, understand and see their part in what is going on. Sometimes two therapists will work with a family in order to maintain an objective view of a difficult situation. This form of therapy can be powerful and useful if all members agree to attend but can fall apart if a recalcitrant family member refuses to pitch up.

Sometimes a child will need medical attention because of physical symptoms that arise from emotional disturbance. Doctors, like teachers, have more than enough to do. While they hit targets, keep abreast of medical news, fill in their paperwork and give each patient their allotted ten minutes without being sued for negligence, they are still expected to know their patients and to understand the personal context of their medical problems. We are expecting a huge amount of our GPs and are lucky if we have a regular one to whom we can turn when times are hard.

If a doctor is to help a child who is living through the disintegration of his family life, they need to know the full story. Psychosomatic illness may appear, while an inability to go to school can often result in a visit to the surgery. More dramatic symptoms, such as self harm and alcohol abuse, are seen all too often, and if a doctor does not know that there is misery behind the closed door of their patient's house, they will not be able to do their job. If the medical practitioner understands that a child's heart is hurting, they will be able to help much more than by simply writing out a prescription or sending off for some kind of test. Medical treatment may be needed, but an awareness that depression or fear or sadness could be lurking in the background will mean that the whole child is cared for with a greater degree of sensitivity and efficiency.

Luke exhibited symptoms that had no medical cause when his parents split up, and he fell into such a state of disrepair that his school thought that he might have glandular fever. At fourteen, he found it difficult to sleep, lost his appetite and was beset with fears that something awful was likely to happen to his mother. When he found himself in the doctor's surgery facing a battery of blood tests, he could not face the thought of one more piercing piece of pain, and he refused outright to allow the nurse to take any of his blood. Luke was rude, aggressive and angry in his fear and ran away from the practice looking like a maladjusted teenager. Luke's doctor, however, was able to calm his young patient and was successful with the blood tests because he understood Luke's level of stress and was able to reassure him gently while learning that he did not have glandular fever or any other illness. Luke was ill with sadness; his only medicine was to be tenderness and time.

If a GP is worried about a child who is living in an unhappy home and understands that a family break-up is having a negative impact beyond the norm, they will refer a child to a counsellor, a therapist, a psychologist or a child psychiatrist, who might in turn refer the whole family to therapy. Unfortunately, child psychiatrists are hard to find, have huge waiting lists and are often attached to forbidding hospitals. If one chooses to go through the private sector or has insurance to cover the not insubstantial cost, a GP will provide the referral, the wait will be considerably shorter and the surroundings likely to be less forbidding.

Some children find family collapse more difficult to get through than others. They might be especially sensitive or they might be challenged by learning or developmental difficulties. Child therapists, educational psychologists, psychologists, counsellors, doctors, psychiatrists and centres for family therapy play an important role in helping these children. Professionals can also help if a break-up is so toxic that children cannot possibly cope with the fallout on their own. When the fighting has been vicious and the arguments relentless, when children have been asked to take sides or to witness behaviour that they should not see, when they have not had the space in which to develop because their world has been so unsafe, it is a good idea to turn to an expert. Hopefully, children will find useful guidance and a place of safety and help that can make them strong enough to withstand the negative effects of their parents' behaviour.

Lawyers

Lawyers have an enormous influence over the way in which a divorce is conducted, and their actions have an important effect on the lives of the children. From a family perspective, it is infinitely preferable to choose someone who will try to steer the parties towards a more or less amicable settlement rather than wind them up for a fight. For specialist family lawyers, seek those who are members of Resolution, the trading name of the Solicitors' Family Law Association. Members of Resolution, while being well trained in the more traditional legal practice of ending a marriage for individual clients, should also be able to guide divorcing couples through some less combative alternatives. They will have knowledge of Collaborative Law and Mediation and be able to suggest counselling to those clients who need help in dealing with the emotional impact of divorce.

Mediation is not a legal process but is designed to help couples who have decided to separate or divorce to talk things through. A trained mediator can give impartial guidance to help couples understand

and make choices, and will help their clients reach practical solutions that feel fair to both parties and the family as a whole. Mediation can reduce tension and hostility, keep communication channels open and save on the cost of expensive court battles. It is especially helpful where couples disagree about the future welfare of their children and it can help children by showing parents working together to resolve issues.

Collaborative law is a legal process whereby the lawyers on both sides work together with their clients to create a fair and legally binding solution without the threat of court proceedings. With a proven success rate in the USA and Canada, the scheme encourages couples not to litigate when they separate. Instead of disputes over money, property or children ending up in court, collaborative law allows couples to set their own agenda and work out the best possible outcome in their own divorce through cooperative negotiation. Acrimony, financial expenditure and the time taken to resolve divorce issues can be greatly reduced.

Counselling is an important aid to the legal process, and a good lawyer will know when it might be appropriate to suggest it. Divorce lawyers can have a difficult job, dealing with people who are often at their most unreasonable. Sad, angry, vengeful, trapped, broken or jealous people do not make the best decisions, and their emotions need to be contained before important practical solutions as to childcare and finances can be found. In an ideal world, law firms would have in-house counsellors and therapists to catch the sadness and madness of their clients but, actually, law firms able to offer such a service are few and far between. At the very least, family lawyers should have knowledge of and telephone numbers for trusted professionals to whom they can send their clients when feelings are running too high and huge bills are being racked up because of misplaced emotions.

Law firms that can offer the above will give a good indication that their lawyers are interested in keeping divorce out of the courts and making couples resolve their issues without bitter and costly legal battles. A good lawyer is an expert whose job is to inform their clients, to guide them as to their entitlements and expectations, and try to handle the process of divorce as painlessly and objectively as possible. With experience, strength and sensitivity, they will keep sight of the bigger picture and find the means to end a marriage with as little damage to the newly configured family as possible. Their clients will rarely be pleased with the end solution, as both partners will generally want to keep as much as possible and give as little away as they can. But divorce is not a pleasing process, and the sad truth is that nobody comes out of a broken marriage better off than before. Children will benefit financially and emotionally if their parents are not at loggerheads throughout a protracted and difficult court case, and parents will be much happier and more settled if they do not have to spend unnecessary money and time on dismantling a marriage that has already proved to have failed.

Sadly, expensive and aggressive lawyers still exist, and may still be needed in cases where difficult clients have got stuck in an unfortunate kind of war mentality and cannot follow the process of collaborative law or mediation. The decision to fight every inch of the way means that when letters, phone calls, demands and threats of court action are delivered, the negative emotional drama will escalate. This is not good for the children involved, who need their parents to be as well and as strong as possible. They do not need mothers and fathers who are becoming even angrier and more disillusioned and who are preoccupied with fighting, getting even and demanding more of everything. Aggressive lawyers cause more problems when there is simply not enough money to go round. I have seen and heard of so many cases where couples fight to the bitter end for a Pyrrhic victory that only leaves them with sadly depleted finances.

Rachel chose a Rottweiler of family law to help her to leave her husband. By his very name he upped the ante so that when Rachel's husband was told where she had gone for advice, he felt he had to respond in order to protect himself by seeking similar advice at similar cost. At several hundred pounds an hour, these two parents with three children found themselves on day one in an aggressive fight where decency and common sense seemed to have been forgotten. Court orders flew, court appearances were ordered with no warning, and the emotionally battered and completely furious parents as a result spent their waking hours collecting evidence of their financial history and examples of bad parenting to use against each other.

By her choice of lawyer Rachel had declared war. I watched in horror the mounting cost, the increasing anger and unnecessary manipulation of the children as both parents fought and nobody laid an arm on their shoulder to try to stop them. Eventually, I arranged a session to point out what the high levels of spleen and invective were doing to the emotional lives of the members of their family, let alone to their bank balances. It was not a difficult hour. For the sake of the children, both mother and father were prepared to listen to reason and understood the necessity of ending the vicious fighting. They put into place some simple suggestions about not arguing on the telephone and on the doorstep in front of the children, not interrogating their offspring, and giving their children their attention. Neither mother nor father wanted to hurt their children, but they did want to hurt each other. They had become so involved in their personal battle that they had failed to notice the disruptive and bossy behaviour of their son, the fact that their daughter spent increasing amounts of time locked in the downstairs toilet or that their seven-year-old seemed not to be learning how to read at school.

Kate took a different approach and chose as her lawyer a

woman with children of her own. Kate's lawyer could see that there were neither the finances nor the psychological well being for a prolonged battle, and she was able to guide her client with wisdom and common sense towards a solution that would be the least harmful to the family as a whole. Such was her skill that Kate's husband dismissed his own lawyer and allowed Kate's to conduct the divorce, representing Kate but dealing directly with Kate's husband. She was able to explain the procedure to Kate's husband so that he was fully aware of what was happening, and the costs and acrimony were thereby reduced. Such a case is rare, and such a lawyer is a gift to couples who are suffering from all the other strains of separation.

Children do not want their parents to split up. If, however, divorce is the only option, they do not need it to be ugly. Parents have a responsibility to contain the damage of separation. They will be able to do this better if they choose an experienced, well-trained lawyer who understands that there are no winners in divorce and that the children need to be considered at every turn of the road. Such a lawyer will be well paid, either through the legal-aid system, whereby money laid out is reimbursed, or with funds from the separating couple. His or her knowledge and experience should be listened to and the lawyer should be trusted for the advice that he or she is able to give even though, at times, it will be unwelcome and hard to hear. The lawyer will be able to hold steady in the face of the understandable negative emotions that capture the clients, and will be more objective and better trained than a good friend who does not know the law.

The social services

When it comes to the question of child protection, the members of the social services have a thankless and a difficult task. They are there to provide an essential backstop to children suffering from the worst cases of chaos and neglect. But they are also often overstretched, underpaid and have to venture uninvited into delicate situations concerning the care of children. Worried neighbours, heads of schools, family doctors, the police, therapists, the NSPCC and even relatives can and do contact the social services to report that, in their view, there is a child at risk. Once a report has been filed and child protection becomes an issue, social workers have to be very careful and are not allowed to make mistakes. Various forms of assessment are required, and parents may find themselves subject to an unwelcome level of examination that just might result in their children being taken away.

Some family breakdowns are so poisonous and some parents so desperate and unwell that they begin to fail their children and some kind of intervention is essential. However, the support that the social services offer can vary, and can also depend very much on the personality and individuality of the social worker concerned. A lucky parent in distress will find help and understanding, while an unlucky one with the same issues could find themselves fighting a situation in which social services want to take their children into care. When I have to think, in the last resort, about calling in the social services, this lack of consistency causes me concern. Things tend to work out better when family, friends, teachers, doctors and the community can be persuaded to support a struggling family and the social services are left for the cases where there is simply nowhere else to turn.

When Paula started to go to the gym at night, leaving her two young sons home alone, her neighbour reported her to the social services, and she had to face a case conference to prove her fitness as a mother. Of course Paula should not have left her children; however, she was at her wits' end. She worked all day, picked up her boys from school, did their homework with them, fed them and read them a bedtime story. By the time nine o'clock came round, she felt as if she were going mad. Rather than open a bottle of wine and drown her sorrows, she decided to run them away on a running machine and not remain in her flat with lonely, obsessive thoughts of her husband with another woman. In her own way, Paula was looking after herself in order to keep sane for her boys. If she had had a friend or relative who could have stepped in to offer some support, or if the father of her children had taken more responsibility to give her a break, things might have been all right, but Paula was alone in a strange town as a single mother and a single bread-winner. Already stressed and hardly able to cope, the arrival of the social workers, the very public investigation at the school and the threat that her children would be taken into care finished Paula off and drove her to seek medical help at hospital. Paula's boys lost their mother to a short stay on a psychiatric ward while they were taken temporarily into care. Arguably, the social services had done their job and ensured that two small boys were safe. However, the whole episode left the family unit deeply traumatized, and they came to me looking for help in an attempt to work through their collective feelings of abandonment and fear. If the social services had been gentler and less abrasive, if they could have somehow encouraged Paula to ask for help and given her some help themselves, I feel that Paula would not have ended up in an institution and the boys would not have had to be temporarily fostered.

John also reported that the intervention of the social services made a difficult situation nearly impossible. His wife was a heavy drinker and had been seen driving the children drunk; in addition, horrific arguments were heard by the next-door neighbour. Reports from two independent witnesses resulted in case conferences and threatened court action to take their three children into care. In order to prevent this, John left his job and stayed at home to look after the children. Unable to pay the mortgage, he had to sell the family home and move the children from their schools. Although the mother sought treatment and sobered up, she returned to an embittered husband who blamed her for the collapse of his working and personal life and sued her for divorce. The social workers did their job, followed their training and achieved the necessary result. An unsafe mother was prevented from parenting her children, but the cost to the children and their father was great and the family lost a lot. Perhaps if the parents had been treated with more sensitivity around the issue of alcoholism, John's wife could have found help sooner and John might have found some form of support whereby he did not have to give up work and lose his income.

Paula's and John's cases are only two examples of what can happen. When the social services become involved, visits have to be made, interviews conducted and case conferences arranged. Parents can feel judged and, in my experience, children usually feel uncomfortable and sometimes disloyal talking about their troubles to someone whom they do not know. Care is an unpleasant option and should be avoided if at all possible. But sometimes social workers have to play that card for the sake of the safety of a child. Children from two-parent homes also suffer, but a single parent left alone and unsupported is particularly vulnerable. To them, the intervention of the social services can sometimes feel like taking a hammer to crack a nut. Because of this, and the fact that there is an overall lack of uniform quality of care, and because social workers have to make such quick decisions of such importance, I will do my best to avoid having to use them, but I could not do my job if the social services were not there. When children will not go to school and are under the age of sixteen, when children are allowed to wander in the street at night alone and unchecked, when the belt and the stick are the way of the household, when violence and neglect are part of the package of childhood, I have to threaten parents with the call that issues of child protection require me to make. The very threat usually has a positive effect, and families tend to be shocked into looking after their children in a more responsible and careful manner. If the threat of a call to the social worker is not enough, then social services will be called in and I will ask them to take responsibility for ensuring that a child is safe.

The police

Most children whose parents are going through separation will not get into trouble, but family breakdown does bring stress and is a factor in increasing the workload of the police. They are called in to cases of domestic violence, they are asked to find children who have run away and they pick youngsters off the streets who do not want to be at home. As the final safety net for children who are falling from the high wire of our society, the police are exceptional. I have watched them at work for the past twenty years and, in their care of children, I have never seen them put a foot wrong. They appear to have well-practised methods in place, training is rigorous and they manage to maintain a sense of humour and understanding about the often foolish antics they have to deal with.

When Tom could not bear his parents fighting for one more minute, he stole £5 from his father's pocket, let himself out of the house at midnight and broke into a nearby park to sleep under a bush. When the police found him the next morning they gave him breakfast, a ride in their car and a sensible talk about safety and what could have happened to him. Tom's parents had to think about why their ten-year-old son had left home in the middle of the night, but Tom told me that he had thoroughly enjoyed himself and thought the police were really cool.

Jamie climbed on to the roof of his house and attached himself to the chimney. He would not come down because his mother was drunk and had been shouting at him for something that he had not done. He felt safe climbing away from the debris of a broken marriage and found some power on the top of a roof where no one could get at him. As his therapist, I was called in to try to talk him down, but I did not do nearly as good a job as the young policeman who climbed up to sit beside him and was able to reassure him that, when he came off the roof, there would be some hot food and that his mother would be much calmer.

Lucy was allowed out too often and too late by her mother, who wanted her to have fun outside the unhappy family home. Unsupervised thirteen-year-old girls have always been a magnet for trouble, especially after closing time, and the culture of gangs and happy slapping has not helped to make our streets safer for our children. Lucy and her friends were ambushed and attacked late at night by a group of girls who felt that they were intruders on their patch. The police had to be called, charges were made and the whole lot of them ended up at the police station while their parents were telephoned. Then the police drove many of the girls home at two in the morning, having made sure that a responsible adult was there to receive them.

As with all the other helping professionals, each member of the police force will have their individual way of dealing with situations, and some will be better than others. However, the police do have systems in place which serve to ensure that our children are looked after effectively, and these systems provide the final backstop of safety to children who may run wild or become uncontrollable. For those children who are driven to extreme behaviour by the effects of a disintegrating family, it is good to know that there is someone there who will catch them and treat them well.

Summary

- **Grown-ups** can make a difference by looking after the 28 per cent of children who come from broken homes and supporting their parents.
- **Mothers** need support in order not to feel alone and to have things to look forward to. They also need to look after themselves if they are going to be in any shape to look after their children. This may necessitate a call for professional support, should they feel themselves to be tipping into depression or an inability to cope. Mothers also need to be able to forgive themselves, should they occasionally find themselves behaving in a less than elegant manner. Comfort is a necessity, and behaviour that seems out of character can and should be forgiven.
- **Fathers** also need support from friends and family, but with a different emphasis. Men are more traditionally private in their suffering; it can help if they are encouraged to talk about their problems and be given practical help with organizing parenting and family tasks which may be new to them.
- **Grandparents** have an important role to play. A non-judgemental 'being-there' kind of approach works best for both parents and children. The older generation can help greatly by bringing in new routines, security and fun to replace those that have been lost. It is advisable for grandparents to avoid taking sides in front of the children and making negative remarks about ex-sons- and daughters-in-law. Grandparents can be badly hurt if excluded from the lives of their grandchildren, and it is in the interests of both parents and children if contact and relationships with grandparents can be nurtured.
- **Family, friends and neighbours** can do a lot to help out and mop

up. Emotional and physical support in the early days can be followed up with practical help such as school runs, shopping and sleepovers to help the often exhausted single parent. As time goes by, an accepting, listening ear and time for parents or children who are struggling will give loving stability to the new order.

- **Teachers** are increasingly important players in the lives of pupils who tumble into class with the news that their parents have broken up. It is good practice for parents to tell the teacher privately what the situation is. Their understanding can make a real difference in helping a child through tough times. It is good for teachers to confer with each other, to make some allowances and understand that work and concentration will often slip. However, there are as yet no general guidelines for teachers on what to do, and it is normally left to individual personalities and is dependent on the ethos of the school.

- **Doctors and therapists** can help children who display physical or behavioural symptoms of distress or who are obviously unhappy and cannot be reached by their immediate community. If the situation behind the suffering of a child is understood, his strange aches and pains, inability to get to school or return to wetting the bed will make more sense. Parents or carers should give as much information as possible to professionals so that help can be given quickly and effectively.

- **Lawyers** greatly influence the way in which a divorce is conducted, and their actions have an important effect on the lives of the children. A wise adult will choose an experienced, well-trained lawyer who understands that there are no winners in divorce and that the children need to be considered at every turn. Mediation and collaborative law should be considered, since a conciliatory approach is likely to avoid a build-up of negative emotions and huge bills.

- **The social services**, like teachers, are being asked to mop up the problems being created by the social experiment of single parenting. They provide an essential backstop and safety net for children in real distress, poverty and danger. Issues of child protection sometimes require that they be called in. But, with so much else to attend to, and with regional and individual disparities of care, they seldom have the resources to do the necessary repair work on families. However, the suggestion that the social services may need to become involved can often bring about an improvement in the behaviour of parents who would do better if they put their children at the top of their list of priorities.

- **The police**, in my experience, are excellent when dealing with children and have a high quality of training. Children who roam streets, sleep rough in parks, climb on to roofs and end up involved with street gangs are gently and responsibly treated with an eye to child protection, the need for a 'responsible adult' and a sense of humour that is impressive. Of course, I do not want any child to need police protection or attention, but it is comforting to know that, when it comes to vulnerable youth, the police are consistent, well trained, humane and reliable.

3 · · · · ·

Children: different ages and different stages

HAVING DISCUSSED THE IMPORTANCE of the role of adults in helping young people cope with the worst effects of family breakdown, attention needs to be given to the children themselves and the various stages of their development.

Children come in different shapes and different sizes. They come with their own unique blueprint, and they have their own strengths and weaknesses, foibles and way of thinking, laughing and being in this world. The individuality of a child can be even more magical than that of an adult, in that they have not yet had their edges rounded off. They are fun and fascinating, and it is a privilege to be allowed to join them in the exploration of the workings of their inner world. Once a working relationship with a child has been established, their age becomes an irrelevance; what a five-year-old has to show me in pictures is as important and meaningful as what a teenager might tell me more directly, and often as wise as anything an adult might say. However, if the age of a child can be of little significance in the privacy of our sessions, it becomes hugely important in the real world when trying to work out practical strategies to help a child in trouble. While powerful, negative and frightening emotions are universal and difficult to withstand, different age groups have diverse coping mechanisms and tasks to get through in order to grow up as well as possible during a challenging time. A five-year-old is not going to behave in the same way as a fourteen-year-old when faced with infinite sadness, though both need to know that they are safe and that the adults in their life are in charge.

When a marriage falls apart and a parent leaves the home, negative emotions will fill the household and the life of a child. Sadness, fear, confusion, anger, guilt and/or a sense of abandonment are to be expected. These feelings can be countered by positive behaviour on the part of adults if, despite their own problems and arguments, they can still provide their children with love, integrity, honesty, self care, consistency and structure. From toddler to teen, all our children need us to care for them and to maintain a framework of safety from which they can explore and grow, and which they can eventually leave.

Children need different kinds of care according to their ages and stages of development. Babies, pre-school children, five- to ten-year-olds, ten- to thirteen-year-olds and teenagers have specific developmental tasks that require special consideration. Some guidelines, however, apply to children of all ages.

All children will need:

Honesty and an age-appropriate explanation of what is going on. Children are extraordinarily intuitive and, once they have got an idea that something is wrong, they will ferret out secrets, often get them wrong and then store their interpretation as truth, which may form a dubious database that can afflict their future.

Parents who can look after themselves. Children should not feel burdened by their parents' unhappiness or inability to cope. A child who is not able to live life and join in the healthy pursuits of childhood or adolescence because he or she has to keep an eye on a parent could grow up with a lot more issues that will need to be resolved.

Reassurance that there is nothing that they can do to get their parents get back together again. This sense of responsibility for the state of the marriage of their parents needs to be taken away, so that a child is free to be a child.

An understanding that many children will become nervous and start believing that only bad things happen. If one parent leaves, then they may imagine that the remaining parent might leave as well. Disastrous scenarios seem completely possible to a child who has experienced disaster. Younger children can suffer separation anxiety, while older children find it hard to establish relationships of trust with others since, in their experience, people leave them. Faith in adults may be undermined, and much needs to be done to encourage and allow a child to rebuild trust after their world has been shattered.

Conversation. Children lack the words and the experience with which to talk about loss and grief. Instead of using words they express their emotions through everyday behaviour and through games. There will be different behaviours according to age and some will appear regressive, difficult or unattractive. The behaviour of a child needs to be interpreted by adults just as if he or she were speaking. Conversation can be found in what our children do. If we understand, we will not lose touch and we will keep our children close during a time when it is all too easy for them to spin away from parents who themselves are spinning.

Some forms of parenting and caring are specific to the different developmental stages.

Babies and the first year

From the moment a child is conceived, its mother needs to look after herself in as loving and gentle a way as possible while maintaining good standards of health and fitness. Research from all over the world increasingly shows that foetuses sense and feel when their watery world is safe and calm. Similarly, they are damaged by high levels of anxiety, stress and the unfriendly chemical cortisol which travels with highly charged and negative emotion. Happy endorphins and a happy pregnancy have been shown to create happy babies, while high levels of cortisol and stress are a factor in why some babies are underweight, born early and difficult to manage once they arrive in the world. If this is the case, then family and friends will be doing a good job if they can help maintain the mother's equilibrium and keep her as contented as possible during her pregnancy. However, it is not unusual for a divorce or separation to happen before a child is born, and I have had clients whose parents split up while they were still in the womb. These children have had a difficult journey by the time they come to my consulting room. Usually they will have had very little input from a father and they will have been brought up by mothers who have to be both Mum and Dad. As babies, they might have suffered from the lack of calm maternal attention, quiet gazing and sweet play that is so important, because their mothers were too emotionally distraught or too busy to give it. They also will know that something is missing in their lives and, as they grow, they will realize what it is and be full of questions that can find no words while they wonder why other children have fathers who pick them up from nursery school, toss them playfully in the swimming pool and light candles on cakes to celebrate a birthday.

One of the main problems to be found when working with mothers who have been abandoned while pregnant, or who have walked away from the father of their child, is their unchallengeable lioness-like quality when it comes to managing their children. While it is admirable and understandable for a mother to want to protect her child, there can be a negative flip side when a woman has to be both mother and father. Children can find themselves being parented by a determined, strong-willed and sometimes unreasonable woman who feels that she must fight all of life's battles. Over-protection can prevent a child from growing up with a sense of right and wrong, responsibility or fair play, and in its own way is as troublesome to children as the opposite problem of neglect.

Thomas is an example of what can go wrong when a child is left by his father before he is even born. Thomas's father left him and his mother and went to build a home in another country with another woman and to start life all over again. Abandoned at a time of vulnerability and huge need, Thomas's mother got through her final term of pregnancy and the birth of her child in anger and disbelief. From the moment she put Thomas to her breast, Ella knew that she was alone with her child and that she must fight for him in order for them to survive. There was no money unless she made it, no home unless she found one, and no close companionship possible while she had to find a place in the world for herself and her son. Ella did well. She put a life together which, from the outside, looked successful, and she declared herself to be happy with her lot. Thomas fulfilled his necessary developmental milestones and seemed to be contented as a young child. Problems, however, began to emerge as he grew older. I met him by the time he had gone to his third school. He was only eight, but he saw absolutely no need for rules or regulations and believed that the behaviour expected of everyone else in the world did not apply to him. In his eyes, he was allowed to hit, to take things and to fight anyone who got in the way of his pursuit of instant gratification.

Ella, Thomas and I worked together for three years. It was

81

hard to battle against Ella's belief that she must fight all her child's fights and also love him unconditionally and make up for the loss of his father. She would not allow Thomas to be told off at school or have discipline imposed upon him, and if a teacher requested homework that was late, Ella would rush into the school office with an angry explanation as to why it was impossible for a son who had no father and a working mother to deliver his homework on time. The school came to dread her arrival and, at the same time, they could not get Thomas to cooperate. With no father to counter his mother's loving but destructive behaviour, Thomas floundered and found himself expelled from school after school until, the last I heard, he had given up education altogether. His mother, in her anger at her own abandonment and her belief that she must protect her child, had allowed her son to grow up with no sense of fending for himself or subordinating his own immediate wishes to those of broader society. Though well meaning, she had done him no favours by overcompensating for the absence of his father.

Mothers like Ella will be familiar to teachers, doctors and therapists. They are difficult to help because they are on adrenaline-fuelled red alert. Suggestions may be taken as criticism and requests to comply as an attack. Life has been tough on them, and they lash out to protect their children but cannot relax to enjoy them. Therapy would be a good idea but is rarely seen as such, and kindness and care are not always necessarily welcome. Mothers who have had to fight for their child understandably find it hard to relax, have fun or let go of the tight reins of control. In therapy, they are so well defended that they are hard to help. It is difficult to reach a mother who has already done so much and fought so hard for a child that she feels she has to protect with every inch of her being. She will not be helping herself or her child if she does not learn to become less of a warrior and show a softer side to a world which could support her.

The best way to help children who are caught in the sad situation of having no father and an angry, over-protective mother is to spend time alone with them playing games, painting pictures and making puzzles while talking and musing about nothing in particular and always circling around efforts to get a child to take more responsibility for his behaviour, his life and the things that he needs to do with it. As he gets older, a child will benefit by understanding that he is not a victim in an unfair world and, as he grows up, he will need to learn that he is responsible for himself. Wider society can help these lonely children by issuing invitations to traditional family events such as Halloween and fireworks parties so that they can join in with the hugger-mugger of family life. They will feel included and know that there is somewhere to turn other than to a mother who is obviously doing her best but is not able to provide the boisterous nonsense that belongs to a larger family. I have often seen two-parent families virtually give a home to their single-parent friends, including them automatically in Sunday lunches, fairground visits, walks along the river, firework displays and any other family event that is going on in their lives. This kindness and care, which seems to come so naturally to some families, can provide essential nurture to a young child and enable him to grow up with happy memories and the necessary experience of belonging to a wider world.

When parents break up while a baby is still in the womb or is still very young, there is no experience of co-parenting on which to build and therefore it is hard for both mother and father to look after their child. But, whatever the reason for the break-up and however great the acrimony between the couple, parents should try to work together as parents. The children that I know whose fathers have been allowed to bond with them and remain in their lives, even though they did not live with the mothers from before they were born, are happier, more responsible and more successful than the children who have little or no paternal influence. If paternal involvement is truly impossible, then perhaps the paternal grandparents can be encouraged to take a role in the life of the child. The mother will get a well-needed break, which will make her a better mother, and she will be able to do more with her life and have more time to heal her wounds. The child will have additional role models, plus the bonus of knowledge of his or her paternal history and family roots. Mothers, however angry, will greatly help their children if they can facilitate this type of arrangement and allow their child to play with and be looked after by those who have passed on the other 50 per cent of their genetic inheritance. Sadly, the breakdown of relationships while the baby is unborn can be so toxic that communication between families becomes impossible, with the result that both mother and child lose an important part of their potential support system.

A new mother struggling on her own, exhausted and without the back-up of a supportive male figure who will bring her supper, rub her back, take over some of the burden of the sleepless nights and tell her he loves her and that she is doing a great job will find life, at its best, difficult and, at its worst, well nigh impossible. If ever there was a time for friendship and family support it is now. Shopping, baby-sitting, invitations, telephone calls and a non-judgemental being there will help assuage the loneliness of the mother with a young child who has lost the physical and emotional support of a co-parent as well as suffering from the end of a particular and universal dream. I have also known of fathers who have been walked out on and left holding the baby. They too have to face confusion, hurt and a need to earn a living while sorting out a whole host of things they never expected to have to do, and they need as much help as young mothers when they find themselves having to cope alone. Friends, family and the broader community can do a great deal to help ensure that a mother or father is in a good enough state to provide security, attention, warmth, love, safety, structure and playful humour to their baby. As a consequence, the infant will be able to experience healthy attachment; the world will become a less confusing and lonely place and damage will be kept to a minimum.

Pre-school

There was once a belief that children were 'too young' to know what was going on and that it was better if they were kept away from tragedy, difficulties and unpleasantness. This belief was applied to death, mourning and the loss of a parent through divorce, and society tended to take refuge in the idea that young children did not hurt in the same ways we did and that they were free to play while older children and adults lived with the difficult tensions of the household. Understanding has moved on, and there is now a general view that the younger a child is when she suffers the blow of the loss of a parent, the more damaging it will be to her development. She will be a parent short to help her build her world, and the parent that she does have will probably be too exhausted and tired to give her as much attention as she might need.

As babies in the womb suffer from their mother's distress, so a very small child will pick up signals that life is not as it should be. An emotionally challenged parent will find it hard to play endless games of peek-a-boo and could fail to notice the one-year-old's pleasure in dropping his toy to see it magically reappear on the table again. Repetitive games of exploration and glorious delight in being the centre of the universe are curtailed when that universe is clouded by the impending or actual break-up of a home. Instead of learning that he is safe and interesting and in the midst of a wonderful world, a child who is stuck in the middle of mayhem or being looked after by a sad and exhausted single parent will in all probability learn the exact opposite. He might not feel safe, he is not the centre of the universe and he will not learn to play. This negative life lesson can have a fundamental impact on his developing sense of self. Instead of discovering and building a strong and good ego, he will probably have a deep wound at his core. Not only has he been abandoned by one parent, but he finds himself with a parent who is too busy to play with him. He will be too young to understand what is going on and assume that there is something wrong with him if no one is there to take any notice.

A dramatic example of a child who exhibited signs of near madness due to the behaviour of her parents is Lilly, who was three when her father left her home, although she had witnessed and ingested shouting and violence for all of her young life. Her mother had married a difficult and unhappy man and, although they had three children, the marriage was probably failing from the day it began. Depression stalked the mother while anger infused the father and, as a way of escape from a poisonous stalemate, the mother tried to leave the family home with the children. Lilly and her two siblings had to watch an unhappy drama playing itself out, with the final act involving a broken front door, a golf club and the police being called. The older children could escape from the terror and receive help at school, but Lilly was left alone at home with a mother who was unable to look after her child and curled herself into a ball, whimpering in fear that 'the bad man might come back.' Lilly, who needed a mother who could play with her, feed her, put her to bed on time and read her stories, found herself stroking her mother's back in an attempt to make Mummy feel better. When Lilly should have been in her own bed by early evening, she was still awake at midnight and waiting for her mother so that she could sleep with her arms wrapped tightly around her mother's neck to make sure that she did not sneak away during the night. When Lilly wanted to know where her father was and why she could not see him any more, she was told that he was a difficult and dangerous man and that it would be better if she forgot about him and watched a nice video instead. Lilly's father did not make matters any better. He refused to pay maintenance and would not attend the supervised meetings that had been set up by the court on the grounds that the place was 'unpleasant' and it was demeaning to be watched over by a member of the social services. Lilly lost all touch with her father. He could not be redeemed or redeem himself, and her mother sank into a deeper depression, which lack of money and extreme exhaustion did nothing to help.

Whichever way she turned, Lilly could not find the security she needed. There was no room for love, no time for play, no strong parent who made her feel safe and the memory of a violent and difficult father whom she both loved and was afraid of. All she had in her small life was a mother who could barely cope. No telephone calls were answered, friends dropped away, the rest of the family lived on the other side of the world and the household sank into a stagnant pit of despair. Too frightened to be alone, Lilly kept vigil throughout the night, allowing no one any rest and, when she was not clinging to her mother, she was in the fridge eating up its contents in an attempt to find some comfort.

Lilly was one of the brightest and most extraordinary children I have ever worked with. She was the sort of child who would be alone in the playground and chosen last for games. She was bossy but frightened; she needed to be in charge but didn't know what to do; she was incredibly rude but wanted to be loved; and she was convinced that she was right even though she could not have been more wrong. Things were so bad for Lilly that she took refuge in her imagination, but she created a frightening world. Inside her were monsters that lived in her brain and were eating her head. She could draw them, paint them and make them out of clay. She gave them names and would alternately clamp her hands to her head and wish that they would go or say that they were her only friends and that she wanted to keep them. These monsters kept the reality of her daily life at bay. With monsters she did not need to be afraid that Mummy would not wake up. With monsters she did not have to remember that she had got in the way of the golf club. With monsters in her head she did not have to face the fact that she was lonely. The monsters meant that she did not have to do what she was told because she had a perfect reason why she would and could not go to bed at night and needed to steal the last piece of chocolate cake: the monsters made her do it.

Slowly and carefully, I befriended these monsters. We made them out of clay and gave them hair and faces and physical expression and kept them in a doll's house and worked out which one Lilly wanted and needed and why. And as their needs became explicit, the monsters changed and, one by one, Lilly would choose a little doll to replace the screwed-up, distorted and gnarled figure that wanted love or attention, or to play a game or to go to the park. And as each 'monster' began to talk, I would give it what it needed or look to see if the wider world could help. While Lilly worked with me, her mother faced her depression, found medication and unfurled herself from a place of abject misery. The school that the boys went to took Lilly into their infant class, gave her attention and boundaries and watched her food intake. We were never able to get Lilly's father to cooperate with the process of bringing his daughter back from the edge of madness. But we were able to tell Lilly what had happened and help her make sense of his leaving while letting her know that, although her parents could not get along, her father had once upon a time loved her mother and his daughter very much. Life is still tough in Lilly's household. There is no money, and few friends to support Lilly and her mother. However, therapists, doctors and schoolteachers were allowed to step in, and Lilly is now well and going through school using her exquisite brain in the right way and having friends who are no longer imaginary.

Lilly's story is extreme but not unique. One of the reasons that Lilly suffered so badly was the isolation within her home. Her mother's depression and shame and the fact that the maternal family lived in Australia meant that few people were available to help her. I have seen other families that have experienced violence, traumatic leave-taking and confused relationships, but there has been more support available. The children have fared better and have not needed therapy or medical help to unravel the trauma of their early years.

Sebastian was helped by the outside world when his home life fell apart. When his alcoholic father walked out, leaving only debts and bad memories, his mother found herself so depressed that she had to check into hospital. In one way Sebastian had a rougher ride of it than Lilly; he lost his home and he lost his mother to a six-week stay in a clinic. However, he had invaluable support from both sets of grandparents, a large collection of aunts and uncles, committed godparents and a brilliant headmaster. Sebastian was rarely alone and was invited to join the households of others and so he learnt how to live through a huge extended family that made him welcome. I never needed to see him as a client; because of the sadness of his story his headmaster flagged him up for me to watch and I kept an eye on him in the playground and through his report cards as he made his way through primary school. He was a joy to watch as he played football and ran with his friends; he also produced satisfactory work. His extended family and network did a wonderful job, which involved much more than damage limitation and ensured that he grew up without having to face the type of demons that belonged to Lilly.

When children are very young there is not much that therapy can do unless the broader family is included. Up until the age of five, children are too young to make much sense of what therapy has to offer; personalities are forming and parents and familiar adults are needed to provide a bubble of love and security from hour to hour and day to day. One hour a week is of little use unless the family becomes available to make a difference to the daily life of a small person. I tend to work with as many adults as are prepared to work with me. I ask parents to join me and, if necessary, seek permission to talk to a wider circle. I have met grandparents and older siblings and talked to godparents, aunts and uncles on the phone. I have conferred with GPs and, at times, I have needed to talk to the social services. As I work, I attempt to make a safety basket that is of benefit to the entire family and which will cradle the small child in the way that the loving arms of a mother and a father were meant to do. From this refuge, the child has the opportunity of fulfilling the developmental requirements of his age range. He or she can then move on to primary school not too afraid, not too muddled and not too damaged. Caring and careful adults will have made a difference and, for one person at least, the world will be a better place.

Five to ten

By five years of age children have been to nursery, started school, been through the terrible twos and even threes and begun to develop their own personalities. They will have learnt whether or not their world is a safe place and have unconsciously ingested all sorts of ideas about love and affection and attachment. The five- to ten-year-old age group learn so fast, and their minds expand so quickly. Yet they hold on to a magical quality, so fairy tales are still real, Father Christmas still comes, ghosts live at the bottom of the garden and often bad men want to get in through the window at night. They inhabit their own world, in which imagined things can seem very real; everything is possible, be it good or bad, and it is wonderful to be invited to be part of it when they trust you enough to tell you their magical stories.

Lilly, the extraordinary four-year-old from the previous section, had an unshakeable belief in the reality of the monsters that were eating her brain. In our work together we had to make them even more real before we could diminish their power. She was so young that she could not challenge her vivid imagination with a friendly reality check; for me to tell her that there were no monsters would just have confirmed to her that nobody understood and that nobody would ever be able to help. Children over five are easier to reach; their brains have developed sufficiently for them to understand adult thinking, and they can live in two worlds. They have their own, which is filled with fantasy and magic and, as they grow older, they learn about the adult world, which is necessarily more mundane.

While their understanding is increasing, children in this age group will not yet have the words to express their emotional highs and lows. Instead of telling us that they are happy and excited they will whirl around the garden, jump on a bed, dance in the sitting room and splash in the bath. If we are lucky, they will hold us tight when we put them to bed and tell us that they love us but, usually, they will show us by bringing us things and asking us to watch and to play and to join them. The same holds for the negative raft of emotions that children need to experience. When they are sad or jealous or scared or angry, they will find it hard to tell us but will show us by their actions and their body language what it is that they are feeling. An eight-year-old pinching a younger sibling, a six-year-old throwing his fish fingers across the room, a seven-year-old who will not sleep on her own or let her mother go out for the evening, or a nine-year-old who suddenly refuses to join in the much-loved after-school netball club are all telling us in ways that can be more poignant than language that they are suffering.

Understanding a child's way of expressing negative emotion is an important skill. It takes time for an adult to understand why the orange juice has been tipped over at the breakfast table for the fourth morning running, and effort to sort it out. But time and effort can be in short supply for a naughty child who is making everyone late for school, especially when the household is reeling from the drama of divorce and the adults within it are doing a pretty good job to have everyone dressed in the first place. Sometimes a little extra help is needed in order to understand the negative language of the child. Parents who know when it is time to ask for help deserve respect. Mothers and fathers at the end of their tether who seek advice from families, friends, the community or the professionals within it show that they are coping and have the wisdom to use the resources that are available. It is very easy to give a hand if asked, and it is a delight to be with children who are prepared to include us in their play. To be able to work with the vivid imagination and creativity that is part and parcel of the mindset of the five- to ten-year-old, while guiding them towards an acceptance of their reality, is to be invited to walk with them on a unique and moving journey.

Jessica is a good example of a child who mixed up fantasy and reality and who needed some help unravelling the muddle that she had created in her mind. She had lost her father to another continent when she was seven. Early one morning, he had simply packed his possessions and, without another word, flown away, leaving a young woman to struggle alone with two children, not knowing where or why he had gone. Holly had to move home, find new schools for her children and get a job. While she managed with remarkable strength, she was still unable to protect her children from the fact that their father had abandoned them with no explanation or warning. With her mother able only to give the honest answer of 'I don't know' to the question 'Where is Daddy?', Jessica came up with her own explanation. Rather than face the reality that her father had left her, she decided that he had gone abroad to do an impossibly important job that involved saving the family and even maybe the world. Her father gained James Bond-like status and Jessica created an imaginary hero. However, his mission was top secret and she could not talk about him to her friends or in the school setting. Also, if the world had taken her father from her in order to make it a safer place, then her world was not to be trusted. Jessica found herself living with two opposite myths: one that her father was a superhero, and the other that bad men would come through the window at night and steal her mother. She stopped concentrating at her new school, she would not go to bed and she got up every night in the early hours of the morning, waking her mother up from her much-needed sleep, to check that she was still there.

Beautifully behaved, beautifully brought up, Jessica entered therapy looking like a television advertisement for what girl-shaped childhood should be. Our first few sessions involved discussions about collectable toys, girlfriends in the playground, cooking chocolate brownies, TV programmes and the acute tedium of mathematics. Only Holly's report of the three o'clock in the morning visits and the double and triple checking to make sure that there were no bad men under the bed told that all was not well in Jessica's world, but it took some while for her to confide her nightmares and her dreams. A huge piece of lining wallpaper and a large collection of poster paints helped reach the pain and fear for which Jessica could find no words. She painted a scene that started as sunny and ended up as sad. It was one that made her cry as she worked and explained it to me in her seven-year-old language. A happy seaside holiday memory of sun and sand and blue waves ended up as a picture of a man being trapped deep beneath the water in a cave, with a shark lying in wait in case he should attempt to come out. Jessica put herself into the picture as a small girl in tears who was holding out a rope like a fishing line in the hope that the man in the cave could catch hold and be rescued.

It was not difficult to work out that the man was her lost

father, that she was trying to find him and that her sunny world was not all that it seemed. Tears were shed, and Jessica made the simple statement that 'I am not happy.' The mythical hero of her dreams was overturned, and I called in Mum to cry with her daughter about the end of one particular world and to start to work out how to live as well as possible in a new one. This help included understanding Jessica's night-time antics and gave her encouragement to trust that her mother was not going anywhere, while introducing consequences for waking her mother up and rewards for staying in her own bed. By carefully instilling structure into her disrupted life, Jessica was made to feel safer than if she had been allowed to continue to run the household with her demands that her mother not go out and her habit of midnight roaming. Although Jessica did not want to accept the difficult reality that her father had left her family, she was able to face the problem head on when her mother carefully told her the truth about her father's leaving and his new life. With the sensitive help of her mother, she was able to come to terms with her sad truth, and a little girl who had temporarily spun into a world of make-believe was brought back to earth so that she could get on with her life.

The vivid imagination of the under-tens can be disturbing to the remaining family. Once one parent has gone, the fear of losing the other parent can suddenly become very real, and it is quite natural for children in this situation to go on red alert and watch the remaining parent like a hawk. I have had children come to me because they spend their school days imagining that their mothers have had appalling accidents and that every emergency siren sounds for them. I have seen exhausted parents who cannot even go upstairs to complete a task or get a moment's peace because of a child's fear of being left alone. And I frequently work with adults who have no life of their own because their children are too scared to let them out of their sight.

It does not work to tell the children to stop being silly, that nothing will happen to Mum or to Dad and to just relax and go to bed. Something awful has already happened and children by this point will have learnt a lesson that cannot be unlearnt – that bad things happen and grown-ups cannot stop them from happening.

I deeply regret a promise that I once made. Mia either had a premonition or she knew of a deeper vulnerability in her divorced mother than I had been allowed to see. She trusted me and sought me out to speak of her fears that her mother was going to die and that she would be alone. I joined the ranks of adults who told her that there was nothing to worry about; that her mother was going to be all right and that Mia was suffering from natural anxiety because of the process of her parents' separation. But Clara did die, suddenly and unexpectedly, just after Christmas, and Mia lost her mother just as she told me she would. My empty promise sits heavily in my heart, and I learnt a difficult lesson at the expense of a child when I helped to prove that adults were absolutely not to be trusted.

We cannot tell a child that they have nothing to fear, because we do not know what lies around the corner. We can, however, reassure a child that we will be around for that hour, that day, that week, that month, that year, and we can tell them that we love them and want to spend the rest of our lives with them until they are sick of the sight of us and are ready to up sticks and start to live in a home of their own. We can encourage children to go out, developing their own autonomy while we wait for them in the park, under a tree, in the school playground and at home making their supper. While we cannot promise that nothing bad will ever happen, we can promise that they are the most important thing in our lives and that we have no intention of leaving them or wish to disappear.

When children between the ages of five and ten lose the structure that has anchored them to their world they can spin off with behaviour that is difficult to manage. Boys, particularly, have the potential to cause all sorts of problems in the classroom and in the newly formed separate family homes. When their world loses its roots, a source of authority is removed and young hearts are full of negative emotion; children may respond with uncontrollable behaviour in which hitting, lying and stealing are not unusual and not concentrating is the norm. They can behave as if they have some kind of learning difficulty, such as ADHD, and, if the real causes are not correctly identified and help sought, they may end up with a label in the classroom that does not necessarily describe them.

Josh was eight when I met him and was difficult to manage following the separation of his parents. He could not read and would not write and spent his days at school looking out of the window, pulling funny faces, distracting whomever he sat next to and attempting to make the other children laugh. His behaviour was so difficult, with his pinching and biting and refusal to do what he was told, that the parents of the other children organized a petition to the headmaster asking for something to be done. Rather than expel a child who was already suffering from the effects of a particularly vicious parental break-up, his headmaster sent Josh to me and told me that I had until the end of the school year to change his behaviour. This was a tall order. Here was a child who could not and did not want to read, who wanted to be a cowboy, who obsessively collected weapons to be used on his older sister and who rang his mother if he did not like what his father said and his father if his mother asked him to do his homework.

Not all children enjoy the discipline of learning to read or the grind of letter formation, but nearly all will sit at tiny desks with pencil gripped hard and apply themselves in order to conquer the patterns of words and the shapes of the alphabet. Pleasure is gained by being moved up a book or being told that at last one can write in pen rather than in the blunt pencil of infancy.

Playing comes when the bell rings. But Josh played all the time; there was no break between the classroom and the school playground, and he learnt nothing while alienating those around him. A sunny small boy ended up as the class clown and playground scapegoat whom nobody wanted to sit next to on the school bus and who never got invited to tea.

An educational psychologist's report told me that Josh did not have a learning disability and that he had the capacity to begin to improve his behaviour to a level where he could concentrate on the important tasks ahead. He had to learn to read, to write, to do his homework and to accept that he was not a cowboy hero but a small sad boy who was unable to fit in. His father would not help and called me 'that woman' in a dismissive tone whenever my name was mentioned. While Josh was receiving clear instructions from me in order to remain in a school where he was happy, I was being threatened with legal action by a man who did not believe in therapy or the possibility of emotional disturbance. Once again, Josh found himself caught in the middle of two warring grown-ups. Once again, he did not know whom to believe or whose instructions to follow and, once again, he ended up going round and round in self-destructive circles, hurting nobody but himself and unable to use the good brain with which he had been born. Luckily, his school, his mother and our therapy made a strong team and, together, we were able to impose a system on daily life for Josh that shortcircuited the destructive patterns learnt from the process of the break-up of his parents. He was put into homework club after school and not allowed to leave until his tasks were complete; he got extra tuition which concentrated on catching up with his reading; his mother listened to his plodding sounding out of letters every night and then would read to him from favourite books for eight-year-olds; he was rewarded for working and trying, and lost marks and toys and treats for refusing and screaming and hitting. In order to help him contain his manic energy he had drum and judo lessons and practised within a contained environment rather than being allowed to hit out at random. On Wednesdays, when he went to stay with his father, nothing was expected of him; it was explained to the school that no homework would be done and no catch-up would be possible. Therefore a blind eye was turned to missing prep, and he was not put in the wrong for something that was initially his father's responsibility. With the use of puppets and small dolls we created a theatre show where it became possible for Josh to see that his parents had two different sets of belief systems, that both his mother and his father loved him very much but that they did things differently. From this place of understanding and ultimate comfort Josh was also able to see that he was doing himself no favours by refusing to do what was expected of him, and that it might be a good idea if he settled down to his task and did what he was told. Because he was bright, he learnt to read and write. Because his mother supported me, she took his weapons away and made it clear that it was unacceptable to beat people up. And because Josh improved in his behaviour and in his schoolwork, his father grudgingly thanked the school for stepping in and eventually began to call me by my name. He too joined the team effort to bring his son back down to earth so that Josh could join his peers in their age-appropriate development and not be considered a trouble-maker.

Our primary schools will have a Josh in almost every class. These children find it easier to escape the reality of their lives at home by evading the truth that their parents no longer love each other and the fear that maybe their parents might not love them either. Instead of going down into the depths of depression and despair they go up into the clouds and rush around in a whirlwind of ungrounded activity.

Difficult to manage, impossible to teach, they are a real challenge to the people who are responsible for their well being. They need to be brought down to earth, to be grounded and to be settled, and yet they don't want to be. It can feel cruel to make a young child see the truth, and it is hard to burst a bubble that he has built for his own protection. However, bubbles of unreality do not serve children well if they mean that they cannot cope with daily life. The bubbles need to be burst as gently as possible by careful adults who are able to provide a soft landing and a world in which their youngsters want to live.

Magical thinking, fearful worst-case scenarios and attempts to escape from harsh reality are three understandable coping mechanisms for children in the five- to ten-year-old age group who do not and cannot take on the full impact of what is happening within their broken families. By fabricating stories and refusing to take responsibility, a child can avoid that which is too painful to contemplate and leave adults wondering how best to help.

A further strategy that children can employ and one that combines elements of both denial and fabrication is the use of an exaggerated sense of power. Accepted wisdom has it that children often feel guilty when their parents split up and that they believe that it is something they did which made the parent walk away. In my experience, this sense of guilt in its simple form is relatively rare, perhaps because parents and other adults are now so well educated that they are able to reassure their children that they have nothing to do with the break-up. However, while I rarely find a child who literally believes that he or she has somehow smashed a marriage, I do more frequently encounter children who believe that they can put it back together again.

Rebecca took an interesting approach when she attempted to get rid of the obstacle that stood in the way of her parents getting back together. She was seven when her mother sent her to me because she had taken to cutting neat little holes in her stepfather's clothes. The precise use of a pair of scissors in one so young was a wonder. Small V-shapes had disappeared from worksuit sleeves, tiny holes had appeared under the arms of sweaters, and pyjama bottoms had developed mysterious holes in the crotch. Rebecca's mother had moved into a new house with her new husband, was expecting another baby and had moved Rebecca to a new school. For her, a stable life had replaced a difficult period of single motherhood which had ensued after her previous unsatisfactory marriage ended when Rebecca was only four. On the surface, Rebecca had it all: a better school, a happier mother who no longer had to work every day, a bigger bedroom and a soon-to-be-born new baby whom she had been asking for ever since she could remember. And yet Rebecca was not happy. She was jealous of her stepfather and she wanted her real father even though he played little part in her life, having retreated to study poetry and pursue personal enlightenment on an island off the coast of Scotland.

Although a wedding and a pregnancy should have provided evidence to the contrary, Rebecca held it firmly in her seven-year-old mind that she could destroy the new relationship and return her mother to her father. Thus the scissors and various other strategies, such as spying on her mother's sex life and walking in at inopportune moments, made sense to Rebecca, in her hope that, somehow, her father could replace the man in her mother's bed. It mattered not a jot that her stepfather was a kind man who was prepared to treat her as his own and indeed much better than her real father had ever done. In her play with me Rebecca demonstrated again and again that she wanted to destroy and bury the man whom she felt had stolen her mother and go and find her father and put him back where he belonged within a close and happy family unit. There was no reality in her play; there never had been a happy family unit; if there was any happiness to be found, she was to find it in her new life. She refused to accept her stepfather and wrote notes, letters and emails to a parent from whom she rarely received a reply. She begged and begged that he be allowed to visit her and stay in the new house and insisted that her poverty-stricken father's fare be paid for, and that he arrive and be looked after while her stepfather moved out. When thwarted in her demands she threw tantrums more appropriate to a two-year-old and once scared her mother by disappearing from the house without notice to join other children playing in the park.

Rebecca's mother was pretty much at the end of her tether by the time she came to talk to me. She loved her daughter and worried for her, she did not want to hurt her and she wanted to protect her, perhaps a little like the lioness mums I have already discussed. She wondered whether she should leave her new home and husband but knew that she could do nothing about the new life she carried in her tummy. My view was that she had given of her very best to her young daughter and that it was time for her child to accept her new reality and stop being so tyrannical in her attempts to turn back time and try to find a family ideal that had never existed in the first place.

But Rebecca needed a helping hand in order to accept her present life. Her romantic father lived in a far-off world of make-believe and had been unable to let go of his relationship with Rebecca's mother. He had unwittingly fed his daughter with an idealized version of their marriage and with a belief that they were 'meant' to be together. He had therefore unintentionally given a small girl the ammunition with which to fight reality. If her own father had told his child that her mother and he were destined to be together, it is difficult to blame her for holding on to her deepest wish and therefore attempting to sabotage her new life.

To turn Rebecca around required both parents and the new stepfather to perform a remarkably sensitive task. Her father eventually saw the harm that his fantasy was doing to his daughter and began to dismantle it. Her mother, while understanding the scissors and prepared to sacrifice her own happiness, actually saw that standing up to Rebecca's unacceptable behaviour would eventually do her daughter more good. And her stepfather had the patience to stand back and wait for Rebecca to see him as the likeable person he was rather than the hateful symbol of the father's disappearance. Rebecca began to understand that it was over, that a new life had begun and that her father had left for Scotland because he had wanted to and that that was where he had made his life. She was therefore able to put the scissors away, welcome a baby sister, stop screaming around the house and running away from home and start to build her own life with the adults appropriately in charge.

The dilemma for adults dealing with the difficult behaviour of the five- to ten-year-old suffering child is understandable. When faced with comprehensible misery, it is difficult to be strong and perhaps a little tough, especially when the child is so very young. However, adults will be doing no favours to the small people in their care if they allow them to get away with unacceptable behaviour; if they do not carefully and sensitively readjust the negative magical thinking; if they do not provide a trustworthy and reliable base from which children can go out and explore; and if they do not discuss and diffuse the fear that there is a catastrophe around every corner. With careful management, children whose lives have been temporarily bent out of shape can find themselves back on the right course towards the next stage of their development. Without careful management, these children may begin to ready themselves to make a whole heap of trouble as they enter the turbulent pre-adolescent years.

Ten to thirteen

The theory of child development rarely gives attention to this particular age group. Children from ten and thirteen tend to be bracketed either with the magical, mysterious seven-year-olds who are busy sorting out reality and structure, or with the older adolescents who are getting ready to grow up and away. However, with children becoming more street-smart by the day, there is a lot going on in this age group that can require explicitly targeted help.

At ten, most children are getting ready to move school and, at eleven, they have to do so, with all the attendant worries about being a small fish in a big pond. Boys and girls will be openly ignoring each other in the playground while secretly working out who fancies who, and there will be experimentation with make-up and wondering about sex. These children want mobile phones and more freedom, just as their parents want more evidence of homework and educational achievement. When it comes to life in the home, they will no longer be fobbed off with partial explanations, nor will they believe in the magic of fairy tales. The children will be pretty clued up about the realities and structure of the household and, if there are boundaries, they will know by now where they are. If their parents are unhappy, they will know, if a break-up is looming they will feel it in their bones, and they will try hard to work out what is wrong so that they can find some clarity.

While younger children can be ostrich-like in trying to deny that their parents' marriage is coming to an end, by the age of ten they are more likely to turn into budding detectives in order to make sense of a difficult atmosphere. Parents must be aware that their children – especially girls – are likely to scour around for evidence once they cotton on to the fact that something is going wrong within the household. Phone calls will probably be listened to through half-open doors or secretly at the end of a different extension, mobile-phone messages and emails may be read and conversations in the home with friends may be followed with earnest concentration while heads are bowed over unseen homework at the kitchen table.

Some parents know that their children are allowing them no privacy, while others are blissfully unaware that their every move is being followed by an eleven-year-old private eye. All the children I have talked to over the age of ten whose family is in the process of breaking apart have a keen awareness. It is not they who are in denial about what is going on within the family home but their parents who, in a misguided attempt to protect, give a vague story of half-truths that add confusion to an already messy and difficult situation.

Lucy, at twelve years old, was shocked to find her life turned upside down within the space of a day and took matters into her own hands to find out what was going on. Her father left the family home one Thursday afternoon to sleep in a hotel; her mother, ashen-faced and hardly able to breathe, pretended nothing was wrong and produced the children's favourite meals as if good food would make life OK and take the pain away. At night Lucy could hear unfamiliar roaming through the house and would smell the unaccustomed smell of cigarette smoke drifting up the stairs as her mother tried to find comfort where none could be found. Lucy's mother did not know what was happening; she was hoping against hope that her husband was having a moment of madness coupled with a dramatic mid-life crisis and could only wait to see how her own personal nightmare was going to unfold. What she did not know was that Lucy was watching her and was frightened. Lucy, too, wanted more than anything to know why and where her much-loved father had gone and why a world in which she had felt safe and secure had inexplicably ended. And so she turned into a detective. She listened to the endless phone calls that took the place of conversation and laughter, she opened letters that were not meant for her, she read the emails that her father had left behind and, bit by bit, she made sense of the sad story. Lucy knew before her mother did what was really going on: that her father would never come home and that he was lost in a world that did not belong to the family. Lucy never wanted to be a snoop but, if she was going to get rid of the mad feelings inside her head, then she needed to know where her father had gone and why her mother could not sleep.

Lucy was fortunate in having a godmother who was close to both parents and could assess the situation objectively. With her mother's approval, Melissa took Lucy out to lunch and listened as a sad twelve-year-old told her story of overheard conversations, secretly opened letters and stolen text messages. She made no judgements, and offered no solutions, but allowed Lucy to talk, to express her feelings, to feel better and to make sense of what was going on. Lucy realized that she was not mad or bad for having done this detective work, and understood that not only she but everyone in her family was having a horrible time. Melissa encouraged her by saying that, while separation and divorce are terrible and always painful, they can be got through. She advised that it was her parents' job to find a way through the chaos and that, for her part, Lucy should try to get on with her own life, to find fun where she could and to go out and live as normally as possible. Melissa made her mobile number available day or night, should Lucy want to talk or check out some new evidence. And so Lucy left the lunch lighter, happier and freer of the burden of policing a situation that had everything to do with her but which, in reality, she could not influence. She was still sad, still wished that her father would come home and still worried about her parents, but at least she was free of any sense of having to be on red alert. Melissa was able to explain that the worst had already happened and that she was there to lend a hand while the storm subsided and the dust settled. This was immensely comforting, and yet it was all done with one lunch, some wise and dispassionate advice and a mobile-phone number as a lifeline in case of need.

Children who are busy crossing from childhood to adolescence will usually understand exactly what is going on but might not yet have the vocabulary to say how they feel about it. Half-formed sentences and words that even adults find difficult to speak can accumulate in a layer below the surface and come out in strange and unexpected ways. A child may look as if he is coping with the disintegration of his parents' marriage and often say 'Fine' when asked how things are going, yet his monosyllabic response will probably hide a multitude of feelings that are difficult to shape into words. Girls seem to find their emotional narrative more quickly than boys and are usually easier to chat to. Boys, on the other hand, seem to be happier when busy out and about doing things and can look as if little is troubling them as they perfect a cricket stroke, join in an important football match or collect an absolutely must-have card for a game that has swept the school. But if conversation about their emotional state is not their strong point, it does not mean that they do not have strong emotions; it is just that their emotions come out in different ways.

Illness is a useful tool for all children whose parents are going through a divorce and is the subject of a later chapter. I come across lot of boys between the ages of ten and thirteen with tummy aches. They are so bad that appendicitis is suspected, doctors are visited, time is taken off school and a new worry is added to an already worried household.

Whenever Harry saw his father at a weekend and had to come home on a Sunday night to get ready for school, have his mother check that his homework was done, pack his bag for the week ahead and go to bed early, he collapsed with an excruciating pain across the top of his abdomen. He was not making it up; the pain was so bad that he lost all colour from his face and his eyes filled with tears of pain and fear. He was given hot-water bottles, comforting sips of hot chocolate to soothe his stomach lining and massage to release trapped wind. After four visits to a doctor and as many Mondays off school, Harry's mother realized that the stress of saying goodbye to his father and watching him from his upstairs window as he walked down the garden path actually made Harry physically ill. He could not bear the look of anguish on his father's face as he had to say goodbye, he desperately wanted his dad to stay at home for Sunday supper and help him with his homework like he used to do. He did not want to be in a house where his mother efficiently guided three children into bed with everything ready for the next day but with little laughter or room for the nonsense of childhood. But he could not find the words, nor did he want to burden his careworn mother. And so he swallowed his pain, only for it to come out in agony at ten o'clock at night just when it was time to go to sleep.

Ben was a child whose emotional distress surfaced in different form. His mother no longer lived at home, his father was a doctor who had to work all hours to care for his patients and support his four children. So there was little time for dis-cussion, even if Ben had been able to find the words to tell what was bothering him. When life got too bad, schoolwork too difficult and there was not enough attention to go round, Ben's eleven-year-old legs simply stopped working. One day, he was running in the park; the next, he could not get out of bed. As with Harry's tummy pain, he was not making it up. He was clearly frightened that he could not walk and that his legs would not hold his weight. His father was deeply concerned and not only rang me but booked Ben in for an MRI scan. The scan was a good precaution, but showed nothing. What Ben's

107

legs were saying was that he could not take any more. His father was doing his best, but Ben's school was providing too little help and too many detentions, his mother was failing to keep to her pre-arranged visits and his brother was driving him so mad in their shared bedroom he felt as if he could find no peace. By falling over he was showing the grown-ups that they should look after him better. The cure again came through the right kind of talking with adults who themselves learnt to understand his problem better. Therapy began by talking about how burdened Ben felt and moved on to thinking about ways to find Ben more help. Friends were co-opted to provide sleepovers and teachers briefed to interpret the hidden messages. His father agreed to spend the time he would have had to spend with him in hospital having a pizza in order to discuss the things that were hurting his son. Support and attention worked wonders, and we were able to check that his legs did work by very gingerly making our way through the park to the coffee house. By the time we had had chocolate cake and Coca Cola, Ben was on the way to recovery and we walked back to his house with no mention of wonky legs.

The cases of Harry and Ben are not uncommon. Children need an understanding diagnosis, and it is a good idea to have a medical check just to be sure that nothing serious is actually going on. An understanding adult can provide the key to putting things right by keeping a sense of proportion, letting children know that they are not wrong to have symptoms and feelings during such a difficult time, and offering some relief through diversion, attention and reassurance that they are OK. In the end, a way will need to be found to give expression to these strong and mixed-up emotions. If adults close to the child can sympathetically translate what children are saying, it is easier to give their aches and pains the words that will express what is really wrong and watch the physical ailments dissolve.

School can also be very difficult for children enmeshed in family problems. The demands on them are stepped up at this age, often with exams at eleven and thirteen. There is also the move away from the safety of a known and small primary school into the much more challenging secondary environment. These challenges are big enough but, when a child is struggling with trying to make sense of a family breakdown at the same time, there is a heightened chance that their education will suffer. Academic focus becomes lost when a young mind is preoccupied by worries at home. It is a pity if a child falls at an important educational hurdle because of the stress placed upon them by the difficulties of their parents, but it can often happen if the right steps are not taken.

Bella was the brightest of bright children in a bright school. Half Lebanese and half Spanish, she shone as brightly as her waist-length hair and also played netball and hockey for the school team. She was assured of an easy move to a competitive London day school aged eleven. When her headmistress wrote her optimistic summer report that Bella could and would have the world at her feet, she was not to know what the holidays were going to bring. There was an end to a marriage, a super-fast sale of the family home and the return of Bella's father to the Lebanon, from where he informed his daughter that telephone lines rarely worked and email was an impossibility. Bella returned to school in the autumn with a brave attempt at a crooked smile and little concern for preparations for the forth-coming exams. Her teachers were told what had happened and looked after her in an exemplary way, but the timing was appalling. No one could expect Bella to concentrate or even care very much about her academic future when her daily life made little sense and her mother could not stop crying. When the time came for her to take her exams, she failed the lot and did not even get an interview at the secondary school she had wanted to go to. Bella not only lost her home, her father and her security but, through no fault of her own, lost her friends as they all made their way to schools where she was not wanted.

When life turns upside down at school and at home, some children try to cope with their difficulties by attempting to become better and better at everything, almost as if they are trying to control a life that has spun out of control by being very good. Many children are born with an ability to care for others, and to see this is a real pleasure. However, it is not unusual for children who have had difficult child-hoods to be over-solicitous and try rather too much to be in charge of what is going on. Children of this age can make a cup of tea, run to the local shop, look after a small sibling and be generally useful. They have the cognitive skills to work out what needs to be done, and the ability in many cases to do it. They may think that, if they can get it right, they will be able to stop bad moods, prevent an argument, make a father laugh or stop a mother from shouting. At an extreme, they may think that, by changing the bad atmosphere on the surface, they can even stop the break-up. I have seen children who walk on eggshells in order to prevent bad things happening, and I see them sacrificing themselves as they watch out for and put others first.

But children who become over-helpful and too good do so at the expense of their own development. They give up their emotional needs in order to look after those of their parents. These children rarely cause problems but can store up difficulties for themselves in the future. When children who should be noisy are trying to be quiet, should be naughty but are doing their best to be good, don't make excessive demands or seek attention and adjust their behaviour so as not to disturb and be a burden, they are shutting themselves away from their true selves and may need some help to rejoin the ranks of other children. Overly good children need encouragement to venture out to play, to join clubs and after-school activities. They need to have fun and let off steam, to shout and make a mess, and they need to trust that the grown-ups in their life can look after themselves and that it is not their responsibility to make sure that other people are OK. Parents can help by finding local activities their children will enjoy and which will get them out of the house and away from the atmosphere. Any kind of sport, drama, time spent with friends, picnics, shopping, cooking, sleepovers with midnight feasts and other gregarious activity are good ways to get the ten- to thirteen-year-old age range moving out and about. If they have got into the habit of staying close to home, they might need more than a little persuasion to get going, but get going they must if they are to stop protecting those around them and enjoy the life that they are supposed to be leading. If a mother or a father is in too much of a state of disrepair to help them and adults close to the family can see a child unhealthily attached to the unhappy adults, they will be doing the whole family a favour if they can take steps to encourage the pre-adolescent into the world of high energy, social exploration and silly naughtiness that they are meant to inhabit.

Tilly lost her twelve-year-old identity when her parents separated after a long and difficult year of shouting, back-stabbing and discussion of who had done what to whom. Tilly's father did not want to leave the family house; he felt that he had earned it and bought it and that it represented everything he had striven for, but his wife no longer loved him and did not want him in her life. Through coldness and control, she distanced herself, and her husband sought comfort elsewhere and his daughter discovered the evidence on his mobile phone. Divorce was on the cards, and the atmosphere at home became even colder and completely lacking in love. Tilly's mother, already bitter and unhappy, became more so, while her father fell to bits and would cry at the end of Tilly's bed that his dreams had been shattered. On one side, Tilly felt responsible for trying to cheer her father up; on the other, she did not want to make her mother angry by being seen to support him. Tilly could not win; stuck in the middle of two opposing parents who had replaced love with hate, she could only do her best to please them. She stayed close by her mother in a failed attempt to stop her getting angry and would have supper after school with her father and try to stop him from being so sad. She needed to be two different people for two different parents. Neither was the real Tilly; she had become the adult and, as such, was forgetting to have a childhood. Luckily, her teacher spotted that her pupil no longer smiled, that after-school clubs had been dropped and that Tilly had given up playing with the group of girls who had once been her great friends.

When Tilly arrived to work with me, she had no idea of who she was. She felt guilty that she had been the one to find the text message on the mobile phone, she felt afraid of her mother's anger and sad for her father. She was exhausted with trying to sort out her parents, and she knew that she needed to get ready to go to secondary school. She did not feel that she had any friends, she did not know how to have fun and she had no idea what she liked to do. While her mother and father did not love each other, they had no problems with their love for their children, and they were prepared to meet me to discuss the sadness that had been spotted in their daughter. Once they realized that they were hurting Tilly by their constant and open warfare, they joined together to put things right. Several family sessions followed, in which her father learnt that he had to keep his sadness for elsewhere, stop leaning on his daughter and become a male role model who could cope and stand up in the world. Her mother quickly learnt that her anger and bad moods did little to help, and that she herself needed therapy to get over her resentment and bitterness that life had not turned out as she had wanted. With her parents on the right track, attention was turned to Tilly and what she wanted to do. Although she resisted, both parents insisted that she rejoin her clubs and made phone calls to reinstate the sleepovers and weekend dates that had slipped away. Fun was made a priority and, although important schoolwork needed to be completed by the time Tilly was thirteen, she was walking arm in arm with her friends on a Saturday afternoon through the market stalls of London while keeping her parents up to speed as to her whereabouts on her new and shiny mobile phone.

Children of this age need to work hard and to play hard. They will not be free to get on with their lives if they are emotionally stuck in a situation they do not understand and if they are worried about their home. Adults should tell them the truth clearly and trust that they will be able to cope. Children will be helped to cope if their story is understood without too much fuss and bother, if they are not made wrong for having feelings that come out in peculiar ways and if they are encouraged to get out and about. Their lives need to be organized for them, in that they are not old enough to make their own plans, they do not have the money to pay for their fun, they are too young to be without boundaries and they need to be dropped off and picked up by the parent turned chauffeur. It is best if the parents can keep themselves in good enough shape to do these things but, if not, other adults can substitute, and sometimes do better by being an objective and available confidant helping to guide the child through a difficult time.

For the ten- to thirteen-year-olds, adolescence is just around the corner. They need to understand what has gone on, even if it is not all happy, and they need a sense of structure and authority around them. If these things can be given to them, they will feel safer, even if their world has been rocked by the collapse of their home life. They should be ready for the challenging developmental tasks that belong to the world of the teenager.

113

Teenagers

Teenagers can be difficult, impossible, wonderful, awkward, lazy, amusing and preposterous. They have a difficult developmental job to do in that they need to learn who they are, what they think, who they like, who likes them, sort out sex and grow up and get away from their parents without breaking necessary family ties. While they are doing this, they will not take much notice of admonitions to clean a bedroom, empty a dishwasher or try harder at their homework but will spend hours and hours trying on new outfits and sculpting their hair. Curfews are there to be broken, money is there to be asked for, school bags are there to get lost and parents are there to make them safe enough so that they can be pushed away. It is best to accept the phone calls that go on for hours, the rudeness, the tears, the obsession with social pecking orders and the total daytime exhaustion that is miraculously replaced by excessive energy just as it is time for the general population to start to go to bed. Teenagers are doing their job by being sulky, rude, difficult, evasive, exhausting and exhausted. It is very tiring to be the parent of a teenager. Couples who are mostly in agreement when it comes to childcare find them hard to manage. It is much more difficult for both the adults and the adolescent when the family has broken and the centre has failed to hold.

Adolescents are battling on at least two levels. They have their cognitive faculties, which need to work out the important daily doings of their life, and they have their emotional life, which can feel exciting but overwhelming. Emotion and intellect weave around each other in a dance that attempts to make sense of almost every-thing, from the meaning of life to whether or not a friend is going to return a phone call, and a teenage head can give and receive a com-pletely different message from a teenage heart. Some of the clumsiness that belongs to this age group is because they are work-ing out how to execute the difficult task of putting different aspects of themselves together to form a coherent personality which is acceptable to themselves and to the society in which they have to live. When their world is side-swiped with serious difficulties in their parents' relationship, it can be really hard for them to continue with their developmental journey. Instead of learning how to join head and heart, the split becomes greater, as a teenager will attempt to get on with his life but be full of doubt and fear, wondering about whom to turn to for support and for answers to the important questions that he needs to ask about growing up. To lose the very structure that he is meant to trust and fight against at a time when he is meant to be getting ready to go out into the world is a blow.

Teenagers very often look as if they do not care that their family life is crashing to the ground. While their feelings are hidden deeply, it is important for them to go out and about with their friends, to forget the atmosphere at home, to get a rest from worrying or just to have a good time. I find it almost a therapeutic rule of thumb that the less a teenager seems to care on the surface, the more he will care underneath and will need help to give voice to emotions that can otherwise threaten to overwhelm him. But, rather like finding the route to the feelings of an autistic child, it can be difficult to find a way to communicate with an unhappy adolescent. Teenagers must have privacy and be allowed to be secretive. They are intensely aware that they need to look as if they can cope, and they can become furious if a well-meaning teacher puts a friendly hand out and asks in the school corridor if they are OK. When their family is splitting up, they will deal with the fallout in their own way, and only they will know what that way is. They can react badly to attempts to give comfort. When I have taken matters into my own hands and decided that 'it would be good for them to talk,' I have been met with a combination of a cornered boxer and a blank wall. The best way to help teenagers is to trust them. They will find their own way to express their pain and their hurt and sometimes they will find solace in a way that might cause raised eyebrows, sleepless nights and endless worry to the parent population. Some write beautiful poetry and lyrics to songs which show the true nature of their wounds. Others run away to friends and maybe drink too much or spend too much time on the streets at night, just hanging around with people who ask few questions but seem to understand. And some teenagers act out in ways that cause real concern. As with understanding Harry's tummy pains or the legs that no longer worked for Ben, it is important to accept that an adolescent's behaviour makes sense and then to think about ways to change it so that he or she is more comfortable.

Seeds for difficult teenage behaviour as a result of an acrimonious separation can be sown much earlier in the life of a child. The consequences of a difficult divorce and shaky parental foundations can lie dormant in a child's psyche until the turbulence of adolescence brings them to the surface. Although a divorce might have happened long ago, a child might not find the words to say or the weapons with which to fight until she reaches adolescence.

Imo was sent to me because of her antics at her fifteenth birthday party, but her parents had divorced when she was ten. One night, five years after her parents had left each other, she had an illegal party and filled her garden with the drunk and disorderly young of her neighbourhood. Her mother and stepfather were away and things got dramatically out of control. An ambulance had to be called and there were at least three alcohol-related admissions to the local hospital. While Imo was being treated for alcohol poisoning, a nurse noticed that her wrists were lacerated with the marks of the self-harmer. It was time for Imo to get some help.

Imo's mother was stylish and beautiful. She liked the fine things of life and needed to work to keep her status, her house, her fine car and her figure. Her daughter, however, was unhappy. After a brutally combative divorce, Imo had ingested all sorts of negative information about her father and had come to accept her mother's belief that he was a bad man who did not love his daughter. She had too much information and knew of every missed monthly payment, of his spending too many nights drinking and of his relationships with other women. Imo's mother did such a good job of making her ex-husband wrong, and Imo's father had done so little to attempt to put it right, that Imo did not want to see him. But she did want to see her mother, the only parent on whom she felt she could rely. However, Imo's mother wanted to holiday with her new husband and spend time at a job that involved travel and late-night dinners.

Imo was one of the most neglected children that I have ever worked with. She cooked her own supper, put herself to bed in an empty house, bought her own school uniform and, once, while I was working with her, took herself off for an X-ray to sort out her broken arm. She had broken it by running into a wall at full speed on purpose, 'because it was fun'. She called it 'moshing', and also ran into bushes and groups of people because it made her feel 'more alive'. Imo had fantasies of running in front of buses and cars; a part of her wanted to be dead and a part of her wanted to scream 'Look at me' to the people who were meant to be taking care of her. But her mother would not look, and she would not let her father see. Only I, as her therapist, knew what she was up to. When she arrived alone, cold and tired on a winter's evening, I wanted to wrap her up and take care of her myself. I listened to how she had walked out of lessons, fought with teachers, eaten four packets of biscuits instead of dinner, gone to the dentist on her own and filled in forms by herself for her passport. We tried to talk to her mother, but the attempt to make things better made things worse, as Imo's mother felt that she was being criticized and wondered why she was paying good money to be told off when she worked so hard. I tried to persuade Imo to see her father, who very much wanted to re-establish contact, but she refused to see him or read his letters. And so Imo was on her own. Behind the bravura, the hard little face, the tight London voice and the moshing and the joshing was a lonely, angry, frightened girl who had no option but to be tough. Her behaviour made sense and, for the first time, with me, she was able to speak about her life without being called ungrateful or difficult or all of the things she was used to hearing about herself. I called her brave and let her know that I was impressed by the fact that she kept going, and told her that I thought that she might be over-responsible rather than irresponsible. We wondered if somewhere, somehow, she might be able to find some support so that she did not have to fight all her battles on her own. She found a teacher whom she liked and who was prepared to sponsor her through the difficult times at school when she felt like giving up and walking out, and she found comfort from her best friend's mother by explaining her predicament and telling her how she felt.

I could not change Imo's mother; she did not want to change. I could not make Imo see her father; the damage had been done, and her teenage brain was stuck with the sense that she had made of their relationship. What therapy could do was make Imo see that she was sad and not bad and that she had reason to be. When she realized this important truth, she stopped running at bushes and walls, she stopped cutting her arms and she decided that she might study for her GCSEs rather than muck around in class. Her face changed and the brittle armour of make-up was dropped and a softer girl/child emerged who began to seek solace among her friends and found fun in music and going to gigs with others from her school. By discovering for herself the difficult emotions behind her behaviour, by giving them words and being understood for having them, Imo was able to stop being a truly difficult adolescent. When her head understood her heart and what it needed to say, Imo had a chance.

A difficult aspect for a family with teenage children that is going through the process of family break-up is that, by the time children are fourteen, they can pretty much decide whom they do and don't want to see. Adolescents are old and bold enough to choose where and when and how and with whom they spend their time. If, as in the case of Imo, there has been vilification, unfinished business, difficult behaviour, too much information, unreliability and hurt, then it is very possible that a child will refuse to see a parent.

If this is the case, then teenagers themselves will suffer, because they need both parents; they need them to provide male and female role models, to anchor them in the world of their genetic history, to provide the 100 per cent umbrella of love and structure they were meant to be born into and to be able to turn to the other when one is unavailable. When an adolescent finds himself choosing one parent over another, he will not only have the firm ground for his own natural development kicked from under his feet, but he will find himself a parent short when it comes to surviving the teenage years. Practical stuff such as lifts in cars late at night, extra pocket money for much-needed teenage paraphernalia, support at a school play, dinner after parents' evening, input about academic choices and potential universities, exercise in the park and fun holidays may be lost to him while all his friends are able to enjoy what he cannot have. Emotionally, he only has 50 per cent of the eyes and ears that were meant to look out for him and, if the parent that he lives with is busy, distracted or elsewhere, then he finds himself alone. Without the healthy dynamic of two parents working together to manoeuvre, cajole and coax an adolescent through the daily responsibilities of his life, there can be a large hole in the safety net that is needed to protect him.

There was no way to help Mike when he really needed both parents to look after him but had a father who failed dismally in his responsibility. He was sixteen when he had to go to rehabilitation for drug addiction. I had been watching his

119

downhill path for two years and had been unable to change its direction or make any headway with a boy who seemed bent on his own destruction. He was no stranger to the police with his truancy, his drug-dealing and his creative antics with graffiti, and he was within a hair's breadth of being taken into care when his mother sent him to me. No adult in Mike's life could get near to making the slightest bit of difference. His teachers had given up, his mother could not manage him, he had no fear of the police and he looked at me during our sessions with a wide, lazy smile that told me I bored him to death and he was only sitting in the chair because he would get too much hassle from the rest of world if he did not. Mike was able to escape all attempts to get him to behave because he had his father as back-up and he had chosen to live with him. Mike's dad was a drug addict and sent Mike on drug-related errands and told him that his mother was a nag and the rest of the adults were desperately dull. When we told Mike off for stealing or spray-painting, he laughed in our faces and left us furious and impotent. A beautiful boy whom I remembered from football in the park had turned into the sort of teenager one is scared to meet in a dark alley. Mike, with his natural naughtiness, could drive a horse and cart right through the gap in his parents' marriage and choose to live with the adult who looked more interesting but was a hopeless father. All structure was lost, all discipline negated, all moral and ethical values put to one side, and Mike suffered while failing to learn anything that would help him to grow up.

The whole family suffers when a child who is over fourteen chooses to live with one parent and cuts contact with the other. One adult will have little freedom and too much responsibility; the other will be hurt and powerless. Mother and father will feel angry and alone and will not be able to turn to the one person who could and should help guide their child through the minefields of adolescence.

Siblings will have been set a difficult example and will either wonder whether to follow suit or wish that their brother or their sister were less demanding or unhappy. I have met parents in my consulting room, in the psychiatrist's office and in the court to try to help them find a way back to their child but, once a child has gone, it can take all of their teenage years for them to come back. It is as if their developing brain gets stuck in a painful and negative groove and no amount of discussion can persuade them that their truth is not necessarily *the* truth and that there are always two sides to a story. It takes time for a child who has been badly damaged and on the receiving end of the toxicity of the end of their parents' relationship to work things out and achieve the objectivity, wisdom and courage to undo the mythology of years. The parent who has been abandoned also needs superhuman amounts of understanding, patience, love and forgiveness to stay steady and wait for their offspring to return. It is awful to know that a child is out in the world busy with life and yet not have a chance to share in it. I often see fathers who still have to pay for the maintenance of their children who cannot even be sure of recognizing their own son or daughter, and I have spent hours talking to mothers whose children will not come home.

Tough as it is to be rejected, a parent needs to take responsibility for the fact that the seeds of their rejection will have been sown by their own behaviour. A parent who behaves badly will not set a good example and often needs to apologize, while it is best if the other parent does not fan the flames of anger and disappointment. Too much evidence of alcoholism, infidelity, drug use, cruelty, anger or unreliability will cause hurt and a loss of respect. It is best if difficult behaviour on the part of either parent can be explained in as non-judgemental a way as possible. Drug abuse and alcoholism are signs of illness, affairs show that a marriage was not too healthy, bad moods and unreliability can be a sign of depression. If the parent who is exhibiting the difficult behaviour is unwilling or unable to talk to the children, then the other needs to put their own feelings aside and

121

talk objectively about what has happened. By not condemning their ex-partner and by presenting a framework which can be compassionately understood, a parent will be giving their child the possibility of accepting, forgiving and holding on to both their mother and their father and being able to accept both sides of themselves at the same time. While this might seem like an impossible task when facing the dark emotional storm that usually precedes and goes with parental break-up, it is one that is well worth attempting. A teenager who is able to love and respect both parents whatever their faults and peculiar behaviour will be much happier and more psychologically healthy than one who has to turn his back on someone that he wants and needs to love.

Ruth was badly damaged by her decision at fourteen to turn her back on a parent and ended up having to seek psychiatric treatment. Her father amused himself with other women during one long summer when he was alone in town. His antics were well reported to his wife, and she packed his bags, changed the locks and sued for divorce on the grounds of his adultery. Ruth was party to every piece of evidence and witness to her mother's fury and distress. Her father did not help when, instead of accepting that he had made a mistake, he inflamed hostilities by telling his daughter that he would not have done it if her mother had been any fun to be around. Ruth chose the only course of action that she could think of; she came to my consulting room and modelled her father out of plasticine. She then furiously scrunched him up into a small round ball, went into the garden and threw him as hard as she could at the wall. Ruth could not be persuaded to think about allowing her father into her life; at her tender age she could not bear to think of the information that she had been given; her father was disgusting, disgraceful and perverse.

In an ideal world, Ruth's father would have behaved in a different way, but he did not need to lose his daughter. If his wife had not been so full of anger, if he had apologized, if he had asked and listened to the answers as to what he could do to put things right, he could have maintained a relationship with her. Instead he ended up paying maintenance for a daughter he could not see and talking to lawyers and psychiatrists who could not help. Ruth's teenage years were spent achieving top academic grades and developing an eating disorder to get a perfect figure to hide an appalling sense of low self-worth. She was an unhappy girl with only one parent and a distasteful distrust of 50 per cent of her genetic make-up. By the time she was eighteen she wanted to see her father but did not know how to hold out her hand and was frightened about what she might find. She came back to me and told me she wanted to look at the plasticine ball again. Luckily, her father was still waiting, and she was able to work warily and slowly towards a relationship, but four years of important emotional development had been skewed in the wrong direction, and her adolescence had been much more painful and difficult than necessary.

Imo, Ruth and Mike showed symptoms of distress, but by no means all the teenagers who come to me for therapy are suffering from the fallout of a broken home. Many are children from seemingly well-adjusted, functional families who have both a mother and father to look after them. Distressing as it is to have a child on drugs, binge drinking, out all night or on a website learning how to cut their thighs, the child is, in a way, merely displaying some extreme symptoms of what it is to be an adolescent in the western world of today. Arguably, all adolescents could at some point in their developing teenage years give their parents problems with differing degrees of severity, and we need to expect the odd bit of turbulence. When it comes to family breakdown, it is usually the problematic behaviour of the adults that becomes the issue. If parents do not join at the hip, if they have vilified each other to the point of no return, if they allow their teenage child too much power before it becomes too late, if they do not have a clear structure and agreed rules for co-parenting, then a troubled teenager will have nowhere to turn. At that point symptoms that frighten and are difficult to manage may spiral out of control and the safety net that we are meant to provide as parents might prove to be broken beyond repair.

If it is my experience that maladjusted teenagers do not necessarily come from broken homes, it is also my experience that broken homes do not necessarily produce maladjusted teenagers. I have known many people of all ages who have coped with the difficult emotional process of the end of their parents' relationship and who have grown up beautifully.

Lucy, who opened too many letters and emails that were not hers to open, entered adolescence as her parents' marriage broke above her head. She kept going to school and became cross with any teacher who attempted to invade her privacy; she went out and about and sometimes forgot to call home; she found a social life in which many other children had experienced the break-up of a family; she loved her father and forgave him for falling in love with another woman; and she respected and admired her mother for keeping the show on the road when times were tough. Her room was always untidy, she never had any money, the telephone never stopped ringing and she went on a gap year and off to university full of a sense of adventure and with a pretty strong idea about who she was.

Sebastian, too, who had seen his father drink himself to death but who had been guided by the holding hands of inspirational adults throughout the collapse of his parents' marriage and the tragedy of his father's illness, went on to become one of the nicest people I have ever met. He managed to maintain a true love and affection for his father while understanding the truth about his condition, and he grew up with a strong sense of right and wrong, fun and mischief and an ability to shine and do well.

I have known many other teenagers who have coped with wisdom and with courage as their parents have muddled along towards the dissolution of a family home, and I have seen them go on to make successful and happy lives. The single most important factor that has kept them on the rails is having the support of an adult or adults who have been there to listen, love, advise and care.

With teenagers, as much as with other age groups, a breaking family is a time for sensitive grown-ups to make their presence felt but not impose it. Grandparents and friends who like young people can play an important part, with invitations to art exhibitions or strange theatrical events, lunch near a busy shopping street in a café of their choice, a quick word while giving them a lift to a friend's so they do not have to take a bus. This kind of thing will show them that someone is interested in their life and will do a great deal to get rid of the teenage, and often true, idea that adults are dull and rigidly stuck in their ways. If an interested and interesting adult provides the opening, teenagers will start to talk pretty quickly and, if they find the conversation useful, they will come back for more. Once an adolescent starts to talk about what is really going on, they find it hard to stop. Their take on life is interesting, bizarre and fresh, and their feelings are deep and desperate and immediate. Whatever one feels when one is exploring the workings of a teenage inner world, it is difficult to be bored when they tell us how it is. As we listen, we will be able to understand and discover what it is they need to make them safe and help them on their journey.

All teenagers need to feel secure; it is their job to push against the family and walk on the edge of danger. If their family goes through a divorce, their safety net is unlikely to remain intact and, in extreme cases, an adolescent might do one of two things. He might draw back from the edge of life and stay safe, or he might hurl himself over a precipice and end up in varying degrees of trouble.

125

The teenager who stays safe will look as if he is a good and perfect child who causes little worry to those whose job it is to look after him. He will probably get through school without any bother and be a blessing at home, where he will look out for those around him. He will not draw attention to himself and will look as if he is unaffected by his parents' separation. However, in the process he may be neglecting his own need to develop and push against the boundaries of adolescence. He may miss out on the important task of finding out who he is and who he is meant to be. There are choices to be made and, if a young person does not occasionally wander up to the edges of his life to check them out, creativity, joy and a deep feeling of being truly alive may be lost to him. He will be at risk of moving into adulthood with a limited sense of who he could be and therefore may live a life that is less than he was meant to live. And, deep inside, his spirit may resent its loss of freedom and could fight back by making trouble later. Depression is a sign that hidden, untapped energy is wanting to be free, alcoholism or addictive behaviours show that unheard voices need to talk and difficulties with relationships may indicate that feelings have been too deeply buried. A teenager who stays safe will not rock the boat during adolescence but might find that he needs help as he moves out into the world as an adult.

At the other end of the spectrum from the 'too good' teenager comes the complete horror who causes problems for all concerned. Truancy, self-harm, stealing, disappearing, drug-taking, binge-drinking, lying, eating disorders, sexual promiscuity, panic attacks, depression and mute hostility are all weapons in the arsenal of such an adolescent which can be effectively used to make a point. These behaviours are often illegal, frequently dangerous and deeply worrying to those who are either watching or on the receiving end of them. When a child falls over the edge and becomes a danger to himself and to others, then something has to be done. In serious cases a family doctor will refer a child on to an adolescent psychiatrist and may suggest a course of family therapy, but it can take time to get help from the NHS, and parents will very often feel that time is something they do not have. In addition, resorting to the hospital, family therapy and teams associated with the social services can sometimes feel frightening, and a gentler and less invasive approach might be better. Therapists and counsellors can be found working in the private sector, while there are many charitable organizations, books, websites and helplines that are useful when searching for ways to help one's teenage child.

The break-up of a family need not be a disaster for its teenagers. If the adults can keep their heads and guide their offspring, they will find they do not stray too far or behave much worse than their contemporaries. Compassionate and objective explanations are better than screaming fury or icy contempt. If an adolescent understands why a mother or a father has gone and why the relationship can no longer work, he will not judge and will find it easy to forgive because, in his heart, he wants to love both parents. Everything should be done to ensure that a teenager does not need to exercise his right to walk away and that he has a mother and a father to guide him. Parents, although living apart, should decide rules together about monthly allowances, phone bills for mobile phones and weekend and weekday curfews, and work together on other matters such as education and health. Other people are important as life widens out and offers new possibilities. Teachers can help, as long as they are sensitive and careful about how and where they offer guidance; friends and relatives can give time and show interest in a life that is just starting to take off; medical help and counselling can be found if they are needed; and the gang of teenage friends can be a great support group to encourage an adolescent away from the atmosphere in the family home and into normal adulthood.

The teenage years are particularly difficult for separating parents to deal with because children are living on the edge and often react with great depth despite an impassive exterior. Parents should resist the temptation to think that a teenager will be old enough to sort his feelings out for himself and must still regard the child as being in

127

their care. While in need of freedom, teenagers also need love and structure so that they can continue their journey of individual development. Parents need to pull together to provide the support for their teenager's schooling and social life. If the circumstances are so bad that this is beyond them, then they would be wise at least to find friends and professionals who can provide a substitute.

Summary

All children going through the break-up of their family need:
- Age-appropriate explanations of what is going on
- Parents who can look after themselves
- Reassurance that there is nothing that they can do to get their parents back together
- Understanding
- Someone to talk to

Parents need to devise different strategies for the care of their children according to the different developmental stages of childhood.

- **Babies and infants** need parents who are able to care for themselves and who will allow others to look after them. In that way they will be able to provide the tender love and constant attention that will allow a child to grow up feeling secure about their place in this world. Parents should remember that the very young thrive if they feel that they are the centre of a wonderful universe and that it is at this time that an important sense of self-image is formed. Parents need to be aware that becoming too protective and attempting to be both mother and father because of having to go it alone can undermine a child's ability to look after himself and take responsibility for his own actions later in life.
- **Five- to ten-year-olds:** This age group learn fast, their minds expand quickly and yet they hold on to a magical way of thinking.

They will not yet have the words to express their emotional highs and lows, so understanding a child's way of expressing negative emotion through the vocabulary of behaviour is an important skill. Adults face a dilemma when dealing with the difficult behaviour of five- to ten-year-olds. It is hard to be tough when a child is miserable because of the break-up of his family home and yet behaviour such as physical aggression, refusal to go to school or failure to learn or to concentrate in class needs to be dealt with. Parents and other adults need to combine sensitive wisdom with a firm, loving hand in order to stop these still-young children from spinning out of control or into depression.

- **Ten- to thirteen-year-olds:** By the age of ten, most children will be acutely aware of difficult atmospheres and will usually understand exactly what is going on but might not yet have the vocabulary to say how they feel. While sitting on difficult emotions, they will also have to face increased academic demands and a move to a more challenging secondary-school environment. But focus can get lost when a young mind is preoccupied by worries at home, and some children may need a watchful eye cast over them to keep them academically on track. Some might become over-helpful and too good at the expense of their own development as they enter adolescence and forget that it is their job to play hard as well as to work hard. Parents and other adults can help by explaining as honestly as possible what is going on and providing a sense of authority and structure along with the means to join in with their friends and the encouragement and freedom to have a good time.

- **Teenagers:** Adolescents are battling on at least two levels as their emotions and intellect weave around each other trying to make sense of a complex world. With parental separation, a teenager will have to face an additional burden to his developmental tasks in that he will not necessarily know to whom to turn for support or who to ask about the important questions of growing up. It can be difficult to find a way to communicate with an unhappy adolescent and, as with other children, their conversation is more often in the behaviour that they exhibit than in the words that they use.

Seeds for difficult teenage behaviour may be sown much earlier in the life of a child, and the consequences of a difficult divorce and shaky parental foundations can lie dormant in a child's psyche until the turbulence of adolescence brings them to the surface. By the time children reach the age of fourteen, they can choose whether or not to see their parents and can vote with their feet to stay away from a mother or a father. If this happens, then teenagers will suffer, because they need both parents to survive the tricky teenage years.

At least half of the adolescents that come for therapy do not come from broken homes, so it is important to remember that teenagers can be difficult in their own right and not lay all the blame for difficult behaviour at the feet of a breaking marriage. Equally, there are many teenagers who do not behave badly at all when their parents split up and seem to manage their life with an impressive composure.

Separated parents need to join at the hip, provide a clear structure and agreed rules for behaviour and co-parent their teenagers so that they can navigate the turbulent waters into adulthood. The single most important factor in keeping an adolescent out of trouble is to have the support of adults or an adult who is consistently available to listen, love and advise.

4 • • • • •

Difficult times, difficult physical symptoms

THE DIFFERENT DEVELOPMENTAL STAGES need to be taken account of by parents seeking to limit the impact of separation or divorce on their children. It is also important to be aware of, and able to interpret, a whole range of different symptoms which children may use instead of words to tell us that something is wrong.

Tummy pains, headaches, nervous tics, bed-wetting, increased incidences of asthma and eczema, sleep disturbance, depression and a host of other physical problems can be part and parcel of the emotional drudgery of divorce and separation. Children who cannot find the words to tell us what is wrong, who do not understand how frightened or sad or angry or confused they are, or who cannot make sense of what feels like an incomprehensible world, will eventually find a way to call for help. If we ignore the aches and pains that have no medical provenance or turn our busy backs on a child who cannot sleep at night, we will not be listening to the important things they have to say. A symptom in a child can be their way of opening an important conversation. If we do not listen, they will have to speak more loudly and, if we still do not hear, they will eventually have to shout so

131

loudly that their whole world will know that there is real trouble.

Therapists love to talk about 'somatizing' symptoms. By this we mean that, instead of expressing discontent, anger, rage, sadness or even exhaustion, human beings place it within their bodies to come out in different ways. Hence we may have irritable bowel, migraines, depression, insomnia, high blood pressure, skin complaints and a whole host of medical problems that could perhaps be cured by dealing with the emotional content of our lives in a healthier and more positive way. Books are written about it, diets are prescribed and lifestyle 'gurus' make suggestions which are meant to help us find our equilibrium. Some of the suggestions and a great deal of the medical research are helpful and can make a huge difference to the physical problems that beset the modern adult population.

If we believe that we as adults hide our emotional difficulties and let them come out as physical symptoms, then how much more should we understand that children can do the same? As adults, we have the education and experience to go and find out what is wrong with us when something is amiss, but children can suffer symptomatic stomach complaints, headaches, inability to sleep and depression and have to ask the very people who could be inadvertently causing their problems for help. However, once help is found, children are likely to find relief quickly from their ailments as they will not yet have had time to become too entrenched.

Tummy pains

Tummy pains can be useful for children of all ages who cannot or do not want to find the words to tell us what is going on. It is as if the desperate emotions that are hidden deep within a child's body can find some release if they are translated into real pain for which there might be a cure. I wrote in the previous chapter about how I have come to expect stomach pains in children between the ages of ten to thirteen, of Harry who would cripple up on a Sunday night and could not move his poor cramped body because of the agony inside him. I have also had an eight-year-old client who was surgically cut open in a quest for a physical answer to an emotional problem. Stomach aches can also be used as a convenient excuse for not going to school or doing something that a child does not want to do. And they can be caused by a physical problem and in need of medical attention. It takes a wise and careful adult to work out the best course of action when faced with the pale face of a child who swears blind that he is truly ill and is regularly bent double in pain. Once a visit to the GP has been made to check whether there is a specific medical problem and has turned up nothing, it is then up to responsible adults to check the veracity of the crippling condition and to take steps to deal with it. If it is dealt with correctly, an almost miraculous cure can take place, and children who swore blind that they were on the verge of hospitalization will suddenly forget that their tummies (or their heads, or their legs) ever ached at all.

Paul was a Sunday-night-tummy-pain child whose face went white and whose eyes filled with tears when his father began to leave the house. Paul hated the fact that his father did not live at home any more and longed for the every other Friday when he spent the weekend. But joy was replaced by misery when Daddy packed his overnight suitcase and got ready to go back to his rented bedsit. By six o'clock on a Sunday evening, Paul would have become silent and sad and, although he was eleven years old, he would retreat to the corner of the sitting-room sofa and chew the corner of a blanket that he had had as a baby. As the evening drew on, his stomach would begin to hurt until he was curled in agony, whimpering in pain and begging to go to hospital, convinced he would not be able to make school the next morning. Paul's mother became so concerned that she thought about stopping the weekend visits so that her son did not have to go through such regular agony. For justifiable personal reasons, she would have been delighted to stop the arrangement, but she knew that children need their fathers and, with the family life in temporary freefall, could think of no other way of comfortably allowing her son to see his dad. Instead of banning her ex-husband from the family home she brought Paul to therapy.

Paul needed to talk, but he could not find the words to speak about his sadness and he did not know who he could talk to. His mother was an efficient, brisk, no-nonsense kind of woman who had decided that by keeping the show on the road and not showing her grief she would protect her son and do the best she could. But, in the anonymity of rush-hour traffic, she cried alone in her car, and Paul did not even know that his mother was sad. Paul's father was a bluff, sporting kind of fellow who would always find a way to look on the bright side. Nothing was ever too bad, there were always people worse off and every cloud had a silver lining. While admirable in its place, the supremely British ability of showing a 'stiff upper lip' can hurt children. Paul was terribly, terribly sad that his parents had split up, but he could not find anyone to be sad with. Instead he was encouraged by his parents to get on, do his schoolwork, play his cricket and his football and not make a fuss, because divorce happens and 'Anyway, it probably is a good thing as it means getting two lots of presents at Christmas and birthdays.'

Many children will baulk at being taken to see a stranger, and I have often gone to children's homes or schools for an initial session to attempt to show them that I am not frightening, am on their side, can keep secrets, and to explain why they might want to come and talk or play. Most unhappy children want to be listened to, and they usually agree to come and 'interview' me in my consulting room to see if they might be interested in coming for a session or two. If a child needs help but resists the idea, I would encourage therapists and anyone working with children to move towards the world of that child rather than sit and wait for a small person in trouble. Luckily, Paul had enough self-awareness to understand that he needed to talk to someone and came happily to my consulting room. Sand-play therapy helped Paul. Most art therapists will use this way of working, and it has proven success in getting children to understand their situation objectively, give expression to their feelings and come up with solutions which may make life better. A wooden box full of sand, either dry or wet, is made available to a child, along with a whole host of figures and objects which can be chosen to tell a story or to represent an incident. Paul was able to show me the reality of his life by playing in the sand. He did not see his mother as coping miraculously well; he saw her as angry and brittle and difficult to be with. He picked a figure of an old battle-axe crone reminiscent of one of the witches in *Macbeth* to represent her and could see none of the hidden softness that was obvious to me when I met her at our initial interview. By battling on, Paul's mother removed the tender side of herself from her son, which made him feel that he could not turn to her and tell her that he was unhappy. Paul's father appeared as Bob the Builder and was placed dunce-like in the corner and repre-sented as sad and rather stupid. There would be no point in turning to him for help with powerful and difficult emotions as he would not know what to do with them. His father would simply suggest a bracing walk by the river, as if some fresh air were going to get rid of a stomach full of bad feelings and a head full of difficult questions.

When Paul had had six sessions alone in the therapy room and I was fairly sure that we had begun to uncover the depth of his feelings and the real rawness of his emotion, I asked his parents to join me in a session with their son. With Paul's permission, I showed them his unflattering representations of his mother and father and explained why it was that he saw them this way, what he wanted and what he needed to change. In an instant, his mother saw with horror that her brave front was keeping her son away from warmth, comfort and truth and was able to open her arms to hold him so that they could cry their hearts out together about the fact that life had gone so terribly wrong. It did Paul's father no harm to have to watch the reality of what his leaving had done to his child and, although uncomfortable, he was able to stay and ask what he could do. Of course Paul requested through his snuffles and from the safety of his mother's arms that his parents get back together, but the sad reality was that the split was for ever and I gently reminded my young client that this was not a possibility. Paul and his mother and father were able to move on to discussions about how to deal with Sunday-night tummy and other issues that had been bothering a small boy with no one to talk to. I only needed one more session with Paul after that meeting. In it, he was able to show me that things were much improved. His sand play showed me that his mother had rounded out to become a kind, Beatrix Potter-type character full of care and ability to look after her child and, although his father still stood in the corner he was replaced by the figure of a doctor, which showed me that things had got better and he had won back some much-needed respect from a young son. Paul's mother told me that the Sunday-night stomach pains had been replaced by a Sunday-night need to stay up and watch TV, but I was able to trust that she was perfectly capable of imposing her own boundaries and that she did not need me to deal with the normal requirement of a young man to stay up past his bedtime.

Girls are just as susceptible to tummy pains when finding symptoms that will tell us that all is not well in their world. By the time they are twelve (and sometimes younger), crippling period pains can add an extra twist and there can be further plausible excuses for not going to school or having a little lie down and giving up on life. If a teenager is suffering from heavy bleeding and extreme tenderness, she needs to be taken to a doctor and maybe to a gynaecologist to check that there is nothing wrong. If the girl is given a clean physical bill of health, her menstrual cycle is not an excuse to miss out on life. There is effective over-the-counter pain relief which may be taken before the start of a school day or an important activity, and the school nurse should be well equipped and can provide analgesic and an objective assessment as to whether a girl needs to be sent home or not. I have had at least a dozen girl clients who have attempted to use 'the time of the month' as a reason why they should avoid the activities that life has to offer. Girls whose parents are going through the process of separation will be full of difficult feelings, and having a messy period might be the last straw when faced with a busy day. If a child has only just heard that her parents are splitting up or she has had to face some difficult news to do with the break-up of the family home and she has a bad tummy at the same time, then sensible compassion and parental care would suggest that she be allowed to stay at home until she feels better. However, girls need structure; they need education, a life outside the home and friends to turn to. If they are allowed to give up and give in on a regular, monthly basis, they will lose consistency, fail to learn self-discipline and probably fall behind with their schoolwork.

Sophie's mother left home when Sophie was eight years old and gave custody to the father with little fight and apparently no regret. Unfulfilled by being a mother and unhappy in her marriage, she left the country and, after that, was rarely to be seen by her daughter or her ex-husband. Sophie's father Michael had had very little experience with young girls in that he had only had a brother, had been to an all-boys school and married when he was young. When Sophie hit adolescence he had little idea of how to bring up a teenage girl and certainly had no idea how to cope with the tricky subject of menstruation, let alone any confidence in having a conversation about the facts of life with his young daughter. He left such topics to the care of her school and hired help. Schools today can generally be trusted to impart sensitive information about human biology and sex in a practical, humorous and useful manner. This seems to be more acceptable to young people than having to listen to one's parents make an embarrassing hash of trying to explain something that they already know. What schools cannot do is teach a father how it feels to have a period and how to work out if he should or should not send a child out to get on with her day. Poor Michael was completely ill equipped to cope with Sophie's monthly drama and thought it was normal for his daughter to miss at least four days of school and be excused from tennis lessons and other sporting activities which would have done her the world of good.

Without a woman to guide either of them, Sophie was able to pull the wool over her father's eyes and give up on life for nearly a week on a monthly basis during school term. By the time she was fourteen she had learnt that she did not have to do anything that she did not want to do, that she did not have to face up to life's challenges and that sometimes she could stay in bed all day. When I met her she was having 'the wrong time of the month' at least every two weeks and Sophie's school insisted that she come to see me because of her frequent absence and the sad fact that a bright child was being allowed to ruin her potential by never turning up. Sophie's tummy pains had turned against her.

Therapeutic work with Sophie was not easy; she had stolen the power that should have belonged to her mother and had learnt to run rings around her confused father. I had to stand up to her and fight her for the control that did not belong to a young girl. I also had to teach her father that stomach ache and period pains do not mean staying in bed for days at a time, and encourage him to have the backbone to challenge his daughter and accept that she should join the rest of her peer group in getting up in the morning and going to school unless she had a temperature. Both Sophie and Michael became my clients as I and teachers from the school worked to change the status quo. Sophie hated me for dismantling her cosy world and forcing her out of bed. She got no pocket money if she missed a day at school; she had the fourteen-year-old's lifeline of her mobile phone removed if she did not get out of bed and the cables to her computer pinched so that she could not go on Facebook or correspond with her friends from the privacy of her bedroom. If school was missed there were no weekend outings or sleep-overs and, if she was not well enough to play tennis, then she was not well enough to saunter around the shops and coffee bars on a Saturday afternoon. And yet she also understood that I was working for and with her rather than against her and that I was doing what her mother should have done if only she had stayed around.

I had trouble with Michael, too, in that he was not entirely sure that I was doing the best thing for his daughter. He felt so sorry for her motherless state and so guilty that he had been unable to prevent his wife from leaving that he wanted to protect Sophie from all difficulties and bad feelings. In a way it was easier for him to give in to her tears, pale face and convincing stomach pains than to face her wrath and make her cry. As a soft touch who did not understand that the vast majority of young girls make it to school when they have their period, it was easy for a fourteen-year-old girl to manipulate him. But he was not helping his daughter and, in his own way, was killing her with kindness. I had to get as tough with him as I did with his daughter to stop him allowing Sophie to feign illness, and I had to work hard for nearly a year to get both father and daughter to agree to the new regime. The faked aches and pains were doing nothing to help a child find her feet in an already difficult world and they needed to be confronted and the reason for their existence understood.

Harry and Paul's tummy pains were real and difficult to bear. Although nothing was physically wrong and a doctor could have done little to alleviate the boys' symptoms, they were hurting as much and were as raw inside as if their very stomachs were bleeding. Trapped emotion can be worse than the horrible colicky pain of trapped wind and can sit in the stomach screaming out until something has to be done to alleviate the pain. In both cases, the parents of the boys understood that this was not a case of attention-seeking behaviour and took the right steps to help their children. Loving nurture in the shape of hot-water bottles, magic medicine and warm healing hands over the painful area, stories and movies in a parent's bed and anything else that seems to deflect attention away from the pain are a good idea in the short term. For the longer term, a visit to a doctor and a listening ear from a friend, teacher or trained expert will help a child to understand the causes of such trapped emotion and give them more practical ways to deal with their distress. Sophie needed different treatment. In the absence of an understanding mother and with a father who was all at sea with the practicalities of child-rearing, she was able to use her stomach pains to manipulate a situation and run her life in a way that felt attractive and rather clever to a fourteen-year-old girl. In order to live life as was expected of the rest of her age group, she needed to be given firm boundaries, guidance and directives.

Stomach aches in children going through and living with the break-up of a family call for a three-step plan of action. A visit to a doctor is essential to check that there is nothing physically wrong such as rumbling appendicitis, the swollen glands of approaching tonsillitis, the difficult and painful Crohn's disease or a whole host of gut problems which are familiar to specialists. If the child is given a clean physical bill of health, parents can be pretty sure that difficult tummy pains are caused by the emotional factors to do with the break-up of their relationship. Their child has started to say that they do not like what is happening. Care is needed to provide comfort for the pain and encouragement needs to be given so that words can be found and feelings can come out of the mouth of the child. If the child's mother and father are too preoccupied to listen or too hostile to each other for the child to be able to talk to either, then a friend or professional needs to step in to help. And, finally, if stomach pains are being used as effective avoidance techniques, then they should be gently confronted and their power diminished.

Headaches

Children who are living with parents who are going through the process of separation very often arrive in my consulting room complaining of headaches. As with problem stomach pains, they need to be treated seriously, and a visit to the GP is a first port of call, probably followed by a visit to the optician. Bad headaches can be the precursor of a cold or flu, and are to be expected during the winter months in the crowded, warm schools where our children spend much of their day. They can also be caused by too much sunshine, dehydration, excitement or too many hours with eyes glued to the computer. If all of the above are ruled out and a child still looks green around the gills and continues to complain about a tight band of pain around their head and an ache that will not go away, then they are probably in need of the same kind of conversation and help as the children who are stuck with too many tummy pains.

Lucy chose headaches as an avoidance strategy when she did not want to go to school. Too many people were invading her privacy about the very public breakdown of her parents' marriage, and she hated the well-meaning looks and lowered voices of the teachers who were trying to look after her. When her friends asked her how she was, she wanted to duck and run, and she expressed the strong wish that people let her forget that home life was difficult and allow her to get on with a normal life when she had the chance. So hated did school become with everyone asking her what was going on that she started to dread going in and came up with the clever plan that a headache would let her off the hook and allow her to stay at home. Her mother was reeling from the impact of her husband leaving and allowed her daughter too many days off. Only when the autumn-term school report arrived and clearly indicated quite how many days Lucy had missed did the penny drop. Lucy's mother needed to take action before an understandable avoidance strategy became a bad habit. Unluckily for Lucy, her mother had no scruples about reading her daughter's diary, in which she found written down clearly each day that Lucy had faked a headache and got out of going to school. With this misappropriated information, Lucy's mother had the practical knowledge that she needed to boot her daughter back to school with full attendance for the following term. The problem with the caring but intrusive enquiries was sorted out with a simple and private conversation with one or two of Lucy's friends and the head of her year. Lucy was able to return to a new term where no one bothered her and where she was free to get on with living her own life without having to think about the drama that was unfolding at home.

A difficulty facing a separating parent is the need to work out whether their child's headache is real or strategic. Because of the troubles at home, it is likely that the child will already be pale, with dark circles under their eyes, and have quite understandably lost their joie de vivre. Even if intuition says that an illness is strategic, there is something to be said for temporarily allowing a child faked aches and pains, in that it gives them time to recover from the depth charge of a piece of unwelcome news and allows them to regroup before facing life in its new form. However, a real headache caused by stress, tension and unbearable pressure is hard for a child to live with. They will not be able to hide happily in their room watching their television, pleased to have pulled the wool over a parent's eyes, and physical pain will add to the burdens they already have to face.

Tim was brought to see me at the suggestion of his doctor, who could find nothing wrong with his young patient who, although unquestionably often in real pain, showed no physical mani-festations after a whole battery of tests as to why his head hurt so much. Tim's thirteen-year-old brain felt as if it was bursting; no painkiller made any difference and although he wanted to go to school and join in with his much-loved rugby team, he found himself often lying in a darkened room listening to the soothingly familiar tales of *Just William*.

Tim did not want to be in therapy, as he did not believe in it; and he was fed up with adults asking him predictable questions about what was wrong, to which neither they nor he had any answer. It was so obvious that he did not want to talk that the best thing to do with this bolshie adolescent was to present him with a wall of paper and allow him to cover it with spray-paint. As he worked, I asked him questions about his family and his life and suggested that he indicate to me by colour, shape or quantity of paint how he felt. Tim spray-painted a vast and complicated mural of graffiti and showed me more with his emotional and energetic responses than he could have told me in hours of talking. He was angry with his mother for being such a sad, broken victim, he was furious with his father for walking off and leaving him as the eldest child in the

143

household, having to cope with his younger brother and sister, he hated the way he looked and his spots and his size, and he did not understand how he was meant to mix with friends, find girls, get a life and sort himself out when he felt so ill. As Tim worked, he seemed to change from imploded and impacted to explosive and energetic, and he finished that first session with a smile on his face and an agreement to come back to discuss some of the 'stuff' that had appeared all over the paper. He left my studio having told me that he had had great fun and, although I was worried that fumes from the spray-paint would trigger off yet another headache, he returned the next week reporting that he had suffered less from the familiar tight band of pain. Tim needed quite a few more sessions before he was released from the headaches that haunted him. He never sat still for a moment and was always up to some project or other that involved making things out of wood, building bonfires, painting huge murals or discussing with an enthusiastic knowledge the ingredients that he needed to make fireworks. He was an explosive child who needed to let off steam, but his parents' separation and his mother's consequent dependence on him meant that his energy had gone underground and turned itself into an anger which had no escape. His headaches were his safety valve; they brought him to therapy – and even Tim would admit with a cheeky smile that he had fun while he sorted them out. Free of the headaches, he got back to school, returned to the rugby field and began to work out the teenage mysteries of friendships and relationships with the opposite sex.

Headaches need the same three kinds of approach as the pains that get trapped in the stomachs of children. A trip to a medical specialist, including an optician, to rule out a physical problem; tender, loving, compassionate care with the understanding that a bad head is not an attention-seeking device but a prelude to an important conversation and a gentle but firm confrontation if one is pretty sure that there are strategic avoidance techniques going on. Once again, if parents are too split or too unhappy to find ways to reach their child, then a request for some outside help is a good idea. In my experience, a crashing headache in a child will usually suggest trapped anger, while pains in the stomach suggest infinite sadness. However, each child has such a different story to tell that I would do nothing but harm if I held on to such hypotheses as concrete truth. Perhaps anger lives in heads, perhaps sadness lives in stomachs. The child will tell me if I listen and, hopefully, I will be able to send him home to use words rather than symptoms to tell his parents what is wrong.

Bed-wetting and soiling

Bed-wetting and soiling are often seen as symptoms of emotional distress and are considered to be important tell-tale signs that a child is not coping. My experience is slightly different. The children who are brought to me because they continue to wet their bed after an age that is considered acceptable or because they don't make it to the toilet in time to defecate probably already had some type of physical or developmental problem before a breaking home exacerbated it. If a child has problems with bed-wetting, he will wet his bed more if his family is breaking up; if he has a problem with soiling, he will soil more frequently if his head is so full of other thoughts and feelings that he forgets the strategies that he has attempted to learn to get to the loo.

A child who wets the bed just might have a medical problem and needs to be checked out at an enuresis clinic, where helpful suggestions will be offered and guidance will be given. Bladders can be too small, sensory problems might mean that a child does not get the necessary physical signal to get to the toilet in time, or a child may sleep so soundly that he does not wake up. These problems can be dealt with by a change in the child's drinking habits (as much fluid as possible before 6 p.m. and nothing thereafter) and useful props

145

such as the brilliant square-metre incontinence pads that pack into any suitcase and similarly slim pull-ups that go unnoticed underneath pyjama bottoms. Having visited the doctor and bought the tools to make life easier, it is important to be as relaxed as possible about a child's bed-wetting. Adults do not wet their beds, and children grow out of it somewhere along the way. If this fact can be remembered, then everyone will be very much more comfortable with living with a problem that can be annoying and embarrassing.

Adults who are nervous pee more frequently than if they are calm and happy. And so it is with children. When a family is breaking apart, children will necessarily not be happy and their little heads will be full of worries, sadness and fear. It is not surprising if their nervous systems are overloaded. If they are already challenged in the bed-wetting department the first thing to go will be the dry nights. This backward step can be hugely distressing.

When ten-year-old Susan's parents sadly told her that their marriage was over, she returned to wetting her bed, having so proudly thrown away her plastic sheet at the age of seven. So ashamed was she that she lay awake at night dreading the prospect of the end-of-term school trip which she had been looking forward to all year. She stopped concentrating at school, did not want friends over to play and walked around with the cares of the world on her shoulders. Her parents thought that she was reacting strongly to the news of their impending break-up and sent her to talk to me. Of course, Susan was deeply upset – the evidence was in the return to bed-wetting – but what was really bothering her was the fact that she was no longer dry at night. This impacted on her social life and on her plans for the summer holidays. How could she go out and about, share bedrooms, stay with friends and go on holiday with such an embarrassing secret? Her immediate problem loomed large and made everything much worse.

Luckily, Susan was a child who was able to speak and tell me what was bothering her. I was able to reassure her that many children have problems with wetting their beds, that no one does it when they grow up, that it was a perfectly natural consequence of hearing the news that her parents were splitting up and showed what a caring and thoughtful young girl she was, that some of the children going on camp would have the same issue and that there were things that could be done to help. Susan was much relieved, and we called her mother in to give her a lesson in bed-wetting management for ten-year-olds so that her daughter did not have to face shame and fear on top of going through the distress of a breaking home.

Soiling is a more difficult problem. The children whom I have met who still soil after the age of five almost all have chronic constipation or developmental disabilities such as dyspraxia, which means that they are clumsy about wiping their bottoms and do not get the physical sensation that they need to poo until it is too late to get to the toilet. Like the children who have urinary and bed-wetting issues, older children do not usually soil because of emotional issues but have some kind of physical problem, which can be made much worse by stress. It is important to get a thorough check-up from a specialist doctor and/or a psychologist in order to understand why a child might be resistant to using the toilet before blaming one who finds it difficult to maintain hygienic bowel habits. Once a diagnosis has been obtained, adults will be able to give practical help to a child who has trouble keeping clean.

A child who soils will have to think in order to stay clean and should be taught a strategy to get to the loo on time and wipe his bottom properly. He will need to be shown what to do and where and how to do it; teachers can help to support him and baby wipes and clean knickers should be provided discreetly in a backpack so that accidents can go unnoticed by the children in the playground. It is hard work for a child who has this problem when they are running around joining in with the rough and tumble of hide-and-seek, tag or football to remember stuff that comes completely naturally to other children, and it is not surprising if there is the occasional accident. Accidents tend to multiply when a child has his head full of unsolved dilemmas and difficulties. If there is a serious problem at home, it is very likely that a child will be unhappy and confused. He is unlikely to remember his step-by-step guide for bowel control as he deals with more important issues such as news that he will have to move out of his family home, and there is a high probability that his pants will end up dirty and he will end up smelly.

Odd as it might seem, there can be a plus side for children who have problems with their bowels. Some of them will have learnt from an early age that their condition gives them attention and that they can exert power in the household by holding on, not going and eventually going in the wrong place. In addition, by no means all of them hate the experience of having dirty bottoms.

Mark was typical of the many children I see with soiling problems who are experiencing the break-up of the family home. He had a pronounced case of motor dyspraxia and was uncoordinated and clumsy. By the age of seven he could not ride a bike, hold a pen, tie a shoelace, remember where he was meant to be or balance on an adult-size toilet. The developmental disability that he experienced meant that his brain did not get the important signals that tell most of us that it will soon be time to go to the loo. The consequence for Mark was that he had frequent accidents and ran around in dirty clothes that smelt badly and offended the sensibilities of those near to him. His parents did not understand his condition and did not know that he needed special toilet-training techniques and props to help him use an adult-size loo; they had had other children who became potty-trained within a normal time frame, and they just thought Mark was being naughty. He was bribed to go to the loo properly, chased around the house so that he would be caught before he did it in his pants and was shouted at and punished if he did. This all took a huge amount of time and gained Mark a lot of attention. And, with a divorce going on and two other children to be looked after, there was not much attention to go around. Mark began by not being able to use a toilet and ended up not wanting to. He liked the power, the chasing, the attention and the rewards when he gave his parents a present in the toilet pan. He had no intention of stopping, even though he was teased in the school playground and people did not want to sit next to him on bus journeys because he was known to be smelly.

Neither did Mark mind his father's wrath. His father was an angry man who did not want a separation but found himself being sued for divorce on the grounds of unreasonable behaviour. He was allowed his children once a week for an overnight stay but would rarely collect them on the allotted day or at the allotted time. When he did pick them up, he was generally in a bad mood and complained to his children about how much work he had to do, how he should not have had to leave his home, how he was furious with his wife and how life had dealt him a very tough hand of cards. This moaning and groaning would continue, and he would get crosser and crosser at the normal shenanigans of three young children being put to bed in a strange place by someone who did not know what he was doing. When Mark's father started to shout, Mark would bravely look him straight in the eye, go red in the face and poo in his pyjama bottoms; his father would completely lose his temper, and the older sister would phone home and get Mum to come and pick them all up.

Mark had a lot invested in not learning to use the toilet properly. It was going to be hard to teach him to stop soiling, but it needed to be done. It is sad to see a lonely child from a difficult family having a tough time being bullied in a play-ground because he smells, and it is heartbreaking when it goes on for so long that a child gets stuck with a cruel nickname and an appalling reputation. We had to treat Mark in three stages. We had to teach him how to recognize the signals, encourage him to get to a toilet on time and, finally, make him want to give up his difficult behaviour. His parents needed to give him positive rather than negative attention, and his father had to work on not being so angry that his young son needed to soil his pants in order to get away from him.

Bed-wetting and soiling are embarrassing to the children who suffer from them and inconvenient to parents, who have to change sheets and wash clothes. There is often a physical or neurological reason for the problem, and there is much that can be done to help. In times of stress, the problems are likely to get worse or to reappear, while soiling may be used as a weapon to get back at adults who are too angry, have too little time or don't understand. One of the greatest forms of stress of all for a child is their parents splitting up and their home life no longer being stable. Patient understanding, reassurance that the inconvenience will not last for ever, back-up from the school, medical help and therapeutic input for both the child and the fighting parents will help a child over a hurdle that they badly need to jump if they are going to be sociable and happy with themselves.

Asthma and eczema

More and more children are suffering from eczema, asthma and hay fever. Central heating, dust mites, food additives, the daily use of chemicals and pollution are blamed for the rise in these annoying and sometimes debilitating conditions, and doctor's surgeries and alternative-health specialists are full of parents seeking help for their itching, scratching, breathless children.

As many children from fully functioning homes will be suffering from eczema, asthma and other allergies as from broken homes, but all physical problems and medical symptoms are made worse by stress. A child who has the painful redness and broken skin of eczema nestling in the fold of skin at the back of her knee will be less able to cope with the torment of the constant irritation if she is unhappy, tired and unable to sleep. Asthma sufferers will find their breathing problems harder to bear if they are already uncomfortable with what is going on within their homes and if they also find it difficult to sleep at night. As with bed-wetting and soiling, stress does not directly cause asthma and eczema, but it can make the conditions more uncomfortable for those who suffer from them. If one is already having a tough time, it is hard to hurt even more and sleep even less, and children who are suffering with their condition will find it hard to cope. They will need more tender, loving care than normal; more magic cream and distracting treats; more bedtime stories as the asthma inhaler has a chance to work; and maybe more visits to the doctor for stronger steroid creams and puffers if the attacks become more frequent and the symptoms seem stronger. This type of careful attention can be difficult for a single parent to give if they are reeling from their own misery and having to keep a difficult show on the road while looking after other children. It could be a good idea for relatives and trusted friends to step in and take a suffering child for an overnight stay to give parent and child a much needed break from the cumulative misery of family breakdown and a chronic condition.

Facial tics and nervous habits

The nervous system is fragile. When it gets overloaded, it can cause all sorts of problems and produce strange symptoms. Dogs might rub a patch bald in their fur if they are unhappy, cruelly treated or neglected. In the same way, children can pull their hair out, bite their nails to the quick, scratch their knees, bite their lips, pull at skin and develop nervous facial tics. They will do so because they are unhappy beyond words but unable to tell anyone what is going on.

Almost all the less serious self-harming activities, such as scratching, hair-pulling, nail-biting and lip- and cheek-chewing will be used by a child to find some physical sensation that provides an antidote to the pain they feel inside. Activities in which children hurt themselves need to be seen as the beginning of a conversation without words, and adults need to listen while involving the children in the process of stopping the destructive behaviour, which can turn into a nasty habit.

When Sabrina felt that she had no one to talk to about the fact that her father had left her and had a new young baby daughter, she started to rub her knees against bricks in the school playground. This gave her something to do since she felt that she had no friends to play with, and it also gave her a measure of comfort to go to the school office and get kind attention and a sticking plaster. Her strange behaviour made sense as a coping mechanism for a sad, lonely girl. Sabrina's school stopped her grazing her knees against the wall by providing a teacher to whom she could say she was feeling sad and bad. She would be given a lollipop and could sit on the sofa reading a book until it was time for break to end. One might think that this would encourage all of the children in the playground to apply for the same privilege, but children are proud and want to fit in with everyone else. As soon as Sabrina felt safe and protected, she lost the need to self-harm, gave up her sanctuary and her lollipop and joined her friends back in the playground.

Facial tics, stuttering and repetitive eye movements may appear because a child is under stress or they can be part of a child's physical make-up. Speech therapy is excellent for dealing with stammers and speech impediments and should be available via a GP anywhere, and there are extraordinarily good specialist centres in the UK. Facial tics are more difficult to understand. If resistant to therapy, calm understanding and playful humour, they probably need to be checked out by a children's doctor, who might look for something like a childhood case of Tourette's syndrome. However, most children who blink too much, squeeze their eyes tight or repetitively bite their cheeks will stop their unconscious behaviour when life calms down and they are given the right kind of help.

Patricia had a facial tic but was sent to me ostensibly because she was disappointed at the age of seven to have failed a difficult entrance exam to get into a highly academic school. A small, nervous, round-faced girl who could hardly speak sidled into my art-therapy room giving the impression for all the world that she not only did not want to be with me but did not want to be anywhere else either. The poor child stood motionless and lost among a sea of toys that other children would leap into. The only thing that moved was the right side of her face, which twitched involuntarily, as she repetitively blinked her eye, making the right side of her mouth curl at the same time. Not for her the drums or the climbing frame; she needed quiet and sensitivity, and I had to search for a way to reach her that would not frighten her further.

I started by quietly making a pattern in the sand box using shells, pieces of polished glass and bits and pieces that I had collected on the seashore. Here and there I added water or precious beads and sat engrossed in a task that meant nothing but looked beautiful and had the feeling of different textures and thoughts of the rolling calm of the sea. I did not speak but sat on the floor gently pouring sand between my fingers and hiding precious gems under rocks and putting pearls into shells until Patricia, intrigued, sat and joined me and began making her own patterns and hiding her own treasures and helping me to make a picture that needed no beginning, no middle, no end and did not need to mean anything. Children who are sad and lost love to play with sand and water; they like to mould and sculpt and move mountains from one end of the sand tray to the other. They become involved with something unexpected and, as they work, they usually begin to talk. Bit by bit and very slowly, a story emerges which needs to be carefully interpreted by adults, who might not immediately understand and who must often check with the child who is at last beginning to speak.

Patricia's story was much sadder than that of a girl who had failed to get into the school of her parents' choice. She was the child of a bitter divorce that had included fights in front of her about money and sexual infidelity, and she had the damaging information that her father had been having a long-term relationship with a family friend whom she had known from an early age. Trusting nothing and no one, she was moved from her childhood home to a new house where her mother welcomed a live-in lover whom they had little time to get to know. Unfortunately, he was physically violent and would not think too much before slamming a door on her mother's hand and breaking her wrist while Patricia watched as a young witness. At every level in Patricia's life there was mayhem, and yet to the outside world it looked as if her mother and father were coping well with the separation while continuing to put their child first, choose the 'right' school and get her ready for life with the best education possible. Patricia did not need to be with me because she had failed an exam; she needed to be with me because her life had failed her. The only way she could show the way she had seized up on the inside was to allow the world to see how the right-hand side of her face had seized up on the outside.

But Patricia had not seized up completely. Her parents loved her notwithstanding the troubles in their own lives, and she was at a careful school which understood that she could not cope. She had not yet turned her back on love and play, and she wanted to feel better. From the first tentative steps she took when helping to make a pattern in the sand, she worked with me until she was able to build a relationship that she could trust and so be able to talk to me about her troubles. She told me about witnessing violence and how it was somehow worse to hear it from her bedroom than to watch it from the landing, she showed me with battling figures how her parents fought, she indicated that she could not concentrate at school and did not always understand what her teachers were trying to tell her, and she told me that she felt that she had let her parents down. As she talked and played and began weakly to smile, her right eye began to twitch a little less and her mouth stayed still as she concentrated on whatever we were up to in the art room. Eventually I judged that Patricia trusted me enough to talk explicitly about her nervous tic, and she was happy to admit that she did not like it and that she hated it when it was mentioned at school. She asked for help to stop doing it. It surprised her when I suggested she do it more, as trying to do it less did not seem to work. And so we sat pulling funny faces together and seeing who could keep the most grotesque facial expression, at the same time refusing to laugh and continuing a conversation as if there were nothing wrong at all. From there we moved on to a game in which we tried every activity on offer in the play area and banged drums and went down slides and played chess while trying to keep our mouths twitching and our eyes blinking rapidly. We could not do it. More importantly, Patricia could not do it and, also, she began to be able to make a noise and whoop and whoosh down slides and across monkey bars, so unlike the small girl who had sidled into my therapy room silent and afraid only weeks before. By the end of a term of weekly therapy Patricia no longer blinked and grimaced. She was able to play and she was able to speak. Her mother and father cooperated and stopped fighting in front of her, agreed about her contact with each parent so that it was consistent and reliable and learnt to listen to her when she had important things to say. Her mother apologized to her about the fact that she had had to witness violence and promised that it would never happen again, and her father was able to make his daughter believe that he had never stopped loving her, even when she had not got into the school, which had been more about the ambition of a forty-year-old man than the need of a seven-year-old girl. By the time she was ten, no one would have ever known that Patricia had had a major blip in her young life, and she sailed through a competitive exam with a relaxed face and a relaxed personality.

Not all facial tics and nervous habits are the result of stress, and some need to be checked out medically. However, if there is a bitter and difficult divorce going on and parents are finding it hard to keep their children removed from the day-to-day corrosive negativity of a breaking home, there is a high likelihood that tics and habits will be symptoms of a child's unhappiness. A strange habit is usually a symptom of unhappiness and it is the beginning of a conversation. It helps if a child can find someone to talk to who can speak the language of childhood and who might be able to guess what is bothering them. It helps if they can talk about their habit without being told not to do it and if they can find something else to do instead. If adults can empathetically and imaginatively join the discussion, the child should find relief and no longer need to pull at, bite, pick and graze their body, and facial tics, blinking eyes and nervous stammers will diminish.

Sleep disturbance

One of the most difficult and often hidden symptoms for a child to exhibit in a breaking home is an inability to go to or to stay asleep. Life is exhausting when two adults who have children decide to separate. It is never an easy decision and, usually, both mother and father are left unhappy and reeling. Although adults need to look after themselves, they rarely can at a time of maximum stress. They need to eat and sleep, exercise and work, find friends to talk to and discuss with lawyers and other professionals the practical ramifications and consequences of the break-up. In reality, they often sink to a low ebb and, rather than live a healthy life, they turn to alcohol, cigarettes, late nights, chocolate and any other comfort they can find. Sleep usually goes out of the window, as does exercise and serenity. Most of the adults I have met who are separating have stress levels off the Richter scale.

Children feel the same levels of stress and sadness, but do not have adult choices to help them escape from or soothe their feelings. Rather than find comfort in externally gratifying stimuli, children need to act out, play up, implode, explode and demonstrate with physical symptoms that all is not well with the world. One of the most powerful but least talked about symptoms is sleep disturbance, which can present as sleep-walking and sleep-talking, night terrors, a refusal to go to bed and to sleep, or an early-morning waking which brings sheer panic and, in a teenager, very often a conviction that, at that moment, their very life is in danger. At the time when people need a good eight hours' rest in order to recover their equilibrium and mend their shattered minds, nature plays a cruel trick and ensures that they awake at strange, dark hours, get no rest and do not have the chance to regain perspective or hope. When a child is very unhappy, it is likely that their sleep pattern will also go to pieces, and they will be unlikely to be able to cope with the demands that daily life places upon them. Parents will be even more pushed against the wall by concern for their child and the necessity of night-time vigils which leave a whole family exhausted.

In a previous chapter I wrote about Lilly, who stayed on red alert, who was still awake at midnight and slept with her arms tightly curled around her mother's neck in case she too should disappear; and about Jessica, who was convinced that bad men were going to come through the window and steal either her or her mother and so got into her mother's bed at two in the morning. And I know of many cases where children will not go to bed because their parents, in their distress, have lost the power to make them do so; who cannot go to bed because they are afraid that if they take their eye off the ball the remaining parent will walk out of the door; or who cannot stay asleep because their brains are whirring. For these children, sleep deprivation becomes a part of the process of the break-up, and it needs to be dealt with as quickly as possible. A separating family will find it infinitely harder to cope if it cannot sleep, and a child without sleep has small chance of developing well and keeping up with his school and friends.

Before their child reaches the age of fourteen, adults need to be in control of their bedtime and sleep habits. As birthdays come and go, night-time routines will change and the time for lights out will grow later. Other parents, teachers, health workers and parenting books will have rule-of-thumb ideas about healthy bedtimes for different age groups, and each family will find its own system. These family systems are important. A child needs to know what is expected of her, and a parent needs some rest. Children will feel safer if there is routine and structure in their life, and they will benefit if their mother or father is in charge.

Sadly, when a family is going through the process of separation, it can be easy to let routines slip. Boisterous ten-year-olds who do not want to do their homework and certainly do not want to go to bed can be difficult to persuade to behave when a parent has no energy, perhaps has had a glass of wine or two and needs to talk on the telephone about matters which feel much more important than bed-time for a naughty child.

Fred was eight when his parents went through an acrimonious break-up. His mother Sally was left alone with two small boys while their father set up in a bachelor pad around the corner, leaving little money to help his ex-wife. She had to sell the house and work full time. By the time it came to evening, with a long day at the office behind her, a house move to consider, a broken heart and two children to put to bed, she could hardly stagger to run the bath or read her boys their bedtime stories. Fred, naughty and adventurous, saw an opportunity for doing what he loved to do and refused to get off the computer, turn off the television or move upstairs when asked. Sally was simply too exhausted and too sad to fight him. Neither could she see much point in attempting to instil discipline and routine and make herself unpopular when Fred was allowed to stay up until midnight at his father's. And so Fred became an eight-year-old boy who could hardly think during the school day and would lash out in easily provoked anger because of his exhaustion. Sally did her son no favours by being lax with him and allow-ing him to forget to go to bed.

Other children are not as naughty as Fred and have a different problem. They want to go to sleep but genuinely cannot. Worry, con-fusion, not knowing, concern for a parent, being on alert for a row downstairs, an inability to switch off, or non-specific fears about the days ahead will all keep a small brain turning around in an unhappy muddle so that sleep will not come and time ticks painfully slowly by as the house grows silent. Everything suddenly becomes very much more frightening when adults go to sleep and, just as an exhausted parent begins to make his or her way to bed, a small figure will appear asking for and needing comfort. Some children can get to

159

sleep but find themselves waking in the small hours of the morning full of fear that something might be badly wrong.

Different parents will have different ideas about what to do. Some will bring their child into their beds and thus set a precedent that might be difficult to change in future months; others will sit with their children while they go to sleep; and others will just tell their children to stop making a fuss and go to bed and stay there. There is often inconsistency in the way the two members of a separated couple will deal with what can be a serious problem; furthermore, mothers tell me that their children will not leave them alone during the night while fathers tell me they have no trouble with night-time wanderings. A way will eventually be found through the tiring nights and the problem will not last for ever, but it can hurt the entire family while it is going on.

The best way to help a child to get to sleep is for parents to work together and come up with the same expectations and strategies for both households. It is important not to make a child be in the wrong; it is equally important to understand his fears and teach him to get to bed and stay there so that he can find some rest. Bedrooms can be made more comforting with night lights; carefully closed curtains and firmly shut cupboard doors can protect against bad men and black shadows; doors can be left open with a light on outside; two-way baby alarms can be installed so that a child can hear the comforting background noises of adult presence; story tapes can be bought for easy listening; relaxation techniques can be taught; lavender and parents' favourite scents and aftershave can be placed on pillows; a favourite cuddly jumper complete with smells and sense of the missing parent can be tucked into the bed; and star charts with rewards attached can be made for a child who succeeds in staying in his own bed in his own room. It is hard to turn a tear-streaked face away and lead an unhappy child back to bed. But sleep disturbance can become a bad habit and needs to be nipped in the bud by firm but understanding parents who somehow have to find the energy to set the rules and get their child back into bed so that he knows there is no longer any point in night-time wanderings.

Adolescents who are sleepless for the same reasons need different strategies. By the time a child is fourteen she should be able to provide her own comfort and autonomy in her bedroom and not need to keep an entire household awake by staying up after a parent has gone to bed. However, the teenage years are turbulent, full of hormonal and growth spurts, physical and emotional challenges and difficult times. Sleep is one of the most important things that a teenage body needs, and parents should encourage good habits. That said, the teenage pursuit of pleasure often seems to be about staying up as late as possible and going out and about with a huge push at the boundaries of parenting to extend the night-time curfew. Adolescent culture sometimes dictates that teenagers should stay up absurdly late and, if at all possible, not go to bed at all. If we accept that this is the way that many adolescents want to party, it can be factored into the equation of how best to deal with disrupted sleep patterns.

However difficult it might be, it is especially important that separating parents join at the hip about boundaries and expectations of the sleep routines of their adolescent children. Give and take works well and clear guidelines as to expectations and routines help everyone concerned. If a teenager gets to school, produces good enough work, keeps vaguely to household rules, communicates with his parents, has some exercise and finds friends to call, then he will be doing well. He will have earned the right to party on occasion, depending on his age, his school and other commitments. However, if a late night at a weekend means that he sleeps all day and then his sleep is disrupted for the rest of the week, the late nights need to stop until he learns to manage his sleeping pattern. While it is all right to be up late or up all night occasionally, it is not all right to tip into the vampire-like behaviour I see so often in my consulting room where children as young as thirteen go to bed at four in the morning and then wonder why they cannot get up for school. Teenagers need the

161

same good practice as younger children and they certainly need to go to sleep before midnight if they are going to cope the following day. In an ideal world, both parents would agree on bed before eleven for the younger teenagers on school nights, with computers removed from bedrooms to get rid of the powerful temptation of MSN and Facebook; phones would be switched off so that the all-night chatter comes to an end; televisions would be unplugged; and a united discipline would be enforced so that a teenage body has no choice but to get some rest and have a chance to face the daunting task of growing up. Sometimes a teenager simply cannot go to sleep and his body clock seems to go awry; if this is the case melatonin, as discussed below, is a good idea. And if a teenager becomes defiant about his sleep patterns, then his parents can become defiant back and remove the things most precious to him, such as pocket money or a mobile phone, until he establishes good practice.

If a sleep problem becomes chronic, a visit to the doctor might provide comfort, helpful suggestions, a referral to a therapist or, in extreme cases, a diagnosis of depression. Doctors sometimes suggest antihistamine medication for children to try to get them to sleep and to break a difficult cycle. It can be bought over the counter, but I suggest that it is administered under medical supervision while counselling or family therapy is explored. Private psychiatrists are able to prescribe melatonin, which can be bought over the counter in the USA and is used to combat disrupted sleep patterns and jet lag. It helps children to go to and stay asleep and is especially good for adolescents. It has not yet been endorsed in the UK and is not on the list of drugs that can be prescribed by the NHS.

Childhood depression

Seeing the pale faces, dark eyes and worried, pinched expressions of children who are watching their family break apart is hard. Sometimes I want to do anything in my power to get parents back together again so that I can see joy reappear on faces that seem to have had all the light knocked out of them. When I see this unadulterated sadness I wonder whether divorce is worth it and if we should attempt to turn back the clock and stay together for the sake of our children. However, there is no such thing as a quick fix; even if parents were to get back together to remove the haunted and sad look from the eyes of their children, the damage would already have been done, on top of which a child may have learnt the negative lesson that she can get what she most wants in the world by being depressed or sad.

Our quick-fix culture likes to hide negative feelings and pretend that they are not there but, ultimately, it does more harm than good to bury and deny. Sadness is an important part of the kaleidoscopic range of human emotion and, within the context of a breaking home, is entirely normal and needs to be lived with, understood and accepted. Some children will show their sadness by exhibiting the physical symptoms that I have discussed previously, while others will be so unhappy that they might look as if they have lost their energy, their will to live and the very life force that belongs to childhood.

Kit's parents broke up when he was ten. He was a small, wiry boy with a serious face and a secret sense of humour. He had been doing well at school, had lots of friends, had no time for his teenage sister and was busy collecting and swapping football cards and insisting that he had a rise in his pocket money. He slept and ate and complained about homework and, until the horrible day when he sat on his mother's bed and watched his father pack his suitcases, he was a normal boy. With one stroke, his parents took away his security, his happiness and his *joie de vivre*.

Kit became so sad that he turned his back on the world. He no longer played in the school playground and found the rough and tumble of the world of boys difficult to enjoy. His pride meant that he did not want anyone to know about the sad situation in his personal life, and he had an almost neurotic fear that the children in his year at school would find out; it was as if he were ashamed that his parents could not stay together. His work went downhill and he sank to the bottom of the class, he stopped his chess and cricket clubs, he refused to answer phone calls from friends who wanted him out in the park and he would not go to his much-loved Saturday football game. He replaced his healthy disdain of his sister with a clinging desperate need to be with her, and he would not let his mother out of the house.

Sadness was overwhelming Kit, and something needed to be done to stem the tide so that he did not drown. Therapy was a good idea, in that he was given an hour a week just for him where he was not made to feel guilty about feeling so awful. He played in the sand, painted, made things out of clay and threw them around and bashed at drums to express his fury. He was given time to work out the catastrophic sense of doom, gloom and panic that his parents' unwelcome decision had stirred within him, and he was able to make sense of the fact that there was nothing wrong with him in having such strong feelings but that there was a great deal wrong within his household and some things which needed to happen to begin to put things right.

His parents helped him by coming to occasional sessions and listening and taking suggestions seriously as to how they could best help their small, unhappy boy. He asked to be allowed to watch more television until he felt prepared to get back on to the football field, and his mother, who had strictly rationed his TV, agreed that, as a comfort zone, he could turn it on during the week if his homework had been done. The same applied to computer games, and his father bought a PlayStation to keep in his rented apartment so that Kit felt that he would have something to do when he visited a sad and sterile place that never felt like home. His mother understood that her son had an important need for privacy and did not want her talking on the telephone for hours about their situation, so she delayed her phone calls until after he had gone to bed. Kit's appetite diminished, and he no longer wanted to eat the sort of food that had appealed to him. He gave up spicy adult flavours and went back to mashed potatoes, pasta and roast chicken. He needed nursery food, special bedtimes with night-time stories, blankets to tuck him up on a sofa while he watched television and an understanding that he was reeling and could not cope with growing up at the same time as receiving shattering news. His parents allowed their ten-year-old to become young again, giving him treats and careful attention so that he could cry and be sad in peace, away from the watchful eyes of his competitive peers.

Gradually, Kit regained his energy and his composure. Underneath the sadness lurked huge anger, and his parents had to deal with that as he allowed them to know that he felt as if they had ruined his life. They needed to stand up to him so that his wrath did not turn tyrannical, and to have a joint strategy when he behaved badly. Bit by careful bit, Kit was encouraged back to the playground, the football field, the park and his friends. But it took a year of a pale face, aching sadness, lost energy, loneliness and loathing for him to heal. And it took someone who had nothing to do with the break-up of his parents' marriage to listen to him and allow him to be sad and desperate. Kit came to me because his mother believed in therapy, and I was able to help, but I did not need any special skill. A friend, grandparent, godparent, aunt or uncle could have provided the same comfort and place of emotional safety by allowing a small person to be sad and giving him an understanding and listening ear.

Children who are not allowed to be sad or angry and who have to tuck away their feelings in order to survive and cope with the demands of growing up may be in danger of becoming depressed. The Royal College of Psychiatrists estimates that 2 per cent of children under the age of twelve and 5 per cent of adolescents will struggle with significant depression; and that it will often be caused by a traumatic event such as the disintegration of a family home and be deepened by inconsistent parenting. Perhaps best described by Louis Wolpert as a 'malignant sadness', depression brings an overwhelming feeling of hopelessness, sadness and lack of self-worth to all when it visits and needs to be taken seriously by adults and treated by experts.

All children will be sad when their parents break up. However, if the sadness goes on for too long and stops a child from coping with his life, it might be a good idea to think about the possibility of depression. Steps will need to be taken to ameliorate symptoms which in themselves will make a situation much worse and a child increasingly unhappy. Depressive symptoms to watch for in children are:

- Looking unhappy, miserable, unloved and lonely a lot of the time. This will present as an inability to speak or find words for what is going on.
- Frequent health problems and physical symptoms such as the aches and pains already discussed.
- Becoming withdrawn – avoiding friends, family and regular activities and shutting themselves away in a silent bedroom.
- Spending a lot of time in bed but sleeping badly and waking early. This will bring tiredness, irritability and an inability to cope.
- Finding it difficult to concentrate or be decisive. This will probably mean problems with academic work, a loss of interest and enthusiasm and a heightened likelihood of troublemaking.
- Major changes in appetite and weight, with the problems associated with being under- or overweight.

- Unusually irritable, sulky, quiet and introverted. This will exacerbate problems with socializing and will inadvertently push people away.
- Losing interest in favourite hobbies: this will exacerbate the problem of withdrawal from life.
- Feeling guilty or bad, being self-critical and self-blaming, feeling ugly. This will ensure that it is difficult to socialize or get out and about and away from the difficulties within the family home.
- Irritability which may lead to hyperactivity, aggressive or troublesome behaviour. A child is likely to be punished and misunderstood.
- Neglect of appearance and hygiene. This will mean a continued downward spiral away from friends towards negative self-image and criticism from adults.
- Fears of separation and reluctance to meet people. A child will as a result be unable to get on with building his or her own life.
- Contemplating suicide and wanting to die.

If more than three of these problems become evident after the initial breakdown of family life, it is worth contacting the GP and asking to be referred to a psychiatrist. Treatment will usually involve some kind of talking therapy, either with the individual child or with the family as a whole. In extreme cases, and with older children, antidepressants may be prescribed. If medication is to be considered it is important to find an expert who knows what questions to ask and how to translate childhood cries for help. Experience in child and adolescent mental health is essential when it comes to medicating children for depression, as reactions and side effects can be different for each individual and dosage needs to be carefully watched and monitored.

If parents understand that their adult decision to separate might have either caused their children's physical problems or greatly added to their existing symptoms, they will probably feel even more guilty, fraught and despairing about the state of their shattered home. But if they do everything they can to alleviate pain, find the right medical help and make life better for their offspring, they themselves will be able to feel better about what their separation has done to their children. If adults can listen to the physical messages and take action, they will make children more comfortable while showing them that they are understood. The children will learn that there are people who want to listen, and they will feel safer, less trapped and less alone. Importantly, they will also be given essential tools for the development of a better sense of self-worth, and they will understand that, even if their parents have separated and their home life is no longer as they would wish, they are still precious and important to the grown-ups upon whom they depend for their care.

Summary

Emotions that are hidden within a child's body can find some release if they are translated into real pain for which there might be a cure.

- **Tummy pains** are common, especially among boys between the ages of five to twelve. Although nothing may be physically wrong, small tummies can hurt as much and be as raw on the inside as if they were bleeding. Care is needed to provide comfort for the pain, and encouragement needs to be given so that words can be found and feelings can come out of the mouth of a child. If mothers and fathers are too preoccupied to listen, the child should talk to a relative, special friend or professional. If stomach pains are being used as an effective avoidance technique for school or other activities, then they should be gently confronted and have their power diminished.
- **Headaches** need the same kind of approach as the pains that get trapped in the stomachs of children: a trip to a medical specialist; tender, loving, compassionate care, with the understanding that a bad head is not an attention-seeking device but a prelude to an

important conversation; and a gentle but firm confrontation if one is pretty sure that there is an element of strategic avoidance.

- **Eczema, asthma, bed-wetting or soiling** will be likely to get worse or to reappear. As one of the greatest causes of stress for a child is to live through the break-up of his home, he will require patient understanding for his ailments, reassurance that the current bad situation will not last for ever, back-up from his school, medical help and therapeutic input.

- **Minor self-harming activities and nervous habits** such as scratching, hair-pulling, nail-biting and lip- and cheek-chewing might be used by a child to find some physical sensation that provides an antidote to the pain inside. Such activities need to be seen as the beginning of a conversation without words, and adults need to listen while involving the children in the process of stopping any destructive behaviour which may turn into a nasty habit. Facial tics, rapidly blinking eyes and stammers are painful for a child to have to cope with in the classroom and within the context of daily life. Although some need to be checked out medically, it is a good idea if a child can find someone to talk to who understands the language of childhood. It can help if children can talk about their habit without being told not to do it and if they can find something else to do instead.

- **Sleep disturbance** is a powerful symptom of inner turmoil and can present as sleepwalking and talking, night terrors, refusal to go to bed and to sleep or early morning waking that brings sheer panic. Sleep deprivation needs to be dealt with as quickly as possible. A separating family will find it infinitely harder to cope if it cannot sleep, and a child without sleep has small chance of developing well and keeping up with his school and friends.

- **Childhood depression:** Children who are not allowed to be sad or angry and who have to tuck away their feelings in order to survive can be in danger of depression. Depression brings an overwhelming feeling of hopelessness, sadness and lack of self-worth to all those it visits and needs to be taken seriously by adults and treated by experts.

5 ‥‥‥
Difficult times, difficult behavioural symptoms

SYMPTOMS CONVEYING DEEP UNHAPPINESS at parental break-up can be behavioural as well as physical. There can be some surprisingly complex behaviours common to children in these circumstances, and they can be difficult to deal with. Refusal to go to school, violence, aggression, self-harm and a problematic lack of respect for others are often part of the sad story of separation, and will draw in more and more people as the extended family, teachers, health workers, social workers and, sometimes, the police have to get involved.

School

Many children will refuse to go to school when there is trouble at home, either because they want to look after an unhappy parent or because they have the power not to go. Other children cannot concentrate or do not get their homework done, either because it seems pointless or because there is no energy in the family home to have the usual tussles about it. Children may have trouble socially at school

171

because they lack the energy to join the frantic whirl of the playground, or they may become so keen to belong that they try too hard and end up as either the bully or the bullied. They will often not want to go away on school trips and may be tearful or frightened at the thought of leaving the ebbing security of home and the parent who is left behind. Boarding-school children can have a difficult time when parents are separating. Rather than it being a good thing that they are away from the fighting, it is much more common that they become homesick and want to return home to keep an eye on what is going on.

Children find it hard to express their feelings, and wise adults often need to act as interpreters. This is especially obvious in the hectic daily life of a schoolchild, where there is little time to work things out, and huge energy and organizational skills are needed to get from A to B with the right books, the right friends and the right homework at the right time. If a child is feeling overwhelmed with intense emotion, the requirements of the school day can become too much for them, and they are likely to give up or give in to their unhappy inner world. I have written of Lucy, who faked headaches in order not to have to face her teachers, of Kit, who could no longer find the energy to join in with the rough and tumble of the playground, of Bella, who failed all of her exams, and of Josh, who was so confused that he found himself unable to learn. I see endless numbers of children whose problems at school are related to the separation of their parents.

Billy was an example of a child who felt that he needed to be at home to keep an eye on what was going on. At eleven years old he happily left his home in another country and flew to the UK to be educated in a prep school that offered sport, music, drama, art and fantastically good food. Whenever I visited I was impressed by the atmosphere, where children whooshed down stairs, around and about on skateboards and rollerblades at

172

break-time and were allowed to take the headmaster's dog for a walk in the school grounds. It was a happy place, and Billy loved it but, in his second year, things began to go dramatically downhill, and the headmaster called me in to see what might be wrong. By the age of twelve Billy had turned from a chatty, involved, bright-eyed child to a pale, troubled introvert who could not bear school. He attempted to run away on two or three occasions and, when he was brought back, he self-harmed by cutting his hands and arms on sharp stones. He stopped working, gave up playing and turned his face to the wall, declaring that he was homesick.

Billy's parents flew to the UK and booked into a bed and breakfast. Together, they, the headmaster, teachers and I attempted to understand what was happening to an unhappy young boy who seemed to have experienced a complete change of personality. We looked at the possibility of bullying, issues of friendship and the situation in the dormitory and unpicked Billy's daily routine to see if we could find a clue as to why he needed to rub his wrists raw, lacerate his hands and run away, but we could find nothing that made any sense. I wondered about clinical depression and sent him home for the last two weeks of term on the understanding that medical support was sought. During the long school holidays, Billy's parents reported to me that he was fine and that he was back to his old cheerful self. However, when the time came for a return to school and the need to get back on to the aeroplane, Billy launched into a full-scale strike of fury, despair and outright refusal. By now thirteen, he was able to throw a scene of such proportions at the airport that no airline would take him, and he had to return home, with no school to go to and apparently no reason for his worrying behaviour.

I travelled to see Billy in an attempt to find a reason for his uncharacteristic behaviour, and I found it when I entered the house and breathed in the atmosphere. The strained faces of his mother and father, the palpable tension in the air, the dismissive way that the two parents talked to each other and the lack of warmth and sense of cohesion in a house that had a real crisis within it told me that a relationship was in trouble. A long walk by the sea with Billy gave me the important piece of the puzzle that had been missing. Billy's troubles stemmed from his life at home. His parents could not stand each other, and their marriage had run out of love and out of steam. Events were to unfold that would tell us that the mother had had a boyfriend, that this fact had been met with jealous violence and brooding malevolence and that home did not feel safe to Billy. He had witnessed fighting, shouting and tears but, when he asked his mother if she was all right, she assured him that she was fine, that he was imagining things and that he must get back to school and study. But Billy did not want to go back to school and lie awake at night imagining the worst and longing to be home to provide comfort to his mother, who was so obviously in distress.

This intuitive child did not need reassurance that everything was all right when he knew that everything was all wrong. He needed clarity and a promise that his father would not hit his mother when he was away. His parents needed to tell him the truth and show that they were able to deal with their problems without him having to stand watch. Encouraged by the obvious need of their son, Billy's parents sat down and told him what was going on and what was going to happen. They were able to answer his questions about how and when and where, and were able to show that they had already gone quite a long way down the road towards making constructive arrangements about calling a halt to a relationship that was no longer working. Billy was hugely relieved to hear the concrete plan and to know that something was being done about the nightmare, which became so much worse when he was far away and powerless to help. He was able to return to England and went back to school to live and to learn without the heavy burden of needing to stand as guardsman at the gate of an unhappy marriage.

Other children have trouble getting to school because they do not like it, because it does not seem relevant to their daily drama, because their work is going downhill, because they have not done their homework or because it is more comfortable to sit at home and watch television. Like adults who sometimes want a day off, children will attempt to kick against the system and stay at home from time to time. In a breaking home, everyone is unhappy and uncomfortable, and everyone will be exhausted and need a rest. Occasionally, it is a good idea for a child to play hooky and hide under the duvet with favourite food and TV programmes and hugs and cuddles. But if it happens too often and if a parent loses his or her power, worse problems are likely to follow. A sad consequence of a difficult separation and ineffective co-parenting can be a child who is allowed to refuse to go to school.

An extreme example was Jenny, who, by fourteen, was one of the most negatively powerful children I have ever met. Sent home from school because she refused to sit exams or do any homework, and having bitten the ankle of the headmistress to prove her point, she came to the attention of the local psychiatric team and social services. Any grown-up who appeared at her house to find out why she was not at school was greeted with a ferocious frown, and she would lock herself in a bathroom or her bedroom and prove to be quite capable of staying there all day. Her mother could do nothing with her and would alternately plead, bribe or shout outside the locked door in an ineffective attempt to bring her daughter to the conference table, while one glimpse of her father would automatically result in powerful, sulking silence and a withdrawal to the safety of a locked room. Jenny was deeply unhappy in her unstructured isolation and I feared for her.

Jenny's parents had gone through an ugly and complicated divorce which had involved withholding of money, legal wrangles, lots of shouting and enormous anger. The mother earned more than her husband and had to pay him to leave the family home, although he had not behaved well within the marriage. She was bitter and broken to find herself alone with two children and diminished finances while her husband lived with another woman and stepchildren in a house that she had had to buy.

Such was the lack of respect between the two parents that the children found themselves having to choose between their mother and their father. And in reality they had no choice; they lived with their mother and they needed her to look after them. In her understandable role as angry victim, she insisted that her children dislike their father as much as she did. Together, the children lived in an atmosphere of unhappy anger, going out to meet their dad only when they absolutely had to and behaving badly when they did. The father told me that Jenny had 'no manners, no charm and no conversation' and that 'he could not believe that she was his daughter', and, indeed, when I saw the two of them together, I watched a performance of such intense negativity that I doubted that the relationship could ever be put right. But Jenny's mother was no angel; with a broken marriage behind her, she allowed herself to sink into a pit of despair from which she seemed unable to emerge. When I met her she had been divorced for at least four years, but I imagined she was still as unhappy as on the day that her husband had left. She had no life, no interests, had given up her work and was probably suffering from depression. I wanted to help her out of her torpor and tell her that, if she moved, her daughter might move too, that Jenny was only following her example and had learnt that she too could sit down and refuse to do the things that she did not like. The two of them together had become a negative force, a difficult and dark double act that was hard to break and which the father had no power to influence.

Initially, Jenny's parents needed to work out a strategy that would diminish the power of their daughter. Couples therapy proved useful, in that two people who had not been alone in a room together since the final dramatic and painful court appearance were able to talk. Jenny was not to blame for her sulking, school refusal and vicious behaviour although, ultimately, she would have to take responsibility for putting things right. Her parents needed to understand that if they changed, she might follow; if they began to respect each other, she might begin to respect them; and if they worked together to co-parent their difficult child, she might begin to behave. The stakes were high; Jenny was on her way to being educated in a centre for other difficult children. Her mother and father agreed to put their differences aside and learn to work together. They needed to save a child from having too much power but no education, no friends, no discipline, no interests, and problems with overeating due to boredom and a need to obliterate her feelings of not belonging and despair.

Together, they introduced a workable system of punishments and rewards. If Jenny accepted her home tuition and did her homework, she was allowed her mobile phone and TV. If she refused to see her teacher or to talk to me, both were removed. She had to go to bed before midnight and walk the dog for at least an hour a day if she wanted any pocket money, and if she wanted to join her friends on a Friday night she had to earn the privilege by talking to the grown-ups who were attempting to help her. Because she was violent and capable of inflicting damage within the house and on her mother, her father was invited back into the family home on a regular basis. In this way he was able to help and stand firm when difficult new systems were introduced and provide an important male presence that could withstand the slamming doors and hissy fits that so frightened and dominated her mother. As Jenny tried to fight this new and unpopular regime, she found her father standing up to her, and she was unable to hit and scratch and bite if anyone suggested something that she did not want to do.

It was difficult for all concerned to bring Jenny back into the acceptable and normal realms of childhood. Her mother did not want her ex-husband back inside her house, and Jenny did not want her power removed. However, things slowly began to get better. Jenny began to talk to me, so I no longer found myself leaning against a locked door feeding pieces of paper to a sulking child who wanted me to go away. If she wanted her phone, she had to be in the same room as me for our sessions. Slowly, she began to tell me how frightened she was of examinations and how she feared that she was not as clever as her sister; she told me that she thought she was ugly and fat and that there was no hope for her in a school where everyone was prettier than her. She told me that she hated her glasses and wanted to change her hairstyle but her mother would not let her; she told me that she did not know what to talk about during the endless and difficult dinners with her father; and she told me that she wished her mother would stop crying and go out and get a life. Jenny gave me enough information to start to be able to work with her in order to make things better. We arranged for a teacher to give her lessons in exam technique so that she did not freeze, we asked for and got contact lenses and a new hairstyle, we changed the way that she spent time with her father so that they got involved in a physical activity rather than staring morosely at a tablecloth in yet another restaurant and we explained to the school that Jenny was unhappy and sad rather than bad and if she were given another chance and treated gently she would come back and do her best. Her school was amazing in the welcome that they gave her and in the gentle way that they accepted her back into their midst, and I know that Jenny has gone down in its history as one of their real successes, a girl who went from biting the headmistress to becoming a prefect with a string of good exam results and a university place away from home.

Jenny had helpful adults, an understanding school to encourage her back towards life and the social services to push her towards education. But the combination would not have been enough if her parents had not been able to put their differences aside and work together to get their daughter to begin to behave. By coming up with an agreed system of reward and punishment, by joining together to stop the bad behaviour and by refusing to accept any more nonsense, Jenny's parents put into place a new set of rules from which there was no escape.

By no means all children will have such dramatic stories as a result of the separation of their parents, but it might be as well to expect some kind of fallout within school. It is not inevitable, but it is certainly normal for a child to be unable to concentrate, to show signs of increased forgetfulness and find trouble with friendships during this difficult process. Their parents will probably exhibit the same symptoms in the office or the supermarket, forgetting important items or leaving credit cards at home. But adults are able to say that they are having a tough time and a bad day and can put things right or ask for understanding as their minds drift off during what should have been an important meeting. Children, however, cannot explain in front of an entire class that they did not hear the instructions or were not thinking about the question because their mind was on the row they heard at home the night before. Their need for privacy, their worries about what the other children might think and the difficulty of finding words for their emotions mean that they find it hard to speak. Teachers should be told what is going on, and allowances need to be made for work that is handed in late and is not quite up to scratch. Children suffering from academic lapses and social difficulties need a watchful eye and a firm but supportive hand. A homework club, if available, is one option, a tutor or 'homework' mentor can be a good idea until a parent finds his or her feet again; a request can be made to the wider family or circle of friends to come and help engage a child and explain essential points of maths, biology or French, and support can be enlisted to help with museum visits, art projects and the extracurricular activities that are so time-consuming, expensive and difficult to get to for a single parent with other children.

If teachers can understand that almost all of the children who are going through the process of a breaking home will be suffering, and that every child will suffer in a different way, they will do a great deal to help. And if parents hold on to their power and ensure that their children go to school and at least attempt to fulfil the basic academic, sporting and social requirements of their age group, they will do well for them. Although the statistics are against them, with the right support and structure in place, there is no reason why children from broken homes cannot do as well academically as children from two-parent families.

Dragon children

When the basic umbrella of parenting is being ripped to pieces by the emotional storm created by the break-up of a long relationship, there is a possibility that a child will become unmanageable. When parents fight and claw at each other and cannot agree on discipline or basic boundaries, when parents buy love and affection from their children or use them as pawns in toxic court cases, these children grow stronger and stronger and yet more and more alone. They are too young to be in charge, to lay down the rules, to say what they will and won't do, whom they will and won't see, or what they will and won't eat – and yet no one seems to have the power to stop them. If this vacuum of control goes on for too long, then the power within the already broken home becomes utterly distorted and along with the huge problems of divorce will come the huge problems of having what I call a 'dragon child'. I have seen children who will not go to school, who threaten their family with weapons and who let themselves out of the house to roam unsupervised without their parents knowing where they are.

If parents do not agree to find a way to cooperate, if they are too angry with each other or too hurt or exhausted to bother to replace an old system with a new one that will curtail the power of the emerging tyrant, then there will in all likelihood be a high price to pay in later years. This can manifest itself not only in terms of the involvement of the police or the social services, who often come into the picture as dragon children enter adolescence, but also in terms of the despair that the children who have stolen the power which does not belong to them often feel deep inside.

These children do not feel safe as they rant and rave and smash and break and hit and hurt. For every hurt they inflict on other people, they inflict comparable damage on themselves. They do not know it, but they are longing for someone to uncover this damage, understand it and make it better. Children do not want or need to be in charge. They want to be safe, they want to trust the world and they want to be children.

Peter was the best and the worst example of a dragon child who had stolen the power of the household and who needed a year's hard work in therapy to begin to get him back towards any form of acceptable behaviour. He appeared for some help in my consulting room after an evening when he had destroyed his playroom, hit his brother with a cricket bat, thrown his supper at the au pair and packed his schoolbag and run away from home. He had been doing this sort of thing for some time but had never before committed quite so many crimes all at once. When yet another childminder walked out of the house, his parents had to take action.

Peter's parents were a kind, careful, interesting, thoughtful professional couple who loved their children and wanted the very best for them. They ensured that they went to school, ate healthy food, learnt to enjoy sports, had friends over to play, kept contact with the extended family, maintained a close eye on the quantity of computer games played and television watched, checked homework, went to football matches, showed up to school events, played Monopoly, read stories, went on family holidays and, in general, looked after their children in a well-educated, textbook kind of way. The trouble was they could not stand each other.

Two years before I met the family, Peter's father had had an affair, which his mother discovered, and she found that she could neither forgive him nor trust him again. She went on red alert and busied herself with his diaries and email and mobile phone and receipts and combed his whole life for proof of adultery. Unfortunately, she was able to find what she had been looking for and got angrier and angrier with every new piece of evidence. As her anger grew, so did her bitterness and sense of betrayal, and she discovered that not only did she not love her husband any more but she genuinely disliked him and had lost all respect for him. Gone were the happy days when he could make her laugh, when she admired him for his wit or erudition or ability to play a mean game of tennis. Gone were the days when she wanted to curl up with him and watch a movie with a glass of wine. She could not bear to have him touch her, and she moved upstairs to the spare bedroom and watched his activities with pursed lips and cold eyes as all affection died. And yet she felt that separation would not be good for her children, and her husband did not want to leave the family home, so she decided that she would stay, and that he would stay and, together, they would look after the children as best they could.

Unlike other areas of their life, where they had given their best to their children, Peter's parents unfortunately found that this particular recipe did not suit Peter. Although practical and well meaning, their plan to stay together and live in the same house forgot to include a method whereby they could deal with the emotional sub-zero temperature and the fact that they were both utterly miserable. I do not believe that either of Peter's parents understood what they would be asking of themselves or the emotional cost to the family when they came up with the plan of co-parenting the children in the same house. Living with people you do not like is corrosive to the soul and bad for the heart. Day by day, bit by miserable bit, they lost all their joy in life, their ability to laugh and see the funny side and to share anything with anyone and their capacity to be happy. They went about their daily business of working hard and getting the children to the right place at the right time and putting food on the table but their faces showed the strain; the father looked like thunder and exploded at the smallest irritation, and the mother grew thin and worn as she tried harder and harder to make everything all right for the children, which included a mis-guided idea that she should give them everything they asked for.

As the months wore on, an unhealthy family system replaced one that had worked. Peter's father became an irritable and brooding presence in the house. He was so exasperated at the situation in which he found himself and so angry at being unable to find a way out of it that he began to have full-blown

183

temper tantrums, which entailed throwing things, banging doors, pulling the children about by their arms and shouting at his wife. He was so unhappy that he frequently self-medicated with alcohol. By the evening he was in an unreliable mood that could entail falling asleep in front of the news and taking no notice of the children or rampaging through the house asking why their homework was not good enough. His misery, his lack of communication, the open hostility of the woman who had loved him, his inability to ask for help and his clenched-teeth attitude to bringing up his children resulted in these children having a father who confused and frightened them. At one moment he would be shouting and insisting on a rule or a boundary that might not have been altogether clear; at the next moment he would be too depressed or wasted to impose any boundary at all. The children did not know where they were when it came to negotiating his moods. One son learnt to walk on eggshells and work out how his father might be feeling while the other learnt to take him head on. If Peter's arm was pulled, he would pull right back; if a chair was thrown, then Peter could throw one too; and, if voices were to be raised, then Peter could shout as loudly as the best of them. If one face became contorted with rage, so could another, and the pair matched each other in their bellowing and throwing and pulling and pushing. The trouble was that Peter was only seven.

Peter's mother had her own demons to face. As her husband became more and more angry and more and more distressed, she retreated further into a protective shell that became so thick that eventually it was hard to find her. She knew that a piece of her was dying and that she was becoming empty and brittle. She also knew that her children deserved better, better than a rampaging father and a mother who was shutting off the doors to her heart. So she began to try; she began to try too hard. She presented a false self to the world, an all-singing, all-dancing, all-coping mum who could do absolutely anything that was asked. Chairing PTA meetings after a hard day's work and rushing back to check the homework before sewing an outfit for the next school play and baking biscuits for the school lunchbox, Peter's mother found comfort in doing everything right and never stopping for one moment. Exhausted, embattled, unhappy, empty and guilty, she did not have the energy or the courage or the power to say no to her small boy, who began to ask for more and more as his young heart could feel that, in reality, he was getting less and less. She felt that she had to compensate for her husband's temper and poisonous moods and that she must always be fun and kind and say yes. Nothing was denied to Peter. He did not like his supper so he was given something else; he did not want to do his homework so she did it for him; he did not want to wear trousers so she would run upstairs to get him shorts; he threw his shoes out of the window so she laughed and went and got them for him. The list of what she would do for her children was very long; the list of what she would not do was very short; and her children learnt that they could get exactly what they wanted.

Unable to discuss the very different parenting styles that emerged through the bitterness of the end of their love, these parents kept going. Unable to sleep because of unhappiness and needing to work because of fear of the future, they put their heads down and battled on, blinded as to what was happening. The centre of the family had broken, there was no adult present to hold steady in the storm and the children stood in the middle taking every lightning strike and every thunderbolt into the very kernel of their beings. Peter stepped into the vacuum: he started to take charge of what he and his brother could and could not do; he also started to copy his father. An unhappy home was in the hands of a seven-year-old tyrant.

I first met Peter when he was nine. He appeared, all hot and bothered, at my door, with huge brown eyes and blond hair that was damply stuck to his head in the shape of a baseball cap. He did not want to see me, but he had been bribed with a visit to the sweetshop without his brother and, as far as he was concerned, he was on his way for a treat via a quick interview with a grown-up whom he would never have to see again. But I have an intriguing consulting room at the bottom of my garden which lives underneath a large climbing frame made out of scaffolding and scaffolding planks. Children find it hard to stay in bad moods when confronted by drums they are allowed to bash as hard as they want, with toys they do not have to put back, with clay they can mould and paint and whack on to walls without worrying about form or colour or substance or shape. My garden shed gives children an opportunity to say what they have to say in a way they find absorbing and liberating. Spray-paints help with a child like Peter who thinks that he does not want to stay and, on our first meeting, I pinned four huge pieces of lining paper to a wall and asked him to graffiti his feelings about his life. He quickly caught on to the fact that there was something naughty and probably illegal about graffiti art, and that he would be unlikely to get the opportunity to use so many different-coloured cans of spray-paint with such abandon in the near future, and set to work with a happy enthusiasm that was altogether different from the sulky air with which he had arrived.

Without realizing it, Peter told me a huge amount about his life during that first session and gave me enough information to work with in order that I could begin slowly to adjust the family dynamics and work on changing his behaviour. I asked him to put the six spray-paints in order of colour preference and then asked him to spray as I asked a barrage of questions. It became very clear to me that he absolutely hated mushrooms and cabbage, that he loved chocolate and football. Gold was his favourite colour and grey his least. His mother turned out to be a golden sun, his father a grey cloud. His brother was dark-to-middling blue, his computer shone gold next to his mother. School was up near the top of the colour choice but homework was brown, only one up from grey. Sport scored a high scarlet, and spaghetti bolognese joined the ranks of colours that formed his positive rainbow. In less than an hour I learnt that Peter hated his father, was possessively loving of his mother, could just about stand his brother if he lived life on Peter's terms and was a real boy in every other way. I realized that the family needed to reinstate the father and bring him up from grey to at least scarlet if there was to be any hope of curtailing the child's negative power and that, although Peter's mother had done a brilliant job and would be glad to hear that she was the sun in the life of her son, she needed to shine less brightly so that the family could regroup and the father and the brother be given a chance to be invited back into Peter's life in a healthy way.

The temptation of spray-paints brought Peter back, and I kept him with me for a gruelling weekly session for a year. Chess bonded us and, for weeks, we played out our own power struggle. I needed to win because I had to keep his respect; I had to keep the power and I had to keep him coming back. Peter needed to talk. Underneath his belief that he had a right to hit his brother with whatever weapon happened to be around; underneath the belief that he could let himself out of the house and walk around a busy city in the middle of the night; under-neath the belief that he could do exactly as he wanted, he had a much more sinister and frightening idea. He wanted his father to die.

Shocking as it may seem, I have often heard children wish their parents dead. Peter wanted his father to be gone. He was sick and tired of the anger and the rage, he was bored of the bad moods and the inconsistency, he hated to see his mother so unhappy and he wanted her to himself. I was concerned that, with Peter's record of violence, he might one day actually take a cricket bat or a golf club and inflict murderous damage on a man whom he had come to hate.

Peter had become a danger to himself by letting himself out of the house and wandering off on his own. I could understand why he did it; in order to cope with her unhappiness, his mother stayed late at the office and then frequently arranged dates with friends. In order to escape, she ran away from home, and so Peter decided to do the same. If his father asked him to brush his teeth or clear away his plate or do his homework or get off the computer and Peter did not want to do any of the above, he would let himself out of the house and disappear. His father could not leave his younger brother alone and would not have known where to look. When Peter told me during one of our chess games that he had been wandering the streets at past midnight, that no one knew and that he was out looking for his mother, I had to tell him that it was time for us to call a family meeting. I needed everyone with me so that we could contain this small fury and keep him and his brother safe.

My heart went out to Peter's father, who found himself sitting in a room with his head in his hands talking to a strange woman about the most important things in his life. Traditionally, he had remained silent when things had bothered him and had got on by finding a way through his problems on his own. Now, not only did he need to open up and discuss the things that hurt him the most, but he also had to admit failure and hear the painful truth that he had nearly lost his relationship with his son. I give him full credit for turning up to many difficult sessions. He listened to the fact that his angry misery was turning his children from him, that his constant criticism was shutting them down, that his violence and his shouting at his wife was setting them a bad example. He learnt that he needed to find some way to re-establish a working relationship with Peter and have some fun and do some things that would show that he was not all bad and that would also help take some of the strain off the boys' mother. Peter's dad needed to start smiling and stop shouting and to get involved.

The rebuilding process was not easy. Peter's father had to suffer many rejections before Peter would join him on any outing, and Peter's mother needed to allow the two men to have a healthier relationship. Eventually, they went to the golf course together, they went on bike rides, they went shopping and found museums to visit that would back up Peter's work at school. Peter decided to teach his father how to play computer games, and they found one they both really liked. Finally, the sitting room into which no one had dared to tread was replaced by a room that contained the whooping noise of two boys racing cars around hairpin bends on a wide screen or the thoughtful sighs of two men playing chess as I gave back to Peter's father the gift that Peter had given to me when he had allowed me to build a relationship around the game.

Peter's mother had to learn how to say no to her son. If she wanted to take her other child out, then she would and she could and, if Peter did not like it, then he could sit at home with the golf clubs and the cricket bat removed to a place of safety. We had to come up with a list of family rules and boundaries that she had to impose and adhere to. Bedtimes were decided, manners were agreed on, punishment and reward systems were introduced and physical violence became completely unacceptable for both father and son. Peter was furious with me for having the temerity to spoil his fun, but with both his parents in the room working together to curtail his strength, he found that he could do nothing other than attempt to regain power by losing his temper in my consulting room. During one session he turned the chess set over and threw the chess pieces at me; in another he attempted to spray-paint me in the face. I would not budge and took his anger head on but asked his father to be close by in the other room so that, if things got too out of control and I needed help to manage a furious nine-year-old boy, he could step in and protect me. Things at home had to get worse before they got better, and Peter really pushed the boundaries. When his nanny tried to impose a punishment of an early bed and went to read to his brother, his rage was so great that he took a knife to her and broke the skin on her thigh attempting to stab her. When his mother went out for an evening he took a knife to her neck and told her he would kill her if she found a boyfriend. He took it upon himself to answer the telephone and monitored who his mother could and could not speak to, and at one point made a call to South Africa and issued a death threat to a man who had appeared too interested.

Peter's behaviour was so worrying that I sent him to a psychiatrist, invoked the help of his headmaster and suggested intervention by the social services. The psychiatrist was helpful. Peter found his two visits extremely intimidating and had to look at where his behaviour with the knife and the nanny had led him. I was able to threaten him with other visits to the psychiatrist unless he changed. This gave me a useful weapon of my own with which to fight the dragon child. The visit to the headmaster with Peter's mother was useful in that a wise, kind and powerful man came on side, understood the problem and sent a message through the school that a child in trouble needed special care and boundaries. Teachers then insisted on completed homework assignments, correct uniform, punctuality and appropriate behaviour. Consequences were handed out as well as rewards given. Peter found himself not getting away with a trick at school while at the same time his difficulties were understood by men who were able to act as role models. The social services were not needed because once the parents realized that Peter was out on the street on his own at night, they changed their behaviour and his mother came home to look after him.

However, it was important that I was able to call on these professional bodies so that I was supported while I worked with a difficult case which would have been too much to have handled on my own.

The process of therapy enabled Peter's family to find a new way to behave. His parents were brave and committed, turning up week after week. At times they probably felt criticized and hopeless. When Peter attacked the nanny, they must have wondered about the efficacy of therapy, and they did well to understand that he had to get worse before he got better. But, as the months went by, a kinder, more thoughtful Peter emerged. He started to talk to me over our chessboard about things that interested him at school, about friends and problems he had with fitting in, about the negative feelings he had about his brother and about fears that his sibling was more popular and more intelligent than him. He told me that he was afraid that his mother and father were lonely and unhappy and that his father was drinking too much. He told me that his mother might have even less time for him if she found another boyfriend. As his parents and the surrounding world made him safer, he became secure enough to expose his heart, and he showed me that he was not a tyrant and was no longer a dragon child. Like most children whose world has lost its centre, he was afraid.

And so the two-pronged therapeutic approach to bringing Peter back from being a too-powerful dragon child continued. On the one hand, his parents learnt to manage him and, on the other, Peter grew softer and less frightened. As his relationship with his father improved, he no longer wanted him dead and one day forgot that this had ever been the case. During his last session, he spray-painted a cloak with his second-favourite colour to represent his dad, and I was happily able to assume that he now felt protected and safe rather than rained on by the grey cloud of the year before. Peter learnt to be angry without losing his temper, to sulk without running away from home, to be annoyed with his brother without hitting him. He learnt that his mother was not perfect and, slowly and sometimes painfully, he removed her from her pedestal so that he was free to have a real and healthy relationship with her.

Dragon children emerge because they do not feel safe. In order to control their environment, they steal power that should not belong to them and use it in a way that is inappropriate and sometimes dangerous. Not all dragon children are as bad as Peter, and some are worse, especially when they enter adolescence and need to add the teenage battle of growing up to the battle for power in the household. Dragon children are easy to identify: they are the children who one senses are in charge of the adults rather than the adults being in charge of them. They are the children who choose where to eat, who refuse to go to school or play truant when they are meant to be there, who hit their friends and siblings and mothers and think it is OK to do so, who will not get off the computer when they are told, who will not turn off the television no matter what the threat, who will not go to bed or have a shower or brush their teeth or read their book. The more their parents fight them, the more they fight back, until everything is a battle. They make adults feel and look like bad parents, and they look like out-of-control, spoilt kids who are difficult to like.

Whatever the difficulties within a breaking relationship, it is not fair on children to allow them to develop in this way. I have seen children with no friends because they do not know how to share and play; children isolated and alone on the computer because their mother has been too frightened to turn it off and hide the controls; overweight children eating whatever they want, whenever they want, sitting in front of the television with the power to refuse to go to the park or the swimming pool. Children do not know how to look after themselves. They need guidance and rules and an adult to tell them what to do.

There are lots of children who want to be in charge, feel everything very deeply, are angry and defiant if things do not go their way and find it hard to speak but easy to act. These children are usually difficult to manage before the family breaks apart, and they can become nearly impossible to look after when the chaos of separation is in full flow. Parents need to work together to parent these children: this may be a tall order when they are going through the process of divorce and separation but it will prevent problems and provide dividends in the future. If mothers and fathers can work out a basic family policy that works for them and apply it to both households, then dragon children will not be able to divide and rule. Rules about basic behaviour such as bedtimes, homework, having friends to stay, how many nights children are allowed out at the weekend, what time they are expected home, when they can eat sweets and how much computer and television they are allowed need to be in place. If parents are fighting to leave each other, they may not find it easy to agree, and mediation may be needed to help find a strategy that works. Mothers and fathers need to back each other up when it comes to the hard graft of childrearing. If differences can be put aside and rules and rewards agreed upon, then the centre of the family will continue to hold. It will be a different centre, and a sad centre, but at least there will be no room for a dragon.

Fathers should be as involved as possible. In nine out of ten households, children stay with the mother, and the usual process of separation involves the father leaving the family home and the mother becoming the main carer. But dragon children need their fathers to contain them, make them safe and guide them through their difficulties. As they get older, the physical strength of a father is needed to stand up to aggression and temper. Mothers also need to stand up to their children. In the short term, it may be easier to say yes to a child than to say no: yes to sweets after school, yes to not eating the vegetables, yes to a television programme, yes to having friends to stay, yes to sleeping in Mum's bed, yes to a new pair of trainers, yes to going shopping, yes to not going to school because of stomach ache. It is especially easy for an adult to say yes when she is blinded by grief and hardly able to get through the day. Some children are easy to manage and some are not and will push at the boundaries, looking for ways to escape from anything that does not suit them. Mothers need to stand up to these children although they themselves feel like falling down. They need to find a way to keep control so that the power in the household does not shift from the adult to the child. This does not mean that mothers become brittle, inflexible and domineering, and it does not mean they are not allowed to offer good times and treats. It does mean that they have rules, which are hopefully backed up by the absent father, about what is and is not acceptable, and a system of punishments for bad behaviour and rewards for good behaviour.

It takes wisdom to realize that one might need help and courage to ask for it. It is not a sign of weakness to ask for guidance. To grind on relentlessly is exhausting and pointless when looking after children who are becoming increasingly difficult. To imagine that things will get better with time and therefore do nothing when a child is on the edge of becoming a dragon is a risky policy. A militant child who will not do what he or she is told in a household that is breaking apart needs to be managed. If the separation is too toxic or the situation too difficult and a child is beginning to get out of control, then it is very likely that outside help will be needed.

The first place to start is the child's school. If there is trouble at home with homework and getting a child to cooperate, see if the school has the same problem. If it does and the school is willing, get the teachers to work with you on introducing a system of communication so that each side knows what is happening. When as

194

many adults as possible know what is going on, there will be a smaller hole in the child's life, which it will be more difficult for him to fall through.

If a strong, united system of rules and boundaries, paternal involvement, maternal backbone and the intervention of school and friends are impossible to implement or do not help to bring an unruly dragon child to order, professional help needs to be sought. The best way to get support is via the GP or from the school. An educational psychologist could be a necessary pitstop for a dragon child to ensure that he does not have a learning disability which makes him difficult to manage. Family therapy is a useful tool and is available privately or on the NHS, and a referral may need to be made to the Child and Adolescent Mental Health Services (CAMHS) through the family GP.

Peter grew up to become a wonderful adolescent with an original sense of humour, a strong sense of right and wrong, a large character, good academic achievement and a brilliant sporting record. He has not shown any signs of violence or dangerous behaviour since he was nine years old. His parents, who now live happily in two separate homes, stay in touch and tell me that he is ready to take his place in the world. It could have been a very different story if they had not had the courage to put their differences aside and work together. It is likely that he would have become familiar to the police, the social services, young-offender units and other facilities for child and adolescent mental health which are awash with cases of children who have become too strong and are impossible for their families to manage.

Sibling rivalry

Trouble between brothers and sisters does not necessarily follow from parental separation, but if sibling rivalry is already a feature of family life, it is likely to become much worse when separation occurs. When parents are fighting and crying and leaving each other, there will be little time or emotional energy to sort out sibling fights, hurt feelings and indignation. Unfortunately, the adults will probably be exhibiting the very behaviour they feel is unacceptable in their offspring. Children who cannot and will not get on with each other add to the tension and difficulties within a breaking home, and thought needs to be given to how to deal with them.

Not all children like their siblings. Characters clash as a matter of course; some elder children like things to be just so and are outraged when a baby arrives to challenge the status quo. Children can find themselves fighting for scraps of attention as parents are overtaken by external events, or parents can lead by bad example and shout and hit so that the children take their lead and shout and hit as well. Total sibling harmony within a family is a blessing; some discord is normal, but out-and-out warfare, subtle cruelty and bullying should be sorted out. This is especially true in a family that is going through the process of separation, as children who are having a tough time with the behaviour of their parents do not need to be having a tough time with each other.

Duncan and Ben were two brothers of ten and eight who each felt that the other should never have been born and whose behaviour became much worse as the marriage of their parents hit the rocks. Larger than life, powerful, dramatic and funny, they were involved in a vicious dance. Duncan would hit, Ben would hit back and then scream because he was smaller than his brother. A parent would come running to tell one or other of the brothers off and attempt to restore order. The brothers could fight from dawn to dusk and their parents brought them to see me because they were exhausted by the bickering, fighting, appalling language and lack of peace. Individually, the children were charming, but together they were a nightmare. I have rarely witnessed such palpable disregard for another sibling or lack of willingness to change, and I worked with the two boys for well

196

over a term, getting absolutely nowhere. I could not break the pattern or begin to find a way to end the real violence and, with every trick I tried, the boys were fast and clever enough to find another way to torture each other so that they could continue to fight and steal the very oxygen in the house.

Duncan and Ben's parents had gone through a bitter divorce which had taken years to come to a head. The boys had seen fighting, heard shouting and were aware of an undercurrent of violence and lack of respect between their mother and their father. Both parents worked full time and flat out and had little energy for two demanding boys. On their days off, they were more interested in scoring points off each other than looking after two children who needed to be out in the park, on the football field, riding their bikes and letting off steam. Their children should have been anywhere other than cooped up in a small house ingesting the atmosphere of two parents who could not stand each other. Without positive parental input, the boys found a way to get attention, exercise and entertainment. They started a cruel game that involved point-scoring, hyper-vigilance, never giving ground and provoking each other so that their parents had to leave what they were doing and come to look at their children. Sibling rivalry made them feel alive. They were not going to give it up unless they had something to replace it with.

Therapy did not help the boys. Their mother and their father needed to take the responsibility to change. By now established in two separate houses, the parents were in a better space and better shape to help. A series of meetings produced a plan that both homes were able to agree on. The children were separated for periods of time, and both mother and father worked out things to do with the boys that would use up their energy and involve them in a new and healthier lifestyle. Rugby squad on a Saturday was found for Duncan, while Ben decided that he wanted to learn to cook. Both went to judo in order to learn the discipline and self-control behind martial arts, and both went swimming, where they had acres of water in which they could harmlessly rough and tumble and expend some energy. Punishments were introduced for hitting, punching, swearing and pinching each other's things, and each child had to be taught to respect the personal space of the other. Rewards were also part of the package, in that a week without an incident could earn a visit to a restaurant, a special treat with a chosen parent, a ticket to a football game or a chance to stay up past normal bedtime. With both mother and father working from the same rule sheet and wanting exactly the same thing for their children, the situation began to change and the boys found that they could not continue their endless, violent fighting.

Duncan and Ben found that the consequences of their violence were too dull to put up with and that the rewards for ending their vicious games were actually quite fun. They also became too busy and too tired to practise endless furious wrestling moves on each other and began to realize that, while they did not actually like each other very much, they could at least tolerate each other. The two boys can now go on holiday together, Christmas is no longer a nightmare, and Ben has asked to move to the same big school as his brother, while Duncan seems pleased at the idea of having him there.

Boys are like young lioncubs who need to learn to fight and stand up for themselves as part of the package of growing up. While noisy, exhausting and challenging, they are somehow more straightforward to manage than girls, who go underground in order to protect their patch.

Girls tend to be less aggressive yet more subtle when they are jealous of a sibling. They can be cruel and underhand, and it is often difficult for a parent to ascertain exactly what is going on when a daughter is on the warpath. Although the house may superficially be more peaceful than when two boys are thumping each other, there may be an atmosphere which is just as difficult to sort out, especially if there is only one parent available to find a solution to the dripping water torture of female-sibling rivalry.

Rose was born just as her father left her mother, and entered a calamitous world to find a three-year-old sister, Emma, full of fury at her arrival and a mother suffering from both shock and a difficult dose of post-natal depression. Emma was a rigid child who found it difficult to accept change and was never going to be pleased at the arrival of a new baby, and with the difficult events around the birth of Rose, the stage was set for a childhood of sibling rivalry. When Rose was six months old, her mother found drawing pins in her cot; when she was learning to walk, she would be pushed to the ground; as she grew older, her favourite toys would be hidden; and when she grew older still, her homework would disappear from its homework folder on the way to school. Rose could find no peace from her older sister, who was on a permanent war footing. As both girls grew up, negative behaviour became entrenched. There was no possibility of sharing anything or experiencing the normal imaginative play of childhood, and the children developed a subtle pattern of blame and counter-blame that had a depressed mother holding her hands over her ears as the children shrieked, 'But she started it!' and 'It's not fair, you always blame me!' By the time they got to school, the girls found it difficult to form friendships within their peer group. It was reported to me by their headmistress that both Rose and Emma were bullies who picked on weaker members of the class, took things that did not belong to them, had problems with discipline and were greedy for attention, food and anything they could get their hands on.

Therapy was difficult for this family, as there was so little for them to work with. There was no money for outside help, minimum extended family and few friends around to bring any joy or support into an empty home. The father had disappeared into the mist and could only be found once or twice a year, when he would make things worse for his two daughters rather than better. I suspect that he had mental-health issues of his own. Rather than look after his children on the rare occasions that he saw them, he would complain about his life or find himself unable to cope with his daughters' fighting and, at one time, put them, aged seven and four, into an unlicensed taxi and sent them home. The mother continued to be depressed, and her daughters sensed it, Emma painting me a picture of a black, sagging balloon called 'My Mother' and telling me that, when she tried to hug her, there was no one there and when she tried to speak, there was no answer. Rose was too young to be able to find such poignant images or words, but her behaviour told me that she suffered badly.

GPs can refer such families to centres that have well-trained family therapists; or there are colleges for counsellors and psychotherapists who have students who work for very little financial remuneration in order to gain experience. Rose and her mother found such trainee counsellors, and Emma stayed with me. The mother was encouraged to seek medical help for her depression and, as she felt better, she was able to take on board suggestions and ideas so that she could look after her girls. The same kind of strategies, punishments and rewards that worked for Duncan and Ben were put in place but, without a father to help with her children, she needed to think about where she could find alternative support. As the depression loosened its grip, she found that she was not as alone as she had thought. She found a single-parent group to support her and a parenting group to teach her, and she was able to ask her own divorced father if he would have Emma to stay. A man who had had little to do with bringing up his own child nervously stepped in to help and found that he enjoyed the task of building a relationship with his difficult grand-daughter.

It is not easy if one is exhausted, alone, unhappy and broke to bring order to chaos and introduce systems and boundaries that are adhered to and make children feel safe. However, if a single parent does not try to impose control and take back the power that belongs to them, their children will grow too negatively strong and be difficult to manage. Emma was not unlike a female version of Peter in the section on dragon children. Her decision to become boss of the family and never allow her small sister any breathing space made perfect sense. But she grew too strong and suffered when she could find no friends to play with and became the difficult bully in her class at school. Rose suffered, too, as she was cruelly treated by a sister who wished her harm and yet she had no safe haven to crawl to. Her defence mechanism against her lonely world was to behave as if she did not belong in it. She would either endlessly daydream or spin into a hyperactive routine that involved exhausting shrieking and an inability to settle to any task. Neither Rose nor Emma was born difficult, but they were born into a difficult world. Therapy made their life better in that structure was imposed, chaos reduced, support found, their mother became more alive and competent, and bad behaviour between the girls was no longer tolerated. Their sibling rivalry was extreme, and there was reason enough for it to be. It took three therapists, an involved school, parenting groups and a slightly grumpy grandfather to make a difference. Life is still not easy for Emma and for Rose; the wounds they received in early infancy were deep, and their attachment to security is fragile. They will probably always be careful to ensure that the other does not have more of the little they feel to be on offer, but at least their mother has woken up from a deep torpor and is able to look after two daughters who felt that they had to fight each other in order to survive.

Sibling rivalry is a complicated and interesting subject. Books are written about it, university modules are offered on it, and it can be studied from a behavioural, anthropological, psychological or biological point of view. There is a general consensus that problems between siblings will loosen their hold on a family if various guidelines are adhered to.

Families need to accept that not everyone is going to get on.

Favouritism needs to be checked: Children intuitively sense it. If a parent is aware that they have a favourite child, they need to ask themselves why and take responsibility for what their implicit preference might mean to the rest of the family. A mother or a father will need to find a way to learn to love all of his or her children equally, although perhaps in different ways.

Communication is important: Time should be given to everyone in the family to talk and to be heard and understood. Fair negotiation is much easier for a family when sorting out differences of opinion than all-out stubborn warfare where no one gives an inch. Every member of the family (including the parents) should feel that their needs are equally important. Children need help to express their feelings and should not be made to feel wrong for having them.

Praise and attention should be given in equal measure to all of the children: Rewarding achievements, efforts, particular skills and successes goes a long way towards placating siblings hungry for recognition and approval at the expense of others.

Fun and games are important: A family that plays together, goes on outings and gets involved in projects will often be too busy for negative behaviour. It is difficult for children to hate each other if they are involved in physical activity. Friends and relatives can replace the parental figure who is no longer around and provide amusement and distraction.

Follow a consistent plan of consequences and rewards for good and bad behaviour. Individual families will have their own arrangements, but a rule of thumb might be that violence, stealing, tale-telling and lack of respect for personal belongings are unacceptable, while sharing, looking out for a younger sibling, playing nicely and stopping negative behaviour need to be rewarded.

These suggestions are relevant to all families who have children who scrap. They are especially pertinent for children in separating families. When a family is breaking apart, feelings will run high, and there will be less time and energy for talking, playing or praising. Routines will be shattered, and boundaries will seem pointless when there is nothing but an empty centre to protect. At this point, the differences between children who do not get on will, in all likelihood, escalate, and their rivalry will become more extreme, damaging and even dangerous.

As with Duncan and Ben, Emma and Rose, and Peter, steps should be taken to empower and support single parents and keep them in control. Children need to be prevented from becoming entrenched in negative and exhausting behaviour that will make their path into the wider world difficult.

If extreme sibling rivalry is not dealt with, the consequences can be serious. The children who suffer will be unlikely to know how to conduct relationships or deal with authority or have learnt the building blocks needed to form true friendships. They might bully or be bullied. Somewhere in their hearts they will know that something is missing and that maybe there is something wrong with them and their siblings because nobody could or would take the time to sort it out.

Self-harm

Children who self-harm are telling us something about themselves; they are speaking loudly and clearly, and they want us to listen, even if it is sometimes extremely difficult to hear what it is that they have to say. They are full to the brim with unpleasant feelings that will almost always include anger and frustration and, as they delicately draw the pin, the knife, the scissors or the razorblade across their skin, they get satisfaction and a momentary, addictive feeling of relief. Their behaviour can range in severity from, at one end of the spectrum, scratching themselves, to slashing wrists at the other. Sadly, such children, from both two- and single-parent families, are part of the daily caseload of the psychiatrist, psychotherapist, counsellor and school nurse, and what would have led to admission to a hospital ward thirty years ago is no longer unusual. Children who are very young find it hard to give words to their strong feelings, and it is not unusual to find a child scratching their skin or rubbing themselves raw when they are very unhappy and worried about what is going on at home. Older children, while able to speak and to understand what is going on, are likely to inflict more serious damage on themselves, although I rarely see them self-harm during the actual turbulent day-to-day drama of the process of divorce and separation. Cutting seems to come later, when the drama is over and it is time to talk. It can provide a way to express anger, pain and loss; it depersonalizes grief and self-hatred; and it can produce endorphins which help cope with the bad feelings that whirl around busy adolescent brains.

Charlie was a good example of how difficult feelings engendered by divorce can emerge in adolescence and have a dramatic impact long after the event. His parents went through a messy divorce when he was ten, and he was left alone for too long and too often. At fourteen, Charlie found friendship difficult, could not work out the complicated dance hanging around with girls involved, felt he was ugly and stupid and did not know what to do with his anger or his crippling shyness. He did not respect either of his parents and did not feel that he could turn to them for help. He knew that he could and should not fight, and he knew that physical violence would get him into trouble. And so he started to hurt himself rather than other people, by burning his hands with cigarettes and cutting his arms with a penknife. He managed to hide the marks until a school nurse noticed the mess on the inside of his wrists; when she saw more on asking him to pull up his shirtsleeves, she was obliged to ring his parents and the social services, who contacted me to see if I could help.

Charlie was depressed, but his mother did not believe in depression. A busy woman with a hectic schedule that often took her far from home, she decided somewhere along the line that her son was spoilt and looking for attention. Perhaps Charlie had too many material things in his bedroom, but I could not call him spoilt – sadly, I would have described him as neglected. I longed to invite him to join my family and our noisy evening meals when I heard of yet another day he had spent alone roaming the streets with his hands deep in his pockets and nothing to do. Charlie was no angel; by fourteen, he was smoking, drinking and hanging around with boys from the park when he should have been finishing a piece of homework, but he was not a bad boy. If his divorced parents would only come home, bring him in from the streets, talk to him, offer understanding and help with work that was becoming increasingly difficult, he would have been OK. But his parents did not come home, they did nothing about a suggestion to take him to a GP, his work suffered, he fell behind and his unhappiness mounted. In unconscious desperation, he became ruder and ruder at school, swore openly at teachers and presented them with mute hostility and no homework. School did not want to keep him, and I could not blame them: he showed no sign of wanting to learn, was providing a difficult example and distraction for other children and was taking up a huge amount of time in terms of the pastoral care that it was recognized he needed once the staff had noticed his cut arms and his vulnerability. Charlie and I were given until the end of the year to work together; his behaviour had to change or he would no longer be welcome at school.

Charlie lived in the void created by the separation of his parents and, with nowhere to find help, he turned fear and negativity inwards and found comfort in cutting. His arms looked like a battlefield, his face was set in anger; his language was appalling and, if I had not been able to recognize a glint of mischief and sadness in his soft brown eyes, I might have been too frightened to take him on to work with in my own home. Charlie needed to talk and understand his situation and see the part that he was playing in his own unhappiness. He was frightened by how much he enjoyed the patterns of blood that he could create on his own skin and how he liked the ritual involved in marking himself. He knew that he was lost and had to find a way back to some kind of normal behaviour but did not know how to take the steps to help himself.

Work with Charlie was not dull. We played games. We went for walks and, for every week that he did not cut his arms, I allowed him to smoke cigarettes in my garden. Of course, smoking is self-harm in a different form, but Charlie smoked already, and I needed whatever currency I could use to get him to stay and work. There had to be a strong enough bond in order for a child who was about to spin out of school and into real trouble to be able to trust me and respect me enough to listen. I needed to fill the void created by his parents' separation, and I would have done no good at all if I had sat behind my desk and looked like just another grown-up who told him to behave. As the weeks passed, I grew to love Charlie. He was bright and funny and very naughty. And he was prepared to listen and understand that his behaviour was problematic. I found some fairly choice phrases myself to describe some of his activities as we walked along the river, and we laughed at his antics while he promised to think before he pushed his teachers beyond breaking point again.

I felt that I was reaching a lost young man, and that therapy might help steer Charlie away from trouble. The cutting and the burning stopped almost immediately, but his behaviour at school remained appalling, and there seemed to be nothing that I could do to stop a clever boy from getting himself expelled. After about three months of weekly sessions, I got so fed up with Charlie's refusal to take responsibility for his own behaviour that I did something that I have never done in twenty years of being a therapist: I sacked him. I gave him three warnings and then told him not to bother to come back until he was prepared to fulfil some of the reasonable requests from the school. Our relationship was strong, and he trusted me enough to know that I would never, ever have told him not to come back unless I knew that he could change. He did not want to lose the therapy, which had brought a little light back into his life, and he also realized that he did not want to lose his school.

Within a week he changed: there was no more calling out and swearing, homework miraculously began to appear on time and up to standard, he joined the A team for rugby, cut his hair and replaced his permanent scowl with a smile. I got an email from the school telling me that Charlie had turned himself around and, although still naughty, was a delight, with an awful lot of work to do to catch up. With genuine joy and relief, I was able to telephone my client and invite him back so that we could continue to work on the issues that his parents' toxic divorce had created.

Young children whose parents go through a difficult separation will often have feelings which lie buried and unrecognized, but which may lead to trouble when they reach another cycle in their development. Adolescents who are insecure in their attachment to a parental figure, who have felt sidelined in the maelstrom of the separation, who have not experienced enough love or who have had to watch out for the health of a needy parent are likely to be full of difficult and unanswered questions. Relationships and friendships may be problematic, and these children may experience a fundamental lack of peace. They are likely to search for something or someone to make them feel better; they may try alcohol or drugs and be the ones who use too much and too fast. They may use food or lack of food for comfort and control, they may attach themselves to people and find that sex makes them feel better or they may cut themselves to find visible relief from their invisible pain. Most of the extreme cases of self-harm that I have seen involve children who lost the security of a stable relationship with two parents when they were young, who became too involved in the poisonous drama of their parents' separation and who never found any help.

Mary's case is a sad example of a home that shattered when a child was young but did not see the five-year-old pay the price until she was older. Her parents went through shouting matches, fights about money, attempts at reconciliation and an unusual disagreement about who should have the children. Both parents worked, and neither wanted full-time care of their two young girls; they tried to give their daughters to each other and the children were brought up in an atmosphere where they could not have felt less wanted. To add to Mary's problems, her father was a control freak. While making it plain that he did not want his daughter to live with him, he needed to check her homework, her table manners, the friends she had and how she lived. He would imply from the moment that he opened his mouth that whatever she did was not good enough and that somehow she disappointed him. He set himself up as a kind of moral compass and suggested that he knew best and that she should try to emulate his example. And yet his example was lacking in care and in integrity. He had left the marriage because of another woman, but failed to tell his children this. He demanded truth and respect for himself, and yet he lived his life as a lie. When Mary was thirteen, the father's hidden girlfriend became tired of being sidelined, told the children exactly who she was and blew the father's cover.

Mary was heartbroken. She had put her father on a pedestal in order to be able to find comfort from the fact that a good man was out there keeping her safe. With one blow, she learnt that he was not who she thought he was, that he had badly hurt her mother and that he had no right to tell her how to live her life. But, sadly, he had taught her well and she had learnt to be too good. She had learnt to do her best at everything in order to remain welcome in the two households that were essential for her survival. When she found out that her father had lied to her for eight years, she did not know what to do, where to turn or how to behave. Having never shouted at anyone, having never caused a fuss, having never been a bother, Mary shut her misery inside her and continued with her life as if she had never found out. But she started to cut her skin inch by inch. She started on her hands and slowly moved up her arms, with a methodical, surgical stroke that left geometric patterns on her skin. And then she started to mark her chest and cut across her breasts before applying E45 cream, putting on her school uniform and taking the bus to school.

Luckily, her best friend noticed a little of what was going on and was brave enough to tell the school nurse. The nurse rang me and, together, we rang the mother to ask if we could help. Mary started therapy and was glad to find a place to talk. Having landed in a safe place that had nothing to do with either parent, she was able to reveal her suffering, her anger and her impotence. She showed me with sand therapy that she felt as if she were being sucked down and that she would drown if she opened her mouth to attempt to protect herself from her tyrannical father. She drew her panic and an overwhelming feeling of an inability to cope, as if a black hole were pulling her into oblivion, and she told me that perhaps it would be easier if she gave in and simply ceased to exist. Mary let me in on her secret that she ran her life in figures of threes and sevens, and that everything had to be done in sequence. Lights had to be switched on and off seven times before she could sleep, ovens had to be checked three times on leaving the house and a certain amount of steps had to be taken before arrival at a given destination. Unable to control her life, Mary had found a compulsive solution to her problems that made her feel that she was in charge of everything she did. When things did not work out the way that she imagined or wanted, she had no resources to cope with her disappointment and took to the sharp blade of a kitchen knife to give her comfort and a sense of control.

Although Mary's life was difficult, it did not mean that she needed to become a victim and sit alone with her compulsive obsessive behaviour and her sharp instruments. If she could see that it was not her fault that she had been born into a dysfunctional family system, she would not need to be weighed down by it. With therapeutic help, Mary began to shift away from feeling stuck, bogged down and lost in panic. She learnt to question some of her more compulsive behaviours and engage in them less, while replacing them with more positive activities. She realized that her anger with her father was justified and played it out again and again in the therapy room before finding the courage to talk to him in person. Finally, she was able to tell him that she was disappointed in his secrecy and the way in which he lived his life, that she had trusted and admired him and that he had let her down. She pointed out that she did not need to be told off all the time and asked her father to respect that she was doing her best. Their relationship was never to recover from the blow of his discovered deception, but at least now there was honesty between the two. Mary could resume a life in which it did not always feel as if something was wrong, nothing was good enough and her father was always walking away.

Self-harming behaviour will be familiar to heads of schools, teachers, doctors and other members of the helping professions. Teenagers of today are also familiar with cutting, and most of them will at the very least know someone who hurts themselves in order to find relief. A combination of strong, hidden emotion and a lack of adult support often make a young person turn inward rather than outward to express their rage, hurt and frustration. If this is the case, and an adult sees the tell-tale red marks on the skin of a child or suspects that comfort is being found in other negative and dangerous ways, then parents, schools and other carers should be informed and professional help must be sought.

The 'too-good' child

Children, especially girls, can cope with the difficult behaviour of their parents by becoming 'too good'. These are children who walk on eggshells while watching out for bad moods, difficult atmospheres and volatile situations in those around them. They may have had to do this for most of their lives, as this mechanism often develops as a result of a long period of upbringing by unreliable adults. Since a large percentage of relationships between unreliable adults will eventually get into trouble, it is worth looking at these children, the role that they find themselves playing and the price that they might have to pay.

Unfortunately, 'too good' children rarely come to me until the damage has been done, and a long-haul recovery is needed for them to find a way back to their true nature. One reason for this is that they are not immediately distinguishable from other children who are naturally gifted or mature. There are of course children who are natural all-rounders and deserve to be celebrated and admired as they make their elegant way through childhood and into adolescence. I do not worry about them and am sometimes rather jealous that I never had a son in a first eleven who then went on to appear as a star in a school play or a daughter who led her school to victory in the tennis championships while wearing the badge of head girl. These children I accept through slightly gritted teeth as something rather marvellous and, while admiring them, I do not worry. However, when I see golden children who are the product of an upside-down, inside-out kind of life at home, I will wonder. In my experience, a perfect child from an imperfect home life can spell trouble.

Children who live watching out for the reactions of others often end up neglecting their own needs and depriving themselves of the experiences that are essential in order to have a normal childhood. They have been so busy keeping the peace, sorting out problems and listening out for trouble that they have very often not relaxed into who they are meant to be. While they can turn on a sixpence and understand the moods of others, they are unaware of their own emotions and can be strangers to the range of feelings that they will need if they are going to grow up as complete people with a strong sense of self. It is as if these children give up their right to their own emotions in order to look after those of others. But this behaviour is not as selfless as it seems. It is an effective coping mechanism. If a child can stop a parental row in mid-flow, if she can cut her father's anger off before it gets too explosive, if she can put her brother to bed before he annoys her mother and therefore prevent her opening that second bottle of wine, then she will have looked after herself in the only way she knows how. To look after others in the hope that they can look after you is an effective coping strategy and one that works well for children in dysfunctional homes. As with all coping strategies, it does not work when the child has to grow up. It is generally in later adolescence that problems will appear for the 'too-good' child, and these can be frightening and difficult to treat. Full-blown eating disorders or recourse to alcohol or drugs are common, as is the cutting I described in the previous section. Imo and Mary were both examples of children badly hurt by their over-responsibility and lack of a carefree childhood. Both needed a lot of help to stay out of hospital and find a way back to their true nature. The difficulties of a child who is 'too good' because of divorcing parents can take until adulthood to emerge.

> Kay was twenty-eight when she came to see me. Exhausted and unhappy, she felt as if she was living on the brink of a terrifying, dark insanity. Her parents had behaved badly throughout her childhood, and she had been the peacekeeper between two adulterous drunks while they went through a vicious divorce. In order to attempt to make them take more notice of her and appear to love her more, she had danced for her school, acted for her town, excelled academically and been no trouble. At the same time, she kept house and even made her own clothes so she did not have to ask anyone for anything. By the time she came to see me, she had tried so hard to chase the demons away by being perfect that she had brought herself to the brink of an anorexic nervous breakdown.
>
> Therapy helped Kay to drop her perfectionism and led her to start the journey that she had been unable to take as a child. She

discovered that inside she was dying, and she drew herself as a colourless mudfish gasping for breath on the bottom of a polluted lake. By accepting her terrible childhood and by imagining how it should and could have been, Kay learnt that she was allowed to, and indeed needed to, come up for air. The water in her lake changed to clear blue, and she slowly learnt that her perfectionism was just a brittle façade that hid an eating disorder and an inability to be close to anyone who wanted to be close to her. Gradually, Kay began to practise not having to be 'too good' and found that she no longer needed to over-exercise and undereat while working harder than all of her colleagues and never having any fun. She discovered that, by being less than perfect, people came nearer, that relationships had more meaning and that she no longer felt so exhausted or so alone.

Other children I have mentioned as suffering from being 'too good' were also helped by having someone to talk to, someone to understand, someone to witness their suffering and someone to help them find the real person behind the well-structured edifice of being 'too good'. Not all of the well-behaved children in divorcing households need to be whacked into therapy but, when there are signs of unnaturally good behaviour, the first helpful thing that can be done is to find an encouraging and experienced adult who can listen to what is really going on behind a potentially damaging façade.

Summary

- **School:** Many children will refuse to go to school, either because they want to look after a parent or because they have the power to refuse to go. Others cannot concentrate or do their homework. Some may have trouble socially and become either a victim or a bully as they try to find their feet in a world that is breaking around them. School life is hectic, and energy and organizational skills are required to get from A to B with the right books, the right friends and the right homework at the right time. If a child is feeling overwhelmed with intense emotion, the requirements of the school day can become too much for them, and they are likely to give up or give in to their unhappy inner world.

Like adults, who sometimes need a day off, children will attempt to kick against the system and stay at home from time to time. Occasionally, it is a good idea to play hooky and hide under the duvet with favourite food and TV programmes and hugs and cuddles. But, if it happens too often and if a parent loses his or her power, worse problems are likely to follow.

Teachers should be told what is going on and allowances made. Children suffering from academic lapses and social difficulties need a watchful eye and a firm but supportive hand. Friends and extended family can help the child with schoolwork.

- **Dragon children:** Children do not want or need to be in charge; they want to be safe, they want to trust the world and they want to be children. But when there is a difficult break-up, things can go haywire, and some children grow tyrannical. Although too young to be in control, they become able to steal the power that should belong to the parents and can turn into what I call a 'dragon child'.

  Dragon children are easy to identify: they are the children who one can sense are in charge of the adults. The more parents fight them, the more they fight back, until everything is a battle. They make adults feel and look like bad parents, and they look like out-of-control, spoilt kids who are difficult to like. These children are usually difficult to manage before the family breaks apart, and they can become nearly impossible to look after when the chaos of separation is in full flow.

  To imagine that things will get better with time and to do nothing when a child is on the edge of becoming a dragon is a risky policy. Parents need to work together to parent these

215

children: this may be a tall order when they are going through the process of divorce, but it is absolutely necessary. Rules about basic behaviour on which mothers and fathers agree to back each other up are essential.

Fathers should be as involved as much as possible to contain their children and guide them through their difficulties. Mothers also need to stand up to their domestic terrorists. If the separation is too toxic or the situation too difficult, it is very likely that outside help will be needed.

- **Sibling rivalry:** This can add to the tensions of a breaking home, and thought needs to be given to how to deal with it. Not all children like their siblings, and total sibling harmony within a family is a blessing; some discord is normal, but out-and-out warfare, subtle cruelty and bullying should be sorted out. Boys are usually more straightforward with their thumping and fighting and are easier to manage than girls, who tend to go underground in order to protect their patch. Girls can be cruel and underhand, and it is often difficult for a parent to ascertain exactly what is going on. Overt and subtle bullying always needs to be dealt with; this is especially true in a family that is going through the process of separation, as children who are having a tough time with the behaviour of their parents do not need to be having a tough time with each other.

  If extreme sibling rivalry is not dealt with, the consequences can be serious. The children who suffer will be unlikely to know how to conduct relationships, deal with authority or have learnt the building blocks to form true friendships. They might bully or be bullied. Somewhere they will know that something is missing and that maybe there is something wrong with them and their siblings, because nobody could or would take the time to sort them out.

- **Self-harm:** Adolescents who are insecure in their attachment to a parental figure, who have felt sidelined in the maelstrom of family break-up, who have not experienced enough love or who have had to watch out for the health of a needy parent are likely to be full of difficult and unanswered questions. Relationships and friendships might be problematic, and these children can experience a fundamental lack of peace. They are likely to search for something or someone to make them feel better; they may try alcohol or drugs and be the ones who use too much and too fast. They may use food or lack of food for comfort and control, they may attach themselves to people and find that sex makes them feel better or they may cut themselves to find visible relief from their invisible pain.

Children who self-harm are telling us something about themselves. They are full to the brim with unpleasant feelings, which will almost always include anger and frustration, but they tend to delay the actions of self-harm until the turbulent day-to-day drama of the divorce and separation is over. If a void is created by parental separation and a child has no way of finding help, he may find comfort in cutting. What would have led to admission to a psychiatric ward thirty years ago is now commonplace, and nearly all teenagers of today will know someone who cuts themselves in order to find relief. A combination of strong, hidden emotion and a lack of adult support often make a young person turn inward rather than outward to express their rage, hurt, and frustration. If this is the case and an adult sees the tell-tale red marks on the skin of a child or suspects that comfort is being found in other negative and dangerous ways, then parents, schools and other carers should be informed and professional help must be sought.

- 'Too-good' children: These children may end up having as many problems in their lives as the children who wander too closely to the edge. Young people who live watching out for the reactions of others often end up neglecting their own needs. While they can turn on a sixpence and understand the mood of others, they are unaware of their own emotions and may be strangers to the range of feelings that they will need if they are going to grow up as complete people with a strong sense of self. It is as if these children give up their right to their own emotions in order to look after other people. To look after others in the hope that they can look after you is an effective coping strategy and one that works well for children in dysfunctional homes.

It is generally in later adolescence that problems will appear for the 'too-good' child, and these can be frightening and difficult to treat. Adolescents can be helped by having someone to talk to, someone to understand, someone to witness their suffering and someone to help them find the real person behind the well-structured front.

6 • • • • •

Double trouble

FAMILY BREAK-UP CAN GIVE RISE to painful or annoying physical symptoms and difficult behaviour. But it is dangerous to ascribe all problems to the same cause. Sometimes, divorce-related issues can mask other underlying problems in the family or in the child, and some unfortunate children suffer from a real case of 'double trouble' from having to cope with other difficult problems on top of the separation of their parents.

This is especially so when the cause of breakdown in the marriage is destructive behaviour. Alcoholism afflicts as many mothers as fathers. Drug addiction, physical violence or financial irresponsibility leading to economic hardship are other causes which may doubly blight the life of the child. Some parents, through no fault of their own, suffer from crippling depression or serious illness. Whatever the reason, parental inability to take responsibility for their family can seriously deepen the suffering of a child. In these sorts of situations, children will need as much help as possible from those who can shield them from the problems of the parents to help them grow up straight and true.

Some children are troubled by the too-swift introduction of a new partner, or the premature arrival of a stepfamily and half-siblings. Children may be forgotten as a parent thinks that he or she will create an ideal home where everybody is going to be one big, happy family. Unfortunately, the dream is rarely achieved. Second marriages and stepfamilies have a higher incidence of failure than first marriages, so they need to be entered with caution and realism about how difficult they are. I have seen many children over the years who feel that they do not belong, that they cannot find a space in the life of the parent who has moved on or that they do not have a place in the new con-figuration. If children are still suffering from the break-up of their family and are asked to accept a new system in which they do not feel at home, they will face additional difficulties which are hard to cope with when life is already very tough.

Some children have internal hardwiring which means that they are badly equipped to deal with change, hate uncertainty and suffer from acute sensitivity. Life can be difficult even when things are going well. Such children are especially vulnerable and are likely to require specialist help when their world is shattered. Children with learning disabilities, attachment issues and explosive, stubborn temperaments are highly prone to react strongly and badly to the separation of their parents.

When 'double trouble' strikes, the wider network of family and friends is especially needed to distract, befriend, guide, love and laugh with a young life that might have nowhere else to turn. Schools should be ready to lend a helping hand, and professional forces need to be mustered. It *is* possible to provide a safety net; I have seen it done and I have seen children survive when up against seemingly impossible odds. It takes courage and a steady commitment to hold out a hand to a child in real trouble, but it is more than worth it to watch young people shake off their burdens and emerge ready to have a go at building lives for themselves.

Addiction

Addiction is hell for those who suffer from it and for those who live within its orbit. Whether food, sex, alcohol, gambling or drugs are the chosen medication for the individual who finds that he or she needs more than life itself in order to survive, anyone who is addicted to anything will be uncomfortable at the very best, and full of self-hatred and a desire to self-obliterate when the going gets tough. The general medical consensus on addiction is that it is an illness and that alcoholics do not choose to take their downward path, that drug addicts derive no pleasure in spending their waking hours looking for their next fix and that other addictions provide nothing but pain once someone gets hooked into an unhealthy pattern of behaviour. Medical experts, governments and socially responsible institutions throughout the world spend large amounts of time and money on trying to sort out how best to treat a problem that causes serious trouble to the whole of society, fills prisons and hospitals and takes huge resources from the public purse.

Families of addicts face enormous grief, so much so that addiction is called a 'family illness' when the people who live in close proximity to it develop their own unhealthy coping mechanisms in order to survive. When a substance becomes more important than love, reliability, truth, friendship or trust, and when it slowly steals the very soul of the addict, the people around that substance will probably start to behave in all sorts of peculiar ways. Mothers, fathers, lovers, husbands, wives and children are likely to turn detective and listen out for the clink of ice in a glass that means the first of too many whiskies, the metallic sound of the opening of a beer bottle too early in the morning or the sniffing of a drug behind a locked bathroom door. Bank accounts, mobile phone records and private, personal places are given up to the scrutiny of the worried family member who is trying to work out why their lover, spouse or child has turned so strange. Sensible, elegant people find themselves going through rubbish bins to see how many bottles have been consumed or how many screwed-up, empty drug packets have been thrown away. Hours and hours are spent pleading for an addict to give up, change his ways, seek help, go on a course or do anything at all to loosen the vicious stranglehold of a toxic substance. As concerned family members attempt to help, they will probably find themselves assuming the unwelcome position of bore, drag, nag and shrew. As one partner increases his drink or drug consumption, visits more prostitutes, gambles away more money or eats less food, the other is likely to get more desperate and depressed while suffering from an overwhelming feeling of powerlessness. And so the repetitive steps of addiction go on until, eventually, the hellish dance has to stop as one partner finally gets too tired and has to call a halt.

For this reason, addiction is very often a cause of divorce. It can be heartrending to walk out on someone who is ill, and it is heartbreaking to take children away from a parent. It requires courage and tenacity to leave and skill, wisdom and compassion to look after the children. When a parental partnership crashes because of the damage that addiction is causing, the process of separation is likely to be tough. If addictive behaviours endanger children, lawyers will be needed, and it is likely that the social services and CAFCASS (Children and Family Court Advisory and Support Service) will be called in order to ascertain the needs of the children and the truth of the situation. Fights are likely, exhaustion is a given, tears will be shed and the whole saga is wretched. But there is generally still some love left hidden behind the dark cloak of illness, and a good mother or father will want to make that love available to their children, while the children will recognize it and know that it is there. The problem is how to give as much access to the ill parent as possible while ensuring that the children remain physically safe and emotionally supported. Addictions to alcohol and drugs are especially damaging, and my casebook is full of stories of children being driven by drunks, being left unsupervised while a parent is unable to wake up, being forgotten in the back of cars in the wrong part of town while drugs are being bought, and tears and constant emotional backlash as the unreliable parent once again fails to turn up for a prearranged visit or an important school event.

In cases of separation because of addiction, children not only lose the stability of a two-parent family, but they also have to cope with the fact that one of their parents is irresponsible and unreliable. It is a hard lesson and one that children will need help with. The responsible parent will be at the vanguard of the protective forces that need to be mustered, but they themselves will need guidance in order to understand what it is that they are up against and how best to protect themselves while they look after their children. It is difficult to imagine their suffering.

I sat with a father one evening as he waited to hear whether his children had arrived safely at their destination. He had taken his wife to court in an attempt to stop her taking their children in the car. As she had no previous convictions and a clean licence, the law could do nothing to stop her driving her children through the night, even though every one of her friends knew that she should not be behind the wheel.

This small example of the torture that parents go through when they know that their children are at risk and are powerless to stop it encapsulates the terror engendered when out-of-control addictions and childcare are intertwined.

Young children who cannot make phone calls or call for help should not be allowed to be in the sole care of a dangerously addicted parent, and careful thought needs to be given as to how to manage access. Realistic grandparents or other relatives and friends can step in and provide a haven of safety.

I remember two children of four and six who were sent to Italy three times a year to visit their mother, who was addicted to heroin. Their father, Simon, sent them with his heart in his mouth and hardly slept until they returned. However, his children were safe enough, because they went to their grandmother, who accepted responsibility. The children loved her and her food and accepted their mother as an odd, remote kind of person who spent most of her time curled up in a corner gently snoozing or doing a disappearing act to go on missions to find more drugs. As they grew older, the boys were told what was wrong. They were glad to know the truth, had always known it in their bones and immediately made sense of their history. They did not stop loving their mother; rather, they were sad at her suffering and grateful to their grandmother and their father for making sure that at least they could find her somewhere behind her cloud of heroin.

Norah had a six-year-old girl who it was not safe to leave alone with an unreliable alcoholic ex-husband and yet she understood that her child needed a relationship with the only father she had. After a period of intense frustration during which her daughter sat on her weekend suitcase waiting for a father who never came, Norah enlisted the support of her ex-parents-in-law. It was not easy; the elderly grandparents did not want to face the fact that there could be anything wrong with their son and preferred to blame a difficult woman for the end of a marriage. However, they did see that their grandchild needed consistency, love and some knowledge of her paternal inheritance, and they agreed to have their little granddaughter to stay for a weekend a month, during which time it was hoped that her father would get his act together and come and visit.

Simon and Norah and their children were better off than some in that they had relatives who were willing to help. Many families are alone or desperately private and ashamed, and life is infinitely more difficult. If there is no one to provide damage limitation, then outside intervention will be needed. When a parent is obviously unfit, the courts will decide on supervised access, and the social services will step in. There is probably nothing more depressing for members of a family than meeting for a two-hour slot once every two weeks in a neutral place under the watchful eye of an unknown supervisor. The children hate it and the parents hate it. My experience is that fathers who have had supervised visitation orders placed upon them will pretty soon not turn up at all, and that mothers will be so depressed that they spend their time awash with grief and misery. Children tell me that they, too, find these unnatural situations difficult to bear, and that they leave the community hall or local leisure centre with some relief and a longing to get back home to normal life and their prime carer. But these contact orders are often the best that can be done, and the system works as hard as possible to allow a child to keep in touch with two parents in the hope that, one day, things might change and a mother or a father might recover enough to be able to look after their children more independently.

As children grow older and reach an age at which they can under-stand and have the ability to call for help, it becomes easier to find strategies to manage addiction within the separated family.

When Brian walked away from his family, full of crack cocaine and despair, he still loved his children and wanted to be their father but found himself so tortured by the need to use more of everything that it was no longer safe for him to be in charge. His daughter, at thirteen, was old enough to be told carefully about his serious illness, and she was given a list of simple instructions to follow should she be worried about herself or the safety of her nine- and eleven-year-old brothers when they spent time alone with him. The boys were less aware but knew that something was wrong when their father could not wake up in the morning, stayed up all night or forgot to feed them. Brian was not fit to drive the children or to have them alone in his rented bedsit; his mental state and the sheer volume of drugs that he was consuming meant that he was a danger to himself and incapable of being in charge. However, he was not a bad man, he was very ill, and he still sweetly loved his children and they loved him.

When the children's mother attempted to reduce her ex-husband's access to their children, they told her that they needed their father. He was fun, they liked playing the computer games that he understood so well and he read magical stories. Fiona listened to her children and devised a system whereby the children could have a relationship with their father and stay safe at the same time. Friendly neighbours were informed when Brian was going to be at the family home, and Fiona would leave the house, having prepared the lunch and given her daughter the telephone numbers of friends she knew were available and within easy reach. With her mobile phone stuck in the palm of her hand, she wandered through the empty days when her ex-husband sat in her home, but she gave her children a continuation of a relationship with their father. On her return home she would find evidence of cocaine scattered across her bedroom floor and other heartbreaking signs of just how truly ill her husband was. She often sat crying on the edge of her bed, alone and scared that she was doing the wrong thing, and her friends were divided about her decision to give her children access to their father at such great cost to herself. Some told her to practise 'tough love' and attempt to bring her husband to his senses by removing his children from him, but others said that children needed their fathers. To Fiona, it felt true and kind to allow him as much access as possible.

Brian was lucky; he survived his dance with death and crack cocaine and kept his relationship with his children. When he sobered up, he found three kids who had never ceased to love him. Fiona did a good job, but she would have been lost without her neighbours and her friends. If she had been too shy, too proud or too ashamed and kept her problems to herself, or if she had not had a network within which she could ask for help, she would not have been able to allow her children to have a relationship with their father. Because her neighbours were kind and understood, because her friends were prepared to be on standby at the end of a phone line and because her daughter was old enough to understand when and how to call for help, a system was put into place that was safe enough. Having chosen to recover from drug addiction, Brian went on to play a vital part in the lives of his children. His healthy relationship with them has helped them grow into well-adjusted young adults who did not suffer too badly from the double trouble of parental separation and addiction.

Addiction and mental illness can make parents so vulnerable that they fall through normal safety nets and land amongst the homeless and the hopeless. As parents begin and continue their downward trajectory, they will take their children with them. Louise and her husband, Ali, were addicted to heroin and lived their daily life begging, stealing and working out scams to find the means to get their daily fix. Neither trusted the other, and both lived in a violent world, trying to get more of their hellish elixir while regularly falling into bouts of a sweating, shaking cold turkey which rendered them helpless; and they provided no food or heating or basic care for their three children. Arrests by the local police were the norm. The children were watched in the supermarkets as known shoplifters who helped themselves to whatever they could to feed themselves. Parents at their schools avoided their mother as she walked ghostlike into the playground with her hand outstretched for money. Flat after flat was lost as rent remained unpaid and, eventually, the children and Louise landed without Ali in a dirty, damp basement flat with mountains of rubbish heaped against their outside wall and a frightening dog which snarled and drooled at the children as they passed it on the stairs on their way to school.

Louise's mother, brother and sister had spent many hours and hundreds of pounds on housing, feeding and caring for the family, and much thought was given to taking the children from their desperately ill parents and, later on, their single mother. However, the children loved Louise and wanted to stay with her to help protect her from the violence of their father and the horror of her illness. Also, they did not want to leave their schools, where they were happy, had many friends and were looked after by inspirational teachers. The social services told us that they would do everything they could to keep the children with a parent and came up with the interesting statistic that 80 per cent of children of addicted parents fare better if it is made possible for them to remain with either their mother or their father. And so a package was put together that enabled three children to stay together with their damaged mother in their broken home. Schools, social workers, counsellors and extended family worked to provide a safety net that protected the children. The only alternative that the overstretched social services could offer would have been to split the siblings up and send them to parts of northern England to be fostered.

Louise's mother provided money for a deposit to rent yet another flat, while her brother worked the local system to get the rent covered by the council and paid by standing order so that the money could not be used to buy heroin. Once internet shopping became available, a weekly delivery was made of food in order that the children would no longer go hungry, and bills for basic utilities were put on standing order so that they, too, were paid. The headmistress of the school undertook to keep pocket money for the children in her office, thereby ensuring that funds were available for bus passes, stationery and their small daily needs. Sensitive parents of other children were told in the playground of the situation, and mothers stepped in to invite the children home to tea. The headmistress called me in to talk to the children to let them know what was going on and to listen to their heartrending story. This wonderful woman even gave her telephone number as I cast around for people whom the children could call, should they feel themselves to be in danger. Holiday times were spent with members of the extended family, and the children grew to love their cousins while managing to live their own strange lives well enough to be educated and to go on to university and further education. Ali continued to be a nuisance and a restraining order had to be placed on him, as he threatened his own children for their pocket money on their way home from school. Louise found no treatment for her illness while her children were young, and they watched her become a wretched figure who was eventually housed in a hostel for battered women. Her story was tragic. She could not accept the helping hands that were offered to her, but at least her children were saved by the joint efforts of a society working at its very best. Three children who witnessed and directly experienced the multi-layered troubles of physical violence, poverty, addiction, mental illness and parental separation were saved by the careful actions of concerned adults working together. I am still in touch with the children. One has finished university and is moving swiftly up the career ladder of a film-making company, the second is halfway through university, and the third is planning to go to drama college. They read their story and all cried when they saw such sad words about their lives in print. They could not recall it as being quite so bad but did not want me to change a single word. They did, however, want me to add that their mother has taken significant steps towards recovery, they are proud of the way she has turned her life around, they are glad that she is back in their lives and they love her.

Louise's story will be all too familiar to social workers, prison and probation officers, health workers, doctors and schoolteachers. Unfortunately, there is often no back-up available for the children of such tragedy, and they suffer from being split up, fostered or sent to children's homes. There are so many children now at risk that the social services are over-extended and under-resourced. In the case of Louise and her children, the social workers were glad of the involvement of the extended family, a proactive school and a child therapist, and were able to take the children off the 'at risk' register because of the amount of help available. Many others fare less well, and there are many children sadly sliding into the same sort of trouble as their parents because there is no one there to catch them.

Addiction and alcoholism, separation and divorce have no respect for wealth or education. Children from the families of the rich and famous or the traditional moneyed professions are as likely to suffer from the separation of their parents and the experience of addiction as children who are living on the poverty line. Although the fundamental material necessities of life will not be lacking in families where money is not such an issue, it is easier to hide serious problems, and children may suffer by having to live within a toxic family environment that is unseen by the rest of the world.

Anne was the beautiful ex-wife of a famous banker and had two children and what looked like a perfect lifestyle. But she was a secret drinker who opened a bottle of vodka the moment she had completed the early-morning school run and went on drinking until she collapsed incoherently at the end of the day, leaving her twelve-year-old son and ten-year-old daughter to do their own homework and put her to bed, and cover up for her to their rather strict but immensely kind and caring father, Michael. Money meant that childcare and domestic help could be paid for and medical, psychiatric and professional help found quickly when Michael realized the extent of the problem. He brought his children to see me to help them understand the issues that come with alcoholism. The children showed me in their artwork that they understood as clearly as any trained adult and produced figures representing death and the grey pall of depression hiding a beautiful lady who had got lost behind a brick wall of unhappiness. The children blamed the divorce of their parents on their mother's drinking habits and, like almost all children, wanted their parents to get back together, in this case in order that their mother would not drink any more and their father would not look so sad.

These children needed to be given the truth that Anne's drinking had in fact been the reason why the marriage of their parents could not work, and that her illness had made her choose vodka over her husband. A sad and harsher truth was that she was now choosing alcohol over them and the time had come for them to live with their father. Anne was so ill that she did not fight the decision to remove her children and used their absence to drink herself into oblivion. I stayed in regular contact with the family and was able to provide objective answers to questions which the children either did not want or could not ask their father. One Friday night, I had a call from the son to say that he was extremely worried, as he had not heard from his mother for a week. I rang Michael, who went to check the use of her bank card and realized that no money had been taken out. We called for help, and the police broke down Anne's door to find her still breathing but barely alive. She was admitted to hospital and then went on to a treatment centre, where she began to get well and chose to recover from a long illness that had cost her nearly everything. She managed not to drink and began to rebuild her relationship with her children, starting off with sessions in my consulting room, where they felt safe to say the things that they needed to say, and moving on gradually to spending longer periods of time with them alone. By finding them a therapist, their father gave his children the opportunity to understand and accept the complexity inherent in addiction and divorce. The children could not save their parents' marriage, but they could understand and forgive their mother and did not have to blame themselves for not being able to save her, or suffer from feelings of abandonment because she had temporarily chosen the bottle over them.

Children simply hate to see the damaging behaviour that comes with alcoholism, addiction and the often violent ending to their parents' relationship. It makes them scared and sad; it does not earn or deserve respect; and it can place deep wounds in hearts which are too young to be wounded. Destructive behaviour provides a dilemma for those whose job or wish it is to help the children. By its very nature, it is secret and normally conducted behind closed doors. Children often do not want to tell, cannot find the words or, most tragically of all, accept this behaviour as their norm. It is difficult to tread into a private area of life where one has not been asked to go. To confront someone about their drinking can be to lose a friend and be banned from a house where one could have done some good. To name drug addiction can provoke huge denial and misdirected rage in the parent. Concerned adults need to walk carefully if they are to have the courage to reach out a hand to a child who is caught in such a nightmare. They need to remember that a child will always want to love their parent and, if a way can be found to sustain that love while making children safe, then that will probably be the best that can be done until the parent chooses to change his or her behaviour or the child is old enough to choose a different life.

The non-addicted parent, grandparents, aunts and uncles, friends, neighbours and contacts within schools can make a big difference to children who are suffering from the double trouble of addiction and divorce. Children will benefit from practical support by knowing that there is someone available if things get too bad, an age-appropriate explanation that addiction is an illness and does not mean a lack of love, the supervision of contact in a light-handed way and a strategy that ensures that they are as safe as possible. Counsellors and therapists can help children reach an understanding of what is going on, give them a voice with which to speak about their fears and get to the heart of the problem when working out how best to help. Social workers, lawyers and CAFCASS will step in if the problems in the family get completely out of hand and if it is felt that the children are at risk.

Violence

Sad stories of physical abuse meander through too many of the case studies in this book: there was Patrick, who witnessed his mother's wrist being broken by a live-in boyfriend; Lilly, who repeatedly watched her mother being beaten up by her father and who herself at the age of three was hit across the face with a golf club; Peter, the nine-year-old boy who followed his father's example and hit anyone who got in his way; and Ali, who attacked his wife and threatened his children on their way home from school. And I could write of many more heartbreaking incidents in which mothers are hit, slapped or thrown down stairs; fathers have objects hurled at them, are spat at and shrieked at; and children watch and run away, like Jamie, who climbed on to the roof when he could not bear to watch one more moment of fighting. Physical violence is often around in the lead-up to and during the worst moments of a family break-up, but it is rarely talked about and often goes underground, so sometimes I only catch a whisper of the problem. It is one of society's greatest taboos: men should not hit women, women should not beat up men; and children should not be hit by either. Violent behaviour is secretive and difficult to treat. The people who are its victims can be too frightened or too ashamed to address the problem, while the perpetrators are often too angry, too troubled or in too much denial to think rationally about what they are doing.

Information that physical abuse is part of the life of a family needs to be carefully handled.

I remember with regret the time when I had to report the case of Ted, who bore the red welts and angry marks of a belt across his back. Ted had been sent to see me by his school because the teachers could not get him to concentrate or to behave. Initially, his father had been supportive of this, because he wished for academic success and harder work from his son. However, once I realized that Ted was being regularly beaten, I had to tell the headmistress, who, in turn, had to tell the social services. Within a week of the discovery of cruel and habitual physical violence, the father left town and took Ted with him. Ted lost a school where he had friends, a therapist whom he had trusted and a familiar house in which he had grown up, because his father could not admit that his violent behaviour was wrong and that he needed help as a single parent.

Not only is violence often hidden and denied by the perpetrator, but it can be very hard for people to walk away from. There are a puzzling number of women who are beaten up and yet go back into the relationship in the hope that it will be different. I have often seen an unhealthy, repetitive dance whereby violence leads to urgent apology, which leads to a dramatic reconciliation, which results in relief that a passionate relationship is back on track. It is almost as if the non-violent partner is addicted to the other and cannot end the relationship in order to protect themselves.

A sad example of this scenario was when I was working with Olivia, who lived with her mother and her mother's part-time boyfriend. The boyfriend had broken two of the mother's ribs, her arm and her nose in different incidents. Olivia would listen to the shouting, punching and screaming at the top of the stairs and would come to me for a weekly session and describe in detail what she was witnessing. I attempted to work with her mother but could get no further than to be told that she was afraid of loneliness, that she needed her boyfriend and that she was not strong enough to leave him. And so I had to call the social services and get a social worker involved, who supported Olivia's father as prime carer. I found myself being an unwilling witness in court, and had to state my opinion that Olivia would be better off living with her father and out of the way of the constant fights and damaging physical violence.

Domestic violence is the most difficult of the problems that can additionally beset children who are facing the break-up of their family home. To attempt to deal with it may make it worse or more menacingly hidden, and to talk about it may result in punishment or the loss of a parent who, while violent, is also loved. If a teacher, doctor, lawyer, therapist, friend or family member has reason to believe that a child is suffering from physical violence, the social services and the police should be contacted. There are hostels and refuges for battered women and children, and there are intensive family-therapy programmes for victims and perpetrators. Violence goes beyond what is acceptable within any family and specialist help is needed to attempt to sort it out.

Once young people have been removed from violence, they will need to be able to talk about what happened. It is important that they realize that they did not cause it; that it is wrong; that no one is allowed to abuse them; that they are safe and that ways will be found to keep them that way. Therapy and counselling are a good idea, but teachers, family members and good friends can play an important part in talking to a child. If children can understand what happened and make sense of an impossible situation, they will be less likely to be frightened, anxious and confused and will have a chance of not repeating the same mistakes themselves in later life, either by choosing a violent partner or by thinking that it is acceptable to be violent themselves.

Adult depression

Depression is a horrible condition that sucks the energy and joy out of life and can replace all its goodness with unimaginable misery and despair. It is a spiritual, physical and mental illness that affects at least one in ten of the population. Depression seems to want to squeeze every last drop of lifeblood out of its victim until there is no fight left, and it can get so bad that the only hope is to plan a way out. People who have it often find it hard to stay alive, and people who live within its shadow can find it difficult to understand and accept. It is an invisible, sometimes apparently impossible-to-deal-with illness which feels as if it takes the people we love away from us. Depression can be the cause of the break-up of a relationship, and the break-up of a relationship can be the cause of depression. When it comes to looking after children, it does not matter much which comes first: if a child is living with a single mother or father who is suffering from the illness, the entire family will need some extra support.

A parent who is depressed will find everything hard work. It is hard to make it to the shops, plan the meals, reach the school gate, get the children to do their homework and into bed and then to get them up and to school in the morning. There is no joy, no fun, no spontaneity, and yet a depressed parent in sole charge of a child will be doing her very best to appear even half-normal. If anxiety or a bi-polar disorder is also present, then a parent might suffer from unpredictable mood swings, which could include shouting, rushing around and spending precious money at one moment and slumping in a foetal position the next. Whatever shape the depression takes, it is hard for a child to live with, and action needs to be taken if a single parent is attempting to cope with the illness and children at the same time. Signs to watch for in such a parent are:

- A marked loss of or increase in appetite
- Lack of sleep, particularly caused by early-morning waking
- Too much sleep
- Fatigue
- Inability to concentrate
- Tearfulness
- A morbid concentration on worst-case scenarios
- Loss of confidence
- Excessive feelings of guilt or worthlessness
- Reduced pleasure in normal activities
- A grey, lined complexion.

Following the collapse of a long-term relationship, almost every parent will have some of these symptoms for at least the first six months of the process of the separation. But if they persist or become worse and do not lose their grip, then it is likely that a chronic case of depression is being kindled and needs to be treated.

It is difficult to help someone who is depressed until they themselves accept that they are ill.

Fiona suffered from the illness after the break-up of her marriage but could not look for help until she was forced to. She held herself together for the sake of her children and got through the difficult divorce while coping with Brian's cocaine addiction. She believed that her intense feelings of loneliness, fatigue, loss, fear and despair were the normal emotional reactions to the ending of a twenty-year marriage and, while she did everything she could to avoid such dark companions, she could not escape them. Four years after Brian walked away, she found herself unable to function. She reported strange physical symptoms when she came for her session: her eyesight went weird, so she felt as if she were virtually hallucinating in black and white; her mouth felt dry; her tongue felt too big; and she had started to retch with anxiety throughout the long nights in which she could find no sleep. Still she kept going, and played tennis with the children, and put food on the table, and drove the children to visit friends, and crawled through the days thinking that if she just tried harder or did more exercise or found a way to get to sleep, she would be OK. But Fiona was not OK and, finally, early one morning, she rang me and asked for help. By the afternoon she was with a psychiatrist, who diagnosed severe clinical depression. The shock of the end of her marriage, the hard work of being left alone with three children and the financial insecurity and uncertainty about the future had turned her brain chemistry upside down and inside out. Feel-good serotonin had been replaced by the stress-inducing hormone cortisol to such an extent that she was on the way to a nervous breakdown and needed medical help to bring herself back into balance.

The strange thing was that Fiona did not become ill enough to need to collapse until her ex-husband was well enough to take over the care of the children. It was as if she hung on until she knew that she could let go and ask for help. Doctors diagnosed her illness, and friends came to her rescue. She went to stay in the countryside and began to become accustomed to taking pills that, initially, had horrible side effects but helped her recover her equilibrium. She rested and watched television and felt quite helpless, but she was relieved because she had given in, given up and received help, accepting that it was necessary in order for her eventually to get better. Fiona was worried about her children. They had been through so much and had been so unhappy. She was scared that her troubles would add to their burdens and that they would be even more damaged. However, there was a silver lining behind the cloud. Brian re-entered their lives and found himself looking after his children for three weeks and getting to know them again, and they realized that they could depend on him when things went wrong. Their eldest daughter came for a session and told me that she was fine, 'as long as she had one parent who was OK'.

It is often difficult for a person suffering from depression to accept the fact, but it needs to be spotted and dealt with as soon as possible. It takes one away from one's children and needs to be fought using every form of help. When Emma, who was discussed in a previous chapter, drew her depressed mother as an empty black balloon and told me that there was no one there to love her, she got it about right. Children can sense when depression has taken a parent away.

Depression is not shameful; it is a serious illness and should not be kept secret. If the parent who suffers will not or cannot talk about it, then the other needs carefully to flag to important adults in the life of his or her child that all is not well at home. The non-suffering parent, grandparents, family, friends and schoolteachers can talk to children and explain what depression is, how it works and what can be done about it. As in cases of addiction, telephone numbers can be given in case a child is scared or worried about his mother or father; adults can keep a careful eye out and take children for outings and sleepovers to give the adult a rest and the child some fun. Teachers need to be told so that they can help by offering understanding and practical back-up to children if a parent is too ill to sort out the endless organizational details of school life. A child does not need to be told off for not having forms filled in or for having the wrong socks when his mother can barely get him to school in the morning and chaos reigns at home. Medical help should be sought if necessary, even though it may be resisted.

There are many good books and websites that explain the condition, and it can help if the person with depression can find something to read so that they identify with the problem and realize that they are not bad or mad but that they have an illness. The most important thing when wondering how to look after children living within the troubled zone of depression and divorce is not to leave a child too alone. Simple explanation, comfort and a supportive hand will make all the difference.

New partners

The stress on children from a breaking family can be heightened if they are asked to accept a parent's new partner before they are ready; expected to like them if they don't; not told the truth about the importance of a new relationship; or told too much. Successfully introducing a partner is a difficult balancing act, but it is well worth trying to get it right for everyone concerned so that a child does not spin off with yet another bucketful of difficult emotions and is given time to get used to and accept a new order with as little upset as possible.

Some children are barely given the chance to understand that their mother and father are no longer going to live together before they are being asked to meet, like, show good manners to and enjoy being with a virtual stranger. Having had the ground taken from under their feet, they then have new ground built for them which they did not ask for, do not want, have no control over and often wish did not exist. Adults can be quite adolescent in their behaviour when they first fall in love after escaping from the constraints of a marriage and often seem to forget that their children must come first when considering the best way towards their new life. In an ideal world, parents would give their children lots of time to accept the separation and shore up their own relations with their children before introducing them to a new partner.

In my experience, it is usually women who commit the crime of rushing their children into an acceptance of a new order. Men might be guilty more often of infidelity, but once women have fallen in love, they tend to want the object of their affections in their lives as openly and as fast as possible. Men do not, on the whole, have the children living with them after a separation, so they can enjoy a private life that is indeed private. They are therefore able to keep things under wraps while their children and their ex-spouse become accustomed to the idea of the break-up. Women want security and are by instinct home-builders; when they have a new mate they are likely to want him in their home, but they will want their children there as well. In order to get both, I have seen them hurt their children.

There was trouble for everyone when Eddie's mother attempted to get him to accept her new boyfriend too quickly. His parents, Robert and Jo, booked an appointment to discuss how best to separate and look after their ten-year-old son. Jo had recently fallen head over heels in love with someone in her office and wanted to live with him in a new flat while having a shared-residence agreement. Robert, however, wanted to remain the main carer and did not want his son to have anything to do with the new boyfriend until some time had passed and the dust had settled. Jo was adamant that her son would live with her half the time, and Robert was adamant that he would not. Ten-year-old Eddie had been told that his parents were splitting up and knew about the new man in the life of his mother. He also knew that his parents were in total disagreement as to what should happen next. He was confused about where he was going to live and who he was going to live with. He loved his mother, but was furious with her for finding a new boyfriend, and he told me as he hurled toys around my therapy room that he was never, ever going to have anything to do with him. Eddie had made up his mind: although they had never met, he hated his mother's boyfriend with an understandable passion.

Eddie's world fell apart when his parents told him that they were getting divorced, and then continued to smash into smithereens as his mother behaved like a teenager, with little or no thought for her child. Robert asked very clearly that he be given six months' grace before Eddie was asked to meet the new man, and Eddie asked very clearly not to have to meet him at all. However, Jo did not have it in her game plan to be patient and, although she agreed in counselling to bide her time, she played appalling tricks with the result that her child never knew what to expect. Jo would arrange to take Eddie bowling, and the boyfriend would turn up. He would appear in the park, he would appear in the restaurant and once he appeared at the school gate. If Jo spent any time with Eddie, it was likely that it would involve an underhand attempt to introduce the new man into his life. Eddie made Jo promise that the thief who had stolen his mother would not be in the new flat when he went to have a look at it, but he was there for the first tea date when Jo showed her small son the apartment where they were all apparently going to be so happy.

Eddie came for several sessions and always had the same question. He wanted to know why nobody could stop his mother from including her new boyfriend in his life. We were asking the same question, but we could not stop a woman who wanted her way, wanted it fast and would not take any heed of advice. Eddie had a little of his mother's character and decided to fight; he started to run away from his mother if he caught sight of the boyfriend in the background. Jo came for a session to tell me that her son was out of control, that she could not manage him any more, that he showed no respect and that it was unfair on her new love, as he had never done anything wrong. I needed to point out that, in reality, it was Jo who was out of control, and it was she who needed to have a long, hard think about her behaviour. She did not like my message and walked out halfway through the session. However, when Eddie ran all the way home from her flat without paying attention to any rules of road safety or the busy London traffic, she agreed to come back and continue a conversation about putting Eddie first. After her son had literally risked his life to make his point, she was forced to listen to Robert and to others who told her to slow down, take time and have patience. Robert became Eddie's main carer, and Jo began to visit him at his home and to spend Saturdays with him while she conducted her new life in private.

When Eddie understood where he was going to live and who he was going to live with, he settled into the new arrangements and stopped fighting every time he saw his mother. After a year, he met the boyfriend properly, and slowly began to form a relationship with him; and he began to stay with his mother at her flat and go on holiday with her, but only if the boyfriend was not there. If Jo had not pushed so hard at the beginning to get Eddie to accept her lover, it would have been easier for everyone concerned.

When children such as Eddie feel out of control and unimportant and are expected to accept a parent's new partner before they are ready, it is likely that they will play up. What may look like disobedience, lack of respect, lying or a disregard for rules will, on closer analysis, be a cry for help, with a child mirroring his own parent's lack of appropriate behaviour. If parents with new partners want to help a child who is having difficulties accepting the new situation, they need to slow down so that everyone has a chance to get to know each other. At the same time, it is important that a child is not allowed to feel as if he is in charge of his parents' relationships with others. He can be listened to, and his views should be respected, but he must not be able to get rid of people just because he does not like them or the idea of their existence. A mother or a father who sacrifices a chance of love for the sake of their children may end up with an unhealthy, dependent relationship with their offspring. They may also find that they are lonely and resentful or that they have a 'dragon child' who believes himself to be in total control of the personal lives of his parents.

If forcing a new relationship too soon on to an unwilling child after parental separation is damaging (and I would recommend that any child will need, at the very least, a year to be allowed to find her feet), so too is the inappropriate adult behaviour at the other end of the spectrum, when parents completely deny that there is another person involved. Fathers are more likely to commit this error, as their lives are often more private and they find it easier to compartmentalize. Children can sense if something is going on and, as discussed in previous chapters, will turn into ace detectives if they get a scent of something suspicious. Once they have picked up on something, they will find it hard to leave any stone unturned until they have found out what is going on, but it is not good for them to lack trust and to live on red alert. Nor is it good for them to construct a narrative of their life which they later discover to be false.

> Toby was fifteen when he learnt that his father had had his girlfriend since before he left his mother. At the age of ten, he had been told that there was nobody else involved. Because the 'other woman' lived in a different part of the country, it was easy to keep her existence secret, and Toby entered adolescence feeling sorry for his lonely father. When the girlfriend outed herself because she was tired of being hidden away, Toby's world collapsed once again, and he had to come for therapy to work out whom he could trust and who would ever tell him the truth.

Too much information is as difficult for a child as too little. If a parent finds themselves giving details of the ex-partner's love life to their child, they need to ask themselves why they are doing it. Rather than leaning on young shoulders, they would do better to seek adult support and, if they are trying to get a child to take sides, they need to be aware that they are going to hurt everyone concerned.

> Ellen gave her daughter an explicit account of her father's infidelity and used her for support in a difficult divorce. Such was her success in alienating her child from her father that the twelve-year-old refused to visit him, join him in going away for weekends or on holidays. Not only did a young girl lose a father and a father

lose a daughter, but Ellen found that, through her behaviour, she lost her freedom. It would have been better if she had let the adult world know how much it hurt to be abandoned but kept her daughter free of the burden of resentment, anger and outrage.

Eventually, good behaviour on the part of the rejected partner is likely to bring its own rewards. When things have settled down and it is time to get out and about and start to make a new life, it is much more convenient to have children who will go happily to the other parent and not to have to bear the entire burden of childcare alone without ever having a break.

If an affair has been one of the major causes of the disintegration of a relationship, it needs to be included in the discussion as to why a mother and father are splitting up. The parent who is not involved in the infidelity will require superhuman reserves of dignity to pitch this difficult situation right. In an ideal world, the conversation about the fact that two parents are separating would be conducted calmly and clearly with both parents present. It would include the fact that one of the parents has someone else in their life and has chosen to spend time with them. The emphasis does not need to be on the 'marriage-wrecker' but on the fact that the adult relationship between mother and father has run out of steam and that, although they love their children, they do not love each other any more. While such tact and diplomacy may be difficult, it will be useful as the situation calms down and life begins to take its new shape. Children need both their parents if they are going to grow up as well as possible and if one of them has a new partner, it is best if he or she can be slowly accepted into the new configuration.

New partners often have their own children, which adds a whole new dimension to the problems that children have to face when accepting the separation of their parents. If a parent goes off to live in a household with other children, his or her own children are likely to be jealous and resentful and feel displaced as they 'lose' their parent to another ready-made family. Some children will simply dislike each other and would never have been friends under any circumstances and therefore find it difficult to be herded together on holiday and under the same roof. Other children will feel that they are second best as they arrive with their weekend suitcase and have to get used to a whole new system of unfamiliar rules and ways of doing things that do not make them feel at all as if they are at home. The subject is complex, and the issues for each individual are important. Barbara LeBey has written an informative and helpful book, *Remarried with Children,* which looks at problems and solutions for 'blended' families. Mothers, fathers, stepmothers and stepfathers who want to help a child find their feet in a new family would do well to read it, as LeBey manages to convey compassionate understanding for everyone's difficulties while always keeping her eyes on the needs of the child.

Learning and developmental disabilities

Some children living with the tensions of a breaking home may fail academically. They may behave badly, not concentrate, forget their homework, fall behind in lessons and generally give the teacher a very hard time. Parents can find their children more moody and difficult than usual, and the dreaded homework hour after school can become a three-hour pitched battle from which shoddy work is eventually produced that is way below the child's real capabilities. As work falls behind a child's potential and as he is moved to the front of the class and becomes a special case, he will usually also move up the scale to class troublemaker.

While this downward progression is common in children from dissolving households, the real reasons for it need to be checked out. Some children may behave as if they have a learning or developmental disability while the real reasons are the tensions within the home; others may play up but in fact be suffering from a genuine disability which has not been spotted. It is important to try to sort out what is behind a child's behaviour before the wrong assumptions are made and even greater suffering inflicted.

Research has led to much better understanding of learning or developmental disabilities and found that more and more children, especially boys, suffer from conditions that can make learning difficult. It is important to understand that these disabilities impact on children at emotional, behavioural and physical levels so that they sometimes seem almost hardwired to be different from others. It is not unusual for these children to be more sensitive, emotional, stubborn, inflexible, dogmatic and difficult than other children. When such a child faces parental separation, it is likely that they will find the process more difficult to cope with than their less challenged contemporaries and that they will need special guidance and patience to get them through.

Children with general learning disabilities

Children with general learning disabilities used to be called 'mentally handicapped', but terminology has changed to terms such as 'global' or 'general developmental delay' in younger children and 'general learning difficulties' in children of school age. 'General' refers to overall impairment. These children are usually diagnosed early and either need special schools or extra support in mainstream education. Other children are those with a diagnosis that puts them some way along the autistic spectrum and who are described as having 'pervasive developmental disorder'. Parents and siblings will be affected by the unavoidable fact that it is a time-consuming, emotionally enervating, sometimes thankless and often exhausting job to shepherd a disabled child to an uncertain adulthood. If one does not know the characteristics of general learning disability or pervasive developmental disorders, it is difficult to understand the sense of loneliness, the embarrassment in public, the frustration and the total exhaustion that parents suffer as they attempt to bring up their child within a normal family unit.

247

Marriages often suffer from the strain of living with a disabled child, and many do not survive. I have seen single mothers struggling with their children, having either left a partnership because they had no spare energy to give to it or having been left by a man who found that he could not cope. It is heartbreaking, and such a parent deserves and needs as much understanding and support as can be given.

Gloria's child Esther was born with brain damage. Her mother would not give up hope and, understandably, found it difficult to accept the diagnosis. She went from doctor to specialist, osteopath to dietician and school to school looking for an answer to her daughter's problems. Gloria could not bear to hear the words 'brain damaged' or take in the severity of the general learning disability and fought for her daughter while never giving up hope that eventually it would all turn out all right. Gloria's partner was perhaps more realistic and pragmatic about Esther's condition but less loving and accepting of his daughter's needs. The difference in their approach drove a wedge between the two parents and, in their exhaustion and their sadness, they could find no common ground to unite them and no love to get them through. Esther's father left the house when she was seven. He went on to find a new partner and, for his own reasons, decided to cut nearly all ties with his daughter. Gloria found herself entirely alone. She had to earn the money and continue to fight an almost daily fight to find funding, education and support for a child who would never grow much beyond the mental age of eight. Gloria was exhausted and unable to pursue any life beyond that of caring for her daughter, while Esther dreamt of having a father and made up stories about him to reassure herself that he had never really left. While it is easy to understand why Esther's parents could not stay together, it is more difficult to understand how a father could walk away from a daughter who needed him so very badly. If only the parents had received some help during the painful process of separation, he might have been encouraged to stay in touch with his daughter. His negation of his paternal responsibility added to Esther's problems as she grew older and attempted to have the sexual relationships that her adolescent body wanted but her eight-year-old brain could not understand. If only Esther's father had remained available to take some of the responsibility of caring for his daughter and to give her some of the love that she so desperately needed, she would have been happier and less confused.

Specific learning and developmental disabilities

Children with specific learning and developmental difficulties, despite having normal or often superior intelligence, have problems with tasks such as reading, writing or maths. They might have dyslexia, dyspraxia, dyscalculia, language and communication difficulties, attention deficit disorder (ADD), attention deficit hyperactivity disorder (ADHD), or find themselves with a mild version of an autistic-spectrum disorder. Family Doctor Publications in association with the British Medical Association has two superb publications entitled *Understanding Autism, ADHD, Dyslexia and Dyspraxia* and *Understanding Children's Behaviour*, which are useful guides for adults, should they feel that they need more information.

Many children with specific developmental disabilities are often a real handful and can be difficult to manage from the moment they are born. They might have a highly refined sense of justice, a black-and-white attitude to the world with little room for grey, a difficulty with expressing emotion while obviously feeling it very strongly, an inability to see another person's point of view, an ability to argue the hind leg off a donkey, a need to control, a personal sense of unfairness, an inability to see the bigger picture and the extraordinary energy to be able to go on and on and on. Socially, these children may find it difficult to understand cues from other children and are therefore not quick enough in the school playground to join in with others. They may not have enough spatial awareness to understand the importance of personal boundaries and so invade other children's space, and they may have obsessive interests in subjects such as dinosaurs, reptiles, sharks or outer space. These children may also be challenged by having no sense of direction and an inability to organize themselves. As a consequence, they may often be in the wrong place at the wrong time with the wrong equipment in the wrong clothes, having misunderstood just about everything that was required of them. On all levels – academically, socially, emotionally and physically – children with specific developmental disabilities may be challenged by their life and may in turn challenge their parents. Obviously, not all children with learning disabilities will fit this generalized thumbnail sketch, and some have no trouble at all, apart from localized problems with their academic work. However, the ones who crash through my door and need therapy or extra support can be a nightmare to steer successfully through school, and can provoke real problems between parents who may have different strategies for dealing with what seems like an impossible child.

These children are not impossible, but they need different handling techniques to other children and a balance needs to be found between helping them and making them responsible enough to enable them to help themselves. Ross W. Greene's book *The Explosive Child* provides an interesting insight and useful advice, and there are other helpful books listed at the back of this book. If managed well, children with specific developmental difficulties and difficult characters can be some of the most imaginative, original and rewarding individuals to work with; while if managed badly, they can stubbornly give up and go on strike and refuse to do almost anything they are asked and seem to be a real problem to all adults involved in their care.

Ned was a perfect example of a child suffering from the double trouble of having a specific developmental disability as well as a breaking home. His mother and his father split up when he was nine years old, and his father went off to live in another part of town, where he reacquainted himself with the friendships and habits of adolescence. As a successful DJ who needed to stay up all night because of his job, and who thought that lots of alcohol and drugs would help his performance, Alex forgot that he had a young son and partied until dawn in venues all over the world. In the meantime, he failed to send any money to support his family, and Ned's mother was left alone with a chronic-fatigue disability that hospitalized her and left Ned in the care of an elderly grandmother who did not understand her grandson. From the moment he was born, Ned had displayed most of the characteristics that I have described above and had been written off as being 'just like his father', which is not entirely surprising, as specific developmental disabilities are often inherited. He was stubborn, argumentative and difficult to manage and had already had a troubled school history. When his parents separated, he really started to play up in the classroom and instigated fights in the playground. His headmaster understood that family life was difficult for Ned and, rather than put him on an endless round of report cards, detentions and suspensions, he sent him to me with a detailed account of his sad story, understanding that the family's problems and his mother's hospitalization were the likely causes of his disruptive behaviour.

Ned's school history told me that his personal story was not the only cause of his problems. His reports were full of all-to-familiar phrases such as 'he could do better,' 'if only he would concentrate,' 'he is not living up to his potential,' 'he appears bright in class but when it comes to producing written work it is sloppy and not up to standard' and 'Ned lets himself down.'

These phrases tend to recur in the school life of a child with a specific developmental difficulty and are an important clue towards an undiagnosed problem. In addition, teachers' complaints of his shouting out, not concentrating, day-dreaming, constantly fiddling, refusing to do work or hand in homework and trouble with peers in the playground strongly suggested that a developmental disability lay behind the behaviour of a child whose naughtiness was being tolerated because it was known that he came from an unhappy home. Ned went to an educational psychologist for assessment and was discovered to have a high verbal IQ, in which his intelligence proved to be well above the national average, while his non-verbal IQ came out at well below. In other words, while capable of getting to a top university, he was on track to pass hardly any A levels. Ned understood what he was being taught and was probably brighter than the teachers who were teaching him but could never produce what was asked of him. Nobody understood that, initially, he had tried really hard in class to produce neat work that was up to standard, and nobody had noticed when he became disenchanted with the messy results. No wonder he started not to listen, to muck around, ignore the teachers and vent his frustration on children who annoyed him by getting better marks.

Ned not only had a difficult home life but suffered from undiagnosed dyspraxia. His grandmother did not understand his condition and thought that he was just a naughty child who needed a firm hand. His teachers, meanwhile, were asking much more of him than he was able to provide. On top of that, he was worried about his mother in hospital and missing his father. It was not surprising that he played up.

Because of the understanding of a wise headmaster, Ned started on a course of help with practical steps directed at remedying both his aching heart and his specific developmental disability. His grandmother was taught to understand him better and help with organizational, homework and typing skills. His school put in place a special learning programme and, most importantly, he became seen not as naughty and difficult but as challenging and interesting. Somewhere along the line, Ned's school discovered that he had inherited his father's natural sense of rhythm and that he was a talented drummer. He was allowed to use the drum kit when he felt frustrated, sad or angry, and he was encouraged to form a band when he got to year six. By that time, his mother was out of hospital and his father was settled in a flat not too far away. When it came to the school-leaving celebrations, Ned played the drums in public for his mother, his father and his grandmother. I saw a huge grin on his face and I knew of his inner knowledge that he was not a clumsy failure from a dysfunctional family but a special child who had a family that might not live together and might not be altogether perfect, but who could all come and see him play like a dream.

Not all children with specific developmental disabilities have explosive and difficult temperaments, and some will be delightful, easy to manage and suffer no more than the boredom of having to go to extra lessons and replacing an interesting lunch-time activity with a dull visit to the school's special-needs department.

Some children are so clever at hiding their problems and so normal in their outlook on life that they can remain undiagnosed, just like thousands and thousands of children of generations gone by.

Eliza would have gone through her school career with a steady average mark and a good-enough report if the extremely messy divorce of her parents had not led her teacher to suggest counselling. Eliza's mother wanted to return to America with her children when her marriage came to a bitter end, and her father wanted to keep the children in England. This disagreement meant that a court case had to be fought and the children had to be involved and interviewed by CAFCASS and psychiatric experts. Eliza was twelve at the time and had just started to learn French in secondary school, but she found the subject impossible and could not get to grips with a new language and its strange verbs and vocabulary. Although Eliza was usually a diligent and hard-working student, her teacher found her in tears before a French test and presumed that the ongoing court battle was the cause of her distress. Eliza's mother brought her to see me on the understanding that I would help her daughter through the difficult divorce and give her comfort while war raged between the two parents.

As I got to know Eliza, I realized that her parents, although fighting each other for custody and control of their children, had done a brilliant job in keeping them away from the corrosive evidence of their battle. Their daughter was able to tell me of happy weekends with either parent, of visits and laughter with mother and father, and showed that she knew exactly what was going on and that, although she would prefer to stay in England, she did not mind too much if she went to America, as she had family there and she would be able to visit the UK during every holiday. Eliza was not crying in the corridor about her parents, she was crying about her French. She could not do it and did not understand a word. She seemed so very bright, aware and fluent in the way she spoke to me that it was odd that she should have so much trouble. And so I dug deeper into her past school reports, and there I found the tell-tale remarks of 'she could try harder,' 'she does not live up to her potential' and all the other cries that I have heard so often from frustrated teachers as they try to get the best out of children whom they know are bright but who cannot produce the evidence. An educational psychologist's report revealed that

Eliza was dyslexic and extremely clever; she was not a child of average intelligence at all but a clear-minded, clever beauty who had found a way to navigate around her problems until French made a nonsense of her strategies and outed her as needing a little extra help.

Most children with specific learning and developmental disabilities will find school life difficult. Many react either by finding strategies to negotiate around their problems, becoming depressed because they cannot cope or developing behavioural problems because it is all just so difficult. Many of these disabilities can be sorted out. Early diagnosis, understanding and practical help make a huge difference and can give a child the chance to find that elusive potential and make a positive mark on their school life.

Lack of diagnosis, on the other hand, can lead to all sorts of trouble, which might involve refusal to go to school, self-harm, failure to produce work, suspension, expulsion and a continued low level of frustration and unhappiness. In 2005, the Dyslexia Institute reported that 20 per cent of the prison population suffers from hidden learning disabilities and argued for more screening in schools, so that the problem could be dealt with before bad habits become entrenched and it becomes too late to help a child who does not understand.

If a child is having trouble with work, baulking at new subjects or becoming stressed by the introduction of a more rigorous syllabus at the same time as experiencing a parental separation, it would be a good idea to go through past reports and look for the tell-tale signs of unfulfilled potential. While all children can be forgiven for not doing homework, losing concentration and playing up in the classroom when their lives have been temporarily shattered by their parents' break-up, it is important that hidden disabilities are not masked. If a specific learning or developmental disability is suspected, it is important to look for help. Educational psychologists can be found in

255

the private sector, sometimes within child and adolescent mental-health units and within the education system. State schools will refer children for assessment, but such referrals can take a long time, and headteachers necessarily have their eyes on the budget and will often only have funds for more severe cases. GPs can refer the child to child and adolescent mental-health services, while other parents, GPs and teachers will know of professionals working in the private sector who may be expensive but will provide necessary information about a child more quickly than the NHS, where there is frequently a long wait for help. If a learning or developmental disability is diagnosed, schools, parents and other experts need to work together to get a child back on the right track. I have found that fathers often need encouragement to understand, and I have seen many cases where parents disagree vehemently with each other about the care of their difficult child: one thinks that he is naughty, stupid or bad while the other intuitively understands that something is wrong but does not know what can be done to sort out the problem. Unfortunately, the behaviour of children suffering from learning and developmental difficulties can become such an issue between parents that extra stress is heaped on top of a relationship that is already in trouble and can become a reason why parents eventually split up. Children will be helped if all the adults in their life take time to understand their condition. If at all possible, separated parents need to work together to get their child out of an educational hole and away from a belief that they are stupid, out of place, frustrated and somehow out of tune.

Family breakdown is often said to be more difficult than dealing with the death of a parent and is one of the most stressful things a child will ever have to face. If additional external problems such as parental illness, unwelcome new family members, physical violence or economic hardship are added to the problem, or if a child has hardwired learning or developmental difficulties and an original, sensitive character, then life is going to be very tough indeed. Double trouble will make it even more difficult for children to navigate the treacherous waters of family collapse, and they will need as much help as they can get in order to have a chance to be free of the mistakes of their parents and to understand how to manage their lives.

Summary

Some unfortunate children have to cope with complex and difficult situations over and above the break-up of a family home.

- **Addiction** in its many forms is very often a reason for divorce and can become very much worse because of it. Children need special care in order to be allowed to continue to love their addicted parent while being protected from the dangers of the addiction itself.

- **Violence** is often around in the lead-up to and at the worst moments of a family break-up. It is one of society's greatest taboos, is kept secret and is difficult to treat. It goes beyond what is acceptable within any family and specialist help is needed to attempt to sort it out. Children must be able to talk about what has happened and understand that they did not cause it; to know that violence is wrong; that no one is allowed to abuse them; that they are safe and that ways will be found to keep them that way.

- **Adult depression** is a horrible illness that attempts to destroy the lifeforce of anyone who has it. If a child is living with a single mother or father who is suffering from the illness, it is important not to leave a child too alone. Simple explanation, comfort and offers of activities away from the illness can make a big difference.

- **New partners** can add to the stress on children from a breaking family. Adults should not attempt to rush their children into an acceptance of a new order without giving them time to come to terms with the demolition of the old. Nor should they deny that a new relationship exists, thereby destabilizing a child's framework of trust in an already shaky world. Too much adult information should be avoided, and it is better if one parent does not demonize the other and their new partner.

- **Learning and developmental disabilities** impact on children at emotional, behavioural and physical levels and this sometimes makes them seem almost hardwired to be different from others. When such a child faces parental separation, it is likely that he or she will find the process more difficult to cope with than their less challenged contemporaries. These 'difficult' children can also provoke real problems between parents. Schools need to be aware that learning disabilities are often masked by difficult behaviour that is put down to unhappiness within the family home. Adults can help by understanding that children with learning disabilities sometimes find life quite tough, and not all of them set out deliberately to be difficult.

7 · · · · ·

What to do and how to do it

CHILDREN NEED TO FEEL SAFE while they grow up. In an ideal world, their safety would be provided by a united family and they would be loved, educated, looked after, disciplined and encouraged by their mothers and their fathers. When a family breaks apart, the vital safety basket breaks too. Instead of security, children are likely to experience doubt and, instead of consistency, they grow up not knowing what to expect. Instead of experiencing unconditional love, they may feel abandoned and, instead of loving a single unit, they may be unsure to whom they are allowed to give their affection. Instead of finding comfort, they find tension and, instead of joy, they discover sadness.

All of this will lead to difficult questions and impossible feelings that will settle somewhere in their bodies and challenge children as they try to work out the answers. Children will rarely have the vocabulary to talk about what is going on. Their parents are likely to be too busy or too profoundly upset to notice how they are feeling. The wider world will tend to see family break-up as a private matter and therefore fail to offer children a chance to speak. But children need help, especially at that emotional point where they realize that their whole world is about to change. Without help, they are likely to try unsuccessfully to lock away their painful feelings and difficult questions. They will show the world that they are feeling hurt by exhibiting the difficult physical and behavioural symptoms that are typical of children who are living through the divorce and separation of their parents.

The best way in which divorcing parents can help their children is to behave as well as possible and create a different family system so that there is still love, and quality and consistency of care. But divorce is like a serious car crash, and it is unrealistic to expect anybody to walk away from it as if nothing has happened. Men and women with children who have to give up on a serious long-term relationship will be in shock. They will need help from the outside world to find their feet and their equilibrium in order to be the best possible parents for children who will also be suffering.

Divorce is no longer a private matter. With more than a quarter of our children living in single-parent homes, it is a social experiment that does not seem to be going especially well, and everyone who can help should come out from behind a veil of natural reticence and lend a hand. Grandparents, siblings, godparents and friends can do an enormous amount of good by supporting parents in crisis.

When my own marriage hit the rocks and I was left alone with three young children, I felt that my life was saved by the behaviour of friends. I was lucky to have so many who seemed to know exactly what to do. Food arrived, neighbours helped out, friends came with lunch on a Sunday so that my children did not have to eat alone with a mother who could hardly cook, the children were taken on expeditions and invited to sleepovers, we were all invited to France for the first desperate summer by the family of a friend of my daughter, and the telephone never stopped ringing. I knew that, although my husband had left me, I was not truly alone. When I proudly attempted to take my children to Center Parcs for Christmas because I could not face playing happy families with my married siblings or my married friends, I found myself and my children being kidnapped and driven out of town to be cooked for and looked after throughout a four-day family holiday that I was too afraid to face.

Friends, family and neighbours showed me what a difference can be made to the life of a mother who cannot sleep, cannot eat and who can barely get her children to school, let alone get them to do their homework or take any time out to give them any fun. Because of their kindness I was able to stay sane enough to look after three equally shell-shocked children. Life did not grind to a halt, although I wanted it to, and I got through each endless day propped up and egged on by kind people who promised me that the pain would pass, that things would get better and that eventually there would be a light at the end of the tunnel. Although I did not believe a single optimistic word, I did respond to their kindness and kept myself together as people watched over me and my children.

Friends and family can provide the same kind of support for a father who is in shock when his marriage or long-term relationship comes to an end. Practical help is useful as, very often, fathers have nowhere to offer their children to stay in the early days of a break-up. Help with the practicalities of school and children's social life can be welcome, as being in sole charge of children is sometimes utterly confusing for a father who has traditionally left their day-to-day care to their mother. Fathers also need company and comfort. They tend to move more quietly into their distress and stay for longer in a silent misery as they become aware of what they have lost and how much they miss their children. Fathers especially need encouragement to realize that they have a vital and rewarding role to play in the care of their children.

It is practical and in mothers' own interests for them to put negative personal feelings aside and encourage fathers in their competence and confidence so that they are allowed to be the best fathers possible. One recent study ('Making Contact: How Parents and

Children Negotiate and Experience Contact after Divorce': Trinder, Beek and Connolly) found that a shocking 37 per cent of fathers lose contact with their children within two years of divorce. Another (Gill Gorrell-Barnes) found that, in the same two years, a quarter of parents will still be involved in conflicted parenting and that fathers tend to reduce contact in order to avoid further acrimony and defend themselves against their own feelings of guilt and powerlessness. Given that fathers miss their children and that all the available research tells us that children desperately need their fathers, everything possible needs to be done to make fathers feel more comfortable with childcare so that they can stay around and make a difference.

What parents need to do

Expect the children to be hurt and sad and understand that they never want their parents to separate. It is important not to conceal the truth or downplay the impact of the situation in order temporarily to spare the feelings of a child. There is no such thing as an easy way to break up the only family that a child has known, and children need to be allowed to have their difficult emotions. Just as an adult would not respond too well to a suggestion to look on the bright side when their marriage has just ended, so too a child will be confused if adults behave as if it is no big deal. The best gift to give children is permission to be upset and an understanding that it is really hard. It is important to remember that children don't think like grown-ups, that their processes will be out of step with those of the grieving adult and that they don't have the resources to cope with the emotional pain. They are likely to feel powerless and worried, with nowhere to turn except to the very people who made them so unhappy in the first place.

Sadly, many adults miss the point and believe that a child thinks like them, or doesn't think at all, or that their very real distress is merely attention-seeking behaviour. Children do think and feel very deeply, but they do it differently and show their feelings through their behaviour and their physical symptoms. It is desperately important that their parents and other sensitive adults realize what is happening and help children find the words and the tears to express their sorrow.

Carefully choose the time to tell the children. It is important that children are given time to assimilate information of such massive significance. However much fighting or frozen resentment they have witnessed, they will always be shocked when the final announcement is made. I have never met a child who wanted their parents to break up; they always prefer to hold on to what they know, and hope against hope that one day things will be all right again. Children should not have to hear that their world is about to crash around their ears without being given some time and space to process such drastic information.

Choose a time to tell the children when there is not too much planned for the following few days so that questions can be asked, confusions cleared up, tears shed and sleepless nights shared. Bring friends and family over to help with the process so that breaks can be taken from what is a very real tragedy. Children are capable of putting aside their worries for a while if they have a football game to play in the park or a film to see, but their thoughts will return again and again to trying to work out what is going on, what is going to happen and what on earth they should do about it. And while they attempt to work out a future that has lost all signposts, it is important that both parents give them time, are around to talk, answer questions and make themselves available to listen to their fears.

Tell the children together. This step in the process of divorce is probably one of the most important to get right and one of the most difficult. It is so emotionally painful that very few breaking couples manage a good text-book kind of conversation with their children, but it is vital to at least try to do it well and do it together. If a mother and a father can separate their own feelings from the explanation they give to their children and have the conversation as calmly and rationally as possible, their children will be less afraid and better prepared for the future. It is best for parents to admit that they no longer love each other and have grown apart but to reassure their children that they still love them and will always be the only mother and father that they will ever have. It is also a good idea to make it clear to children that, however much the children may want to get their parents back together, it is a final and painful decision that has been made by adults and is not reversible.

However difficult it may be, it is much better if a united front is presented. By doing this, a couple will show that they are taking their parental responsibilities seriously. The children will feel safer if both parents are there to tell them of future plans and to comfort them in their distress; and they will believe the answers to their questions if both Mum and Dad give the same reply. This will help reassure them from the very beginning that their mother and father are going to create a new and different structure that may be unwelcome but nonetheless will keep them safe. With the parents working to end their marriage as well as possible, they will show that they still love their children, are available for them and are not about to abandon them, even when one of them has to leave the family home.

All too often I see a different scenario, where a grieving, abandoned, angry or disconsolate parent tells their children through tears and bewilderment that a mother or a father has left or is about to go. And with the news often comes more information about infidelity, sexual misdemeanours, drug and alcohol abuse and money worries than is good for a child of any age. With one stroke, one distraught parent can so tarnish the other that a child becomes frightened about what is going to happen next and confused about whom they are allowed to love.

If a parent has to tell their children on their own, it is important to do so with great care and with as much support as possible. While they can rant and rave incoherently to their friends about an incomprehensible and impossible situation, it is essential that they hold themselves together when talking to their children and that they find some kind of explanation that makes sense to a child. Addictions can be explained as illness, infidelity can be put down to the sad fact that the adult relationship has come to a natural end, and abandonment can be just about explained away as a mid-life crisis. A wise parent will do this carefully, not for the sake of the partner whom he or she used to love, but for the sake of a child who needs to believe still in the goodness and love of both his parents. When time passes, dust settles and acrimony diminishes, a good mother or father will want their child to have the two parents that are part of their birthright. They might not be able to bring up their child together under the same roof, but shared parenting from different households is perfectly possible and can work well if a child is allowed to love and respect both parents.

Make practical issues as clear as possible and give simple, honest answers to the children's questions. Family breakdown is rarely well organized, and it takes time for the muddle to sort itself out. Initially there are the important questions about residence, housing and contact which need to be explained. Other questions of vital importance to children might be: Can they stay at the same school? Who is going to look after the pets? Who is going to be with them for Christmas and birthdays? Will Mummy or Daddy be lonely? Will there be enough money to pay for food? Some questions will seem entirely selfish, such as 'Will I still get my pocket money on Fridays?', while others will be heartbreakingly difficult to answer, such as when a small child asks again and again, 'When is Daddy coming home?'

The best approach to imparting information that children do not want to hear is to present it as honestly and simply as possible. Some questions will have no immediate answers, and children will have to be content with the fact that their parents are doing their best to sort things out and will tell them as soon as they know. If a family is lucky enough to be able to keep the house for the foreseeable future, then the children will not have to face too much upheaval and will feel secure that they can stay in their neighbourhood with their friends and their schools near by. They will need to be told where their other parent is living, when and how often they can see him or her and how they can keep in contact. If a family does have to move house, it is a good idea to let the children know when they are moving and to involve them in such decisions as decorating their bedrooms or planning the garden. An involved and informed child who knows that life is changing and who is able to feel a little in control of his life will be able to cope much better than a child who does not know what is happening from one day to the next.

Expect to have several conversations and to have to revisit difficult questions and discussions again and again. Children will have lots of different feelings at lots of different times, will never feel everything all at once and will go at their own speed as they process what is happening and what it means to them. It is probably best to see the initial Big Conversation as the beginning of many similar but less catastrophic discussions, and it perhaps would be just as well not to attempt to discuss everything all at once. When children are in shock, they will be unable to hear all of what is said and, just as a patient with a serious illness can rarely remember all the details of an important meeting with a doctor, so it is with children, and they probably will only take in a small percentage of information about impending separation. Not only are children unlikely to hear some of the difficult news, but they are quite likely to deny the parts they find too painful to take on board.

Guy, at eleven, listened intently when his parents told him that his father was moving out of the house and did not seem to be remotely bothered by the news that devastated his brother and his sister. He merely went off to play football and wondered why everyone was asking him if he was all right. It took four weeks and a refusal to go to school one Monday morning before he broke down and told his teacher that he could not bear what was happening at home. His parents had to reconvene and have the conversation again with Guy so that he could listen and ask the questions that he had been unable to give voice to the first time round.

At every developmental stage, a child will need to revisit what happened and reinterpret one of the most important events of their life. As children grow and show different ways of understanding, parents should listen to questions seriously and answer them as honestly and with as much information as is appropriate to their age.

There are some answers that will help children at any stage of their development. Always let them know that:

- They were born out of love.
- They were and still are very much loved by each parent.
- Their mother and father were happy together once.
- The parental separation had absolutely nothing to do with the children.
- The decision to separate is definitive and the children do not have the power to get their parents back together.

Be available so that children don't have to struggle for parental attention. Emotional availability needs to be a given, and is all too often missing when parents are going through divorce and separation. Children need to know that they can turn to their mother or their father day or night if they are in trouble. But some parents are too emotionally distraught and full of negative feelings to have any space for their children, while others are too busy building a new life and sorting out the massive amount of mental and physical work that comes with the ending of a marriage. Children will intuitively know if there is no one to answer their questions, and they may retreat into a dangerous place where no one speaks and no one understands. Feelings will be hidden deep in the darkness of the broken home, and children will be left to cope alone. If a parent becomes unable to give their children the attention that they need, it is important that they seek therapeutic help. In the meantime, they need to ask others to step in temporarily and lend a hand to stop the lonely downward spiral that can become so familiar to the children from a broken home.

Tell them about the good things. All children want to be able to love both their mother and their father, and they get confused during the process of separation if their parents openly hate each other and can only find bad things to say. It is important to continue the positive reinforcement of the initial discussion when the children were told that they were born out of love and that they will still be loved by both their mother and their father. Children are helped to understand themselves and their inner world by understanding their parents. If they are given the chance to have a mental image of a good parent, they will like themselves more and grow up with a better self-image.

Children love to know about when times were happy between their parents and to build a history and mythology that goes beyond the fighting and the difficulties. The more they can be told, the more they will understand, and the more they will be able to like, admire and love both parents. If adults can be kind about each other, they will be giving their children one of the greatest gifts in their control; they will be giving their child the chance of a warm relationship with both a mother and a father.

Make both homes as welcoming and comfortable as possible. Children function best when they feel emotionally and psychologically connected to both homes. If possible, single parents should make their new arrangements as child-friendly as they can. Mothers and fathers can prove to their children that they are all right, in control and able to provide a new and different system of care, which may entail cooking meals together, doing homework, playing computer games, reading aloud or just camping out. Children will consider that they have two homes where they are welcome and happy. It is important that each parent encourages and allows their children the freedom to make the other house their own so that they can move happily between the two and even come to regard having two homes as one of the real bonuses of divorce.

Have the same rules and boundaries for the really important things. No two households will ever be the same, even if the people in charge have previously lived together for twenty years. Table manners may be very important to a father, while a mother may not mind her child eating with his fingers but will be angry if his clothes get dirty. In one house, an untidy bedroom may earn no more than a slight sigh, while in another it may provoke a sharp rebuke and no playtime until it has been cleaned up. Some parents will make their children do all of their homework on a Friday night, while others feel that they deserve a rest after a hard week at school and set aside some time on a Sunday morning. Mothers may be relaxed about TV and computer games, while fathers may apply strict limits to their use. But if rules are explained clearly and children know what to expect in their different homes, they will quickly understand and usually comply as, on the whole, they like to be liked and do not normally want to cause trouble. Separating couples will rarely reach an overall consensus on how to rear their children. This need not be problematic, as long as the differences are made clear to the children and they do not get muddled as they move backwards and forwards from house to house. However, when it comes to the important boundaries that actually make a child safe, then parents need to reach agreement and back each other up.

Children need a few basic rules not only to ensure their safety and their well being but also to give them a chance to grow up with the ability to cope in a competitive world. While it is up to individual families to choose what is and is not acceptable, a general rule of thumb might be that violence and abusive swearing are not OK; that appropriate bedtimes and curfews need to be imposed; that school needs to be attended with schoolwork completed; that diet and exercise are important; and that children sometimes need to help around the house. If parents who live in separate houses can put their differences aside in order to agree on this type of basic behaviour and back each other up in enforcing it, their children will know where they stand. Not only will they feel safe and reassured that they are being looked after by two parents, but they will see that their home life has a familiar continuation to its outer structure, which will automatically help to ease any internal sense of panic. Life will be simpler if children do not have to weigh up differing points of view or try to play one parent off against another. And an important bonus will be that they will benefit from having parents who can continue to regulate a familiar daily life so that they get enough sleep, do their homework, eat the right kind of food, get some exercise and learn enough respect for others so that they too can have the same kind of chances and choices as their contemporaries from two-parent families.

Give children a chance to have their own lives and allow them their freedom. As children develop and grow older, they will begin to find their feet in the world and need to move away from their parental homes. Children of divorce very often get caught in yet another trap that is not of their making. While they will hopefully want to spend time with their parents, they will also want to be completely normal

270

and go out and about with their friends, while exploring the edges of their world away from the watchful eyes of grown-ups. As they enter adolescence, they will in all probability not be remotely interested in staying at home and will be busy on their mobile phones and web pages arranging their own social lives. This is a necessary and healthy part of childhood development and needs to be encouraged. However, if a parent jealously guards their time with their children and insists that it is 'their' weekend or 'their' time, they will either push the children away or stop a child from having the independent life they need. Sharing children is difficult, and it can really hurt if one's precious time with them is further depleted because of their busy schedule. However, a wise parent will be silent about their own needs and give children the encouragement and the freedom they deserve in order that they can begin to get on with their own lives without having to give a backward glance and worry about their poor old parents left by themselves and home alone.

Give children a chance to get used to the idea of their mother and father breaking up before introducing a new partner. Marriages often fall apart ostensibly because there is 'someone else', or someone new will come along pretty quickly after a divorce.

When introducing new partners into the life of the children it is wise to:

- Allow the dust to settle and give the children time to get used to the idea of the separation before introducing them to the person who has been in the background.
- Give children time to adjust to how life has changed before introducing them to a new relationship.
- Wait to introduce children to a new adult until the relationship has moved beyond casual dating.
- Understand that children will have a variety of reactions to meeting new adults.

- Understand that children might not instantly like or approve of someone new.
- Keep some time for children separate from time with a new partner.
- Try to ensure that initial meetings between new adults and children take place in a child-friendly and age-appropriate environment.
- Allow the children the freedom to have their own relationship with a new partner of an ex.

What parents should avoid

Just as it is important to be aware of some of the 'right' things to do when shepherding children through the early days of the process of divorce and separation, it is equally important to take notice of some of the behaviours that do nothing but harm. If parents want to have a good divorce and limit damage to their children, there are basic things to avoid.

Don't fight in front of the children. I have heard too many stories from children of all ages of what it is like to huddle on the stairs while they listen to their parents fight. Siblings will hold on to each other and listen to every word as voices are raised and cruel words thrown with abandon. Others will stand alone in a doorway, hidden and full of fear but unable to go to bed or about their business. In the worst cases, they hear physical violence, and some understand that the fights are fuelled by alcohol. Sometimes children have attempted to separate fighting parents and have been knocked about when they have got in the way of fury that was not meant for them.

Whether the fighting is verbal or physical, children should not have to hear or witness it. It makes them frightened about what might happen next and worried that the parents they love no longer seem to love each other. They do not want to hear the awful things that can be said in the heat of the moment, especially if they are about them. They do not want their parents to divorce, and they do not want to be afraid.

The effects of hearing and seeing too much can be devastating. Children may not want to go to school because they feel they need to stay at home to look after a sad parent; they may stop concentrating and start to fall behind in their schoolwork, thereby increasing their problems; they may become clingy and not want to go out and play. They may sit numbly watching while thinking that they have caused the battle and believe that if they did not exist, their parents would stop their fighting. Worst of all, they may feel that they have to take sides and stop loving one parent in order to support the other. And, because fighting and fury are private and vicious and because children can rarely find the words to explain or people to understand, their fear and confusion sit deep within their psyches, privately undermining their security and their peace of mind.

If parents have to fight, and they probably do, they should fight away from the children. Send them to a grandparent or an aunt or a friend while toxic and painful stuff is sorted out. Go for a long walk in a wide, open space. Row in front of a counsellor; scream at each other through clenched teeth in a restaurant. It is far better to show the true colours of a breaking marriage to other adults and be embarrassed later than to fight inside the family home and cause infinite damage to growing children.

Don't demonize the other parent. Divorce and separation usually bring such emotional turbulence that, for a while, the adults can be relied on to be fairly out of control and not entirely themselves. Most difficult behaviour can be forgiven as a phase, with the understanding that loved ones are really hurt and that they will return to their senses in due course. The one area of difficult behaviour that cannot be condoned is when one parent starts to bad-mouth the absent parent in front of their children. While it is entirely normal to want to win the moral high ground, to have one's point of view understood and to convince the world that an ex-partner has behaved abominably, it is absolutely essential that this kind of strongly emotional language is not heard by the children via telephone calls or at the kitchen table while talking to a trusted friend. It is even more important that the children are not directly exposed to tirades, innuendos, snide remarks or tearful speeches from a mother or a father who feels that their children need to know exactly what kind of ghastly person the other parent really is. A child will come to his own conclusions about his mother or his father and will always want to love both of his parents. It is also important to remember that there are very few parents who have absolutely nothing to add to the life of their children and that an adult who tries to turn a son or a daughter against a mother or a father will, in effect, be stealing part of the natural physical, emotional and spiritual inheritance of that child.

The United Nations Charter on the Rights of the Child (1989) says that a child has a right to access to both parents wherever possible. If one parent corrosively bad-mouths the other he or she will systematically be undoing that right. Children will be totally confused if one parent is demonized by the verbal abuse of the other and will not know whom they are allowed to love or whom to believe. It can be so very sad when children show me in art therapy that they miss their fathers and want to see them but do not dare discuss it with their mothers because they fear a strong, negative emotional reaction. Unfortunately, case studies of children who have had to endure the vilification of a parent run throughout this book. An especially bad example was Imo, who would and could not see her father because her mother had said such appalling things about him. She ended up seriously self-harming herself as a teenager. Another was the dramatically tragic story of Mike, who suffered when his drug-addict father spoke so vehemently and bitterly about his ex-wife, and Mike believed him, locked his heart against his mother and followed the same negative path as his father.

Children know that they are a composite creation of their two parents, and they think that they are part Mum and part Dad. If a child hears that their mother or their father is bad they will feel that they are partly bad as well. There could not be a better way to start the building of a character with poor self-worth and low self-esteem.

If parents want to help their children but find themselves unable to be positive about their ex, it should be an absolute rule that, at least, they do not make negative comments or statements that judge or put each other down. It is also important that one parent does not blame the other for the divorce and that each takes some responsibility for the end of the marriage. If an ex-partner does bad-mouth a parent, it is best if the other adult holds on to all the wisdom and maturity at their command and does not retaliate. Although it will be difficult to stay silent, it will be a short-term victory to get the last word, and be at the expense of the children, who will continue to be torn in two by parents who are intent on winning an ugly battle.

Do not indulge in competitive and fractious post-divorce family management. Negative feelings are likely to remain high as parents work out the arrangements that will create a new system. But when feeling continues to run higher than common sense and parents put their own emotional needs before their ability to think about the needs of the children, there is a problem that needs to be addressed. Things that will only hurt the children are:

- Angry messages on answer phones which are likely to be over-heard by the children.
- Arguments at the time of the hand-over of the children.
- Difficult and contentious emails that will either inflame a parent or be read by a child-turned-detective.
- Refusal to agree on important routines and vital boundaries such as bedtimes, curfews and homework so that one parent has to take all the responsibility.

- Buying of inappropriate presents or provision of expensive holidays while the other parent can afford neither.
- Inconsistency about contact or financial agreements.

Children have to live in a world created for them by adults, and it is better if it is peaceful and well structured. They hate to see their parents arguing, feel helpless when emotions spin out of control and do not want to be involved in the fighting. If there is a competitive aspect to post-divorce family management, it needs to be sorted out so that there is a shift away from a parent needing to be right to joint concern and good intentions for the children. In that way, emotionally driven destructive behaviour will stop, and the children should be able to move between their parents without feeling guilty or uncomfortable.

Unfortunately, sometimes the parent who has residence (and it is usually the mother) has the power to make the other relationship difficult or downright impossible. If children are angry and hurt, they may behave as if they do not want a relationship with the parent who has left and will need encouragement and understanding to re-establish contact. If they have heard too much negativity, they may be either afraid of the absent parent or scared of hurting or making angry the parent with whom they live. It is within adult control to create an environment in which children can change their minds. If a parent can remind their children about the good times, be specific about the qualities of their ex-partner and truly show that they encourage and approve of contact, their children will be free to move towards a relationship with both parents.

Do not make children act as go-betweens. One of the most damaging and impractical behaviours that can come with the process of separation is to use children as message-carriers. Children are likely to tell each parent whatever they want to hear and will be unlikely to be objective. As children have to move between parents with an agenda that they do not understand, they will gradually accumulate a negative emotional experience that is likely to scar. Children who act as go-betweens feel:

- Powerless, in that they have no choice in what they are being asked to do.
- That their loyalties are split because they want to please both parents and can usually please neither.
- Isolated, because they can talk to neither parent.
- Unable to express what is going on because there is no one to talk to and words could not possibly describe the chaos.
- A sense of injustice, anger and self-sacrifice because it is simply not fair that they have to run between their parents to get an answer on any decisions that need to be made.
- As if they are walking on eggshells because they have to be so careful of their parents' feelings.
- An inability to make sense of what is going on.
- Exhausted, confused and fed up.

I remember Sally, and the fact that I needed to give her a train fare to get back to school. Both parents had plenty of money, but neither would budge an inch about who was responsible for the cost of travel in their maintenance agreement. This poor fourteen-year-old lived in a permanent state of not knowing what was going to happen next and was unable to participate in any extra-mural activity because her parents were hell bent on not making any concessions to each other. If she asked for a dress for a party she was told to ask her father, and if she wanted to join a school theatre trip she was told to get the money from her mother. Sally ended up asking for nothing and going nowhere because she could not bear moving between two parents who were too wrapped up in their own fighting to give her what she so desperately needed.

When there is a conflict of interest between parents and neither side will give an inch, it is likely that there will be no room to hear, listen to or take any notice of the children. Although they will need to speak and will have plenty to speak about, they will necessarily bury their painful feelings in order to be able to get on with coping with everyday life. And so, like Sally, these children will end up exhausted and confused while at the same time full of questions, fear, anger, panic and other negative emotions that will make them feel embattled as they attempt to move forward with their lives. It would be far better if parents would seek help via mediation or counselling to create an environment where children can function as children rather than as referees.

Do not let a child have too much power. One of the hardest tasks as a parent is to find a balance between listening to a child, allowing them to feel heard and maintaining appropriate authority. It is especially difficult for parents who are breaking up. They can either feel so sorry for a child that they relax basic rules and boundaries, or they can be so fraught and tired that they fail to keep them in place effectively. Peter's story, described earlier, showed that parental skills sometimes disappear along with the marriage and that children can become too powerful.

In order to prevent children stealing power and becoming tyrannical both at home and in the outside world, it is important to agree on rules and boundaries, as previously discussed. If parents have similar expectations and the same kind of system of rewards and punishments, children will not only feel safer but will be unable to grow too strong. It is also important that parents stand up individually to their children and show that they are in charge. It is not a mother's job always to be liked, nor does a father have constantly to prove himself to be fun. It is a parent's duty to be consistent, fair and responsible and, if that means turning off computers and televisions before midnight and insisting that a thirteen-year-old girl comes home before dark, the parent may be temporarily unpopular but at least they will be showing that they care.

If the balance of power has been upset in a household and it feels as if the children are in charge, it is important to take steps to get things back under control. Tyrannical children are not pleasant to have around as pupils, friends or members of society. But, most of all, they are unhappy in their own skins as they go out and about in the world throwing their weight around and insisting that they have their own way.

Don't burden a child with inappropriate information. Conversations about finances, legal matters, adult emotions and sexual practices are not appropriate topics for children. They will not fully understand what is being said if they are told about such matters and will only pick up frightening fag-ends of conversations if they listen in on telephone calls or discussions that should take place when they are not around.

Money: All that a child needs to know about money is that they will have a roof over their head, that there will be food on the table and that finances are taken care of, even if there is less money than there used to be. After that, it is the responsibility of the parents and the lawyers to sort it out. To include children in such discussions will only muddle or scare them. Most couples who divorce will be at least temporarily financially worse off than before; however, somehow, most newly formed families manage to make ends meet and get through the tough times by cutting back. It is not the lack of money that causes the harm, it is the fighting about it. A further problem that comes with financial hardship in a single-parent home is if a parent has to go out to work for longer hours and becomes less available, while not having anyone else to provide support and back-up. This does need to be discussed so that children can let adults know if they are lonely or bored or nervous when a parent has to work all hours. If this is the case, it would be a good time for the support network of the wider world to step in and help look after children if their single parent needs to work too hard.

Legal matters: These are confusing, have a language of their own and go at their own pace. Adults hate the copious quantities of paper-work and the endless financial declarations which divorce can entail and often get very defensive and annoyed when they receive any legal correspondence that will cost money to answer and make a complicated emotional situation more difficult. Children do not need to know any of this and should be protected from having too much information. A child-friendly explanation of what will be involved and reassurance that it is all a normal part of the sad process of ending a marriage are all that children need in order to understand. Inflammatory legal practice helps nobody, and I often witness legal letters and writs being issued at the most unsuitable times. One client had a writ handed to him on the evening before Christmas Eve, just as he collected his children for the holiday. All legal offices were closed, and there was nothing he could do until the beginning of January except fulminate against his ex-wife and worry about the contents of the writ rather than enjoy his children. Other legal Scud missiles come in via email as mothers are preparing their children for important exams or getting themselves ready for a job interview, and they really cause unbearable heartache and damage. At the very least, it is better if the presentation of legal documentation is done with consideration of what else is going on in the family at the specific moment, and it is important that parents contain themselves in front of their children and wait until they are with their friends to really express their feelings.

Adult emotions: I have stressed again and again that divorce and parental separation are like a bad car crash from which it can be very hard to recover and that I expect mothers and fathers to be in pretty bad shape just as their children require them to be OK. Anger, outrage, jealousy, fear, guilt, sadness, a sense of betrayal, denial, hatred, longing, loneliness and confusion are only some of the intense emotions that will play through the heads and the hearts of separating adults, and they will need to look after themselves as well as possible to get through the most difficult of times. Any comfort that they can find that will make life a little more bearable is probably fine, as long as the comfort does not come from leaning on a child who is too young and too vulnerable to bear the brunt of such strong and difficult emotions. Children do not need to know just how bad their parents feel or they will be in danger of becoming over-responsible and forgetting to have a childhood. Again, it is a difficult balancing act to find the words to explain what is going on, in that it is essential to be human, honest and true but it is also essential not to burden children and make them feel that they have to watch out for a mother or a father.

Sex: When one parent has left because of infidelity, and children understand that the sexual act has taken place with someone other than their mother or father, they are usually horrified. No child of any age likes to contemplate the idea of their parents having sex, and they do not need to be given any details of sexual impropriety. If they are, they will be walking around with difficult, disturbing and distorted images in their heads and a deep inner conviction that there is something wrong with one of their parents. I have had many girl clients who will not see their fathers when they reach adolescence because they were given too much information by their mothers when the whole family was reeling from shock.

Many newly single adults will understandably search for some companionship and comfort that will include a sexual component which is best kept away from the children. In order to reduce insecurity and not ask children to face difficult questions about their parent's sexual activity, it is a good idea to play away from home or take time out while the coast is clear and the children are with their other parent or being looked after by good friends and family.

Don't lie to the children. This is another difficult issue for parents to get right when trying to work out the balance between not giving children too much adult information and telling them the truth. Most children are strongly intuitive and ask any number of difficult questions for which there are no easy answers. It is better if these questions are answered as honestly as possible, although there is nothing wrong with asking for some time or for some help from the other parent before giving a response.

Difficult questions about other lovers, money, house sales or the possibility of the parents getting back together need to be answered carefully and honestly. Something will have made a child ask and, if the wrong answer is given for the right reason, they will realize that they have been lied to, will be even more confused and will not know who to trust in the future.

Most parents lie to their children in order to protect them or to minimize their sadness. But children cannot be protected from the pain of a parental separation, and trying to spare them will only make them more confused in the long term. It is much kinder to tell the truth in an age-appropriate way rather than allow children to live in a bubble of denial which excludes reality and does not allow them to get on with their lives. Some lies are unnecessary and only serve to protect a parent who should know better than to try to outwit a curious child. I have known fathers pretend to be on business when they are in fact on an exotic holiday, having told their children that they are too poor to pay for some household essentials. And I know of mothers who consistently refuse to admit to the existence of a boyfriend even though their children have read their emails and passed private texts to their siblings' mobile phones. These untruths do nothing to help a child and only make him or her furious and unhappy. They also make children doubt their parents at the very time that trust needs to be established and a new order introduced.

It does not seem to be so much divorce and parental separation that cause the problems for children who go through them but the way in which they are executed and the kind of new system that is created. If parents are capable of following the suggestions that will allow for a 'good divorce' and competent childcare, and if fathers can be encouraged to remain an important part in the life of a child, then damage will be kept to a minimum. If all adults understand how much children hurt, how important it is for them to feel safe and how much they need to speak, then everyone will be able to lend a hand and make life better for a generation of children who are the silent victims of a social experiment that does not seem to have gone in their favour.

Conclusion

CHILD-REARING IS COMPLEX AND DIFFICULT. Our world is so busy, and we are so busy too. A lot of us are frightened about our futures, and many of us are worried about our children. While the last hundred years have produced endless psychological studies on the importance of inner security for a developing child, over the same period we seem to have removed their outer safety. Divorce and separation do not help childhood stability, and parents need to replace the broken family system as quickly as possible with a new and reliable structure that involves two parents living in two different homes who can still work together to bring up their children.

Those around the family can do a lot to help children find their feet when their world has been shattered. If mothers and fathers are too broken, tired or unavailable, or if there is a serious case of 'double trouble', then any adult who feels a duty of care for a family, who likes children or who is in some way responsible for a particular child can step in and offer comfort. However carefully one may have to circumnavigate the sensitivities of a brokenhearted parent, it is important to reach the child and hold out a helping hand so that they know that they are not alone.

Children need adults to offer explanations about what is going on and child-friendly clarification to ease the worst-case nightmare scenarios that live all too easily and much too secretly in their heads. Most children will not understand that their desperate feelings are temporary. While they need to have their strong emotions validated, they also need to learn that things will get better, that the pain and confusion will pass and that the nightmare is a process which they, along with many other children, will get through.

Children need comfort when life is so tough and frightening. Comfort can come in many different forms and be given by many different people. Simple things like the gift of a telephone number to be used day or night, carefully written in a small notebook; a coffee, lunch or an invitation to join a family outing; a sleepover with favourite movies, hot baths and cosy conversation; a subtle wink and a nod from a teacher who understands that life has been hard at home or an extra Christmas present – all will let children know that they are not alone, that they have somewhere to turn and that there can even be some advantages to being a child from a broken home.

The community can help if support is lacking at home. Teachers can cut a little slack for lost or forgotten kit and even help with replacement uniform and pens and pencils. They can invite children to or insist that they attend homework club and encourage extra-mural activities. Grandparents can provide comfort and consistency with a weekly tea date if they live near enough, or a weekend away at regular intervals; friends and godparents can take children shopping or away on holiday, and they can be invaluable for older children, who need all sorts of back-up and reference points, which will probably be in short supply from stressed and unhappy parents.

Adults need to understand that the behaviour of an unhappy child is not random. Whether whacking a younger sibling, refusing to go to school, curled up with excruciating tummy ache, scratching eczema until it bleeds, eating too little, eating too much, swearing blind at a parent, refusing to do homework, stealing money, forgetting to come home, lying helpless in a darkened room, cutting themselves or taking drugs, he or she will be telling us something that makes complete sense but that we will find difficult to understand. Children will rarely tell us in words what is making them so distressed, but if we listen to their behaviour and understand that it is nothing more than the beginning of a conversation, we do not need to be so scared and we will be able to help.

There are many reasons that prevent children from using words to tell us what is wrong. They may be protecting their parents in that they want to love both their mother and their father equally and do not want to criticize. They know that their parents are not perfect, that they get stressed, lose their temper, exaggerate, get worried about money, are late for the school pick-up, spend too long on the phone and all the other bits and pieces that are part of normal human behaviour. Children understand us and find us easier to forgive than we do to forgive each other or ourselves. They want to love us and be looked after by us; they do not want to take sides and join in the trashing of a parent, and so they tend to stay silent and clam up.

Sometimes children do not know what to say or how to say it. Everything is so muddled and so bottled up and living so deep down in the well of despair that lives hidden below the tummy button that they cannot make any sense of anything at all. All they know is that they feel desperate and that they cannot take one more thing before they explode all over the place with some peculiar and apparently unconnected behaviour.

Another reason for the mute unhappiness of children is that they cannot find anyone to talk to. There is a conspiracy of silence about how tough it is for children to have to go through the process of divorce, and the adult world prefers to pretend that it is an adult issue. It is not; by their behaviour parents have created a situation of which the children are automatically a part.

If children cannot talk about one of the most dramatic and painful things that will ever happen to them, there is a high likelihood that they will eventually end up in some kind of trouble. Imagine again the child who feels that there must be something wrong with him if his father has abandoned him; who lies awake at night believing that if one parent leaves the other might walk out at any moment. Watch out for children who have learnt to have no respect for either a mother or a father and who have discovered that they can do exactly what they want when they want to. Understand what a child who has overheard conversations about her parents' infidelities or money problems feels. These children need to find someone to listen to them so that they can better understand and also be reassured that they are still loved and not to blame. They need to be taught that their difficult feelings are part of a process from which they will recover. If their fears, feelings and questions are given a voice, there will be a good chance that they can avoid having to carry the negative emotions that live wordlessly in the innermost psychological recesses of a child and so often erupt in turbulent behaviour and difficult physical symptoms.

When children are given the chance to speak, and when they understand that they are heard and understood, it can be like watching shadows leave small faces. When they can find the words to say what annoys, worries, frightens or makes them angry, they gain a freedom from their inner turmoil and become able to rejoin the life that had become hidden from them because of the problems of their parents. It is surprisingly simple to help. If children can find someone to talk to who will hear them without judging, trying to fix, taking sides or giving an adult interpretation to their world, they will have a far better chance of surviving the process of separation. When children have been heard, they will know that they are not the cause of the problems; that it is unlikely that their other parent is going to disappear in a cloud of smoke; that they need to fulfil the same requirements as other children; and that the separation of their parents, while having everything to do with them, is also, in a strange kind of way, none of their business. Even if parents seem unreachable and unreasonable, it is possible for an unhappy child and a wise adult to work out strategies and find support in a wider world so that even the most bereft of children do not have to feel so alone.

Once the conversation is underway, the story has been told, the shock waves have abated, the impossible has become possible and the unthinkable has happened, then children can begin to recover. If parents have not fought for too long and too often, if they have not demonized each other and if at least one parent has stayed in charge and made a safe world for their children, then tears dry, tummy aches abate and football can become fun again. Children return to their worlds a little older, usually much wiser, and carrying wounds and scars that can often make them more sensitive and more interesting than the children who have run carefree.

I have grown to love these children. By allowing us to listen to them, by telling us how bad it is and by letting us support them, they allow us to build up a relationship with them in which they invite us to care. By caring we become interested in what happens to them. While their lives are tough, we can keep a careful eye, and when they stop hurting and start to return to life, we can feel hopeful and glad that our walk together through their darkness has brought them out of the tunnel. As they move into a lighter world they will find that they are not too damaged, confused, angry or alone. With luck, they will rejoin their classes, start to thrive again and be as fit for adult life as their friends whose parents stayed together.

Appendix 1

Conclusions from CIVITAS/NSPCC report, 'Experiments in Living: The Fatherless Family', Rebecca O'Neil, September 2002

Rebecca O'Neill's study concluded that:

Lone mothers are:
- Poorer
- More likely to suffer from stress, depression and other emotional and psychological problems
- More prone to health problems
- May have more problems interacting with their children

Non-resident biological fathers are:
- At risk of losing contact with their children
- More likely to have health problems and engage in high-risk behaviour

Children living without their biological fathers are:
- More likely to live in poverty and deprivation
- More prone to trouble in school
- Tend to have more difficulty getting along with others

- At greater risk of health problems
- At greater risk of suffering physical, emotional or sexual abuse
- More likely to run away from home

Teenagers living without their biological fathers are:
- More likely to experience problems with sexual health
- More likely to become teenage parents
- More likely to offend
- More likely to smoke
- More likely to drink alcohol
- More likely to take drugs
- More likely to play truant from school
- More likely to be excluded from school
- More likely to leave school at sixteen
- More likely to have adjustment problems

Young adults who grew up not living with their biological fathers are:
- Less likely to attain qualifications
- More likely to experience unemployment
- More likely to have low incomes
- More likely to be on income support
- More likely to experience homelessness
- More likely to be caught offending and go to jail
- More likely to suffer from long-term emotional and psychological problems
- More likely to develop health problems
- More likely to enter partnerships earlier, and more often as a cohabitation
- More likely to divorce or dissolve their cohabiting unions
- More likely to have children outside marriage or outside any partnership

The report concludes that these statistics show 'an increase in crime and violence, a decrease in community ties, a growing divorce culture, a cycle of fatherlessness and a dependence on state welfare'.

These findings have just been backed up by a report funded by the Department of Health and published by the Office for National Statistics in October 2008. The researchers studied nearly 8,000 children aged between five and sixteen in 2004 and found almost one in ten had disorders. The children were checked again in 2007. The report said that a child whose parents had split during this time was more than four and a half times more likely to have developed an emotional disorder than one whose parents stayed together. They were nearly three times more likely to exhibit a conduct disorder. Eleven per cent of those children whose families broke up had emotional disorders against 3 per cent among those whose families were still together. Nearly a third of children found to have mental disorders in 2004 still suffered from them three years later.

Appendix 2
The Centre for Separated Families (UK): press release, 12 September 2007

More than twenty million people – a third of the UK population – live with the direct effects of divorce or separation. A minority get help, mainly from lawyers.

Some 33 per cent of respondents reported that either their parents had separated or they had separated from a partner with whom they had children. Given that Britain's population now exceeds sixty million, the survey suggests that more than twenty million people may be living with the direct effects of separation.

Just 33 per cent of those affected by separation have received professional advice, mostly from solicitors, found the survey. Three-quarters of those getting help say they need more support.

As well as calls for more professional help, the survey found strong backing for a change in services so that they offer a more holistic approach to the family, helping both mothers and fathers properly. More than half of those surveyed complained of a lack of attention to the needs of non-resident parents in caring for their children.

Facts on separating families

- There are 150,000–200,000 relationship breakdowns involving children each year. The majority of children have contact with both parents, although the nature and frequency of contact varies.
- Most children want to keep contact with both parents. Their experience of contact varies according to quantity and quality.
- Most parents feel ill-equipped to deal with conflict with ex-partners in order to reach agreement that is in the best interests of children.
- Two-thirds of parents expressed a desire for support to help them understand what is happening to their children.
- The needs of many separating parents are not being met by existing services.

(Source: 'Parental Separation: Children's Needs and Parents' Responsibilities', Next Steps, HMSO)

Useful books

Facing Up to Divorce and Separation

Ahrons, C. *We're Still Family: What Grown Children Have to Say about Their Parents' Divorce*. New York: HarperCollins, 2004

Burrett, J. *To and Fro Children: A Guide to Successful Parenting after Divorce*. London: Thorsons, 1993

Charlish, A. *Caught in the Middle: Helping Children to Cope with Separation and Divorce*. London: Cassell Illustrated, 2003

Department for Education and Skills. 'Putting Your Children First – A Guide for Separating Parents'. www.dfes.gov.uk/consultations/downloadableDocs/planner_draft.pdf

Dowling, E. & Gorell Barnes, G. *Working with Children and Parents through Separation and Divorce*. Basingstoke: Palgrave Macmillan, 2000

Dryden, W. & Gordon, J. *How to Cope When the Going Gets Tough*. London: Sheldon Press, 1994

Emery, R. *The Truth about Children and Divorce*. New York: Penguin, 2004

Focus on Families. 'Divorce and Its Effects on Children'. The Children's Society, 1988

Gottman, J. *Why Marriages Succeed or Fail.* New York: Simon & Schuster, 1994

Hall, P. & Relate. *Help Your Children Cope with Your Divorce.* London: Vermilion, 2007

Helmlinger, T. *After You've Said Goodbye: Learning How to Stand Alone.* San Francisco: William Kaufmann, 2nd edn 1982

Kent Mediation Service. 'What Most Children Say' (pocket guide for parents who live apart). www.kentfms.co.uk (tel. 01795 429689)

Pryor, J. & Rodgers, B. *Children in Changing Families. Life after Parental Separation.* Oxford: Blackwell Publishing, 2001

Ricci, I. *Mom's House, Dad's House.* Canada: Simon & Schuster, 1997

Wells, R. *Helping Children Cope with Divorce.* UK: Sheldon Press, 1988

The Role of Grown-ups

Covey, S.R. *The Seven Habits of Highly Effective Families.* UK: Simon & Schuster, 1997

Faber, A. & Mazlish E. *How to Talk So Kids Will Listen and Listen So Kids Will Talk.* London: Piccadilly, 2001

Gottman, J. *The Heart of Parenting: How to raise an Emotionally Intelligent Child.* London: Bloomsbury, 1997

Gray, J. *Men are from Mars and Women are from Venus.* New York: HarperCollins, 2002

Hartley-Brewer, E. *Positive Parenting:* London: Cedar/Mandarin, 1994

Oaklander, V. *Windows to Our Children.* New York: The Gestalt Journal Press, 1988

Purves, L. *How Not to be a Perfect Mother.* London: Fontana Paperbacks, 1986

Children: Different Ages and Different Stages

Clarke, J. I. & Dawson, C. *Growing Up Again: Parenting Ourselves, Parenting Our Children*. Minnesota: Hazelden, 2nd edn 1998

Eliot, L. *What's Going on in There? How the Brain and Mind Develop in the First Five Years of Life*. New York: Bantam Books, 1999

Figes, K. *The Terrible Teens*. London: Penguin, 2003

Gerhardt, S. *Why Love Matter: How Affection Shapes a Baby's Brain*. Hove and New York: Brunner-Routledge, 2004

Hill, C. & Hill, P. *A Perfect Start*. London: Vermilion, 2007

Hughes, D. A., *Facilitating Developmental Attachments*. North Bergen, New Jersey and London: Jason Aronson, 1997

Hughes, D. A. *Attachment-Focused Family Therapy*. New York and London: W. W. Norton & Company, 2007

Pearce, J. *Tantrums and Tempers*. London: Thorsons, 1989

Phelan, T. W. *1-2-3 Magic – Effective Discipline for Children 2–12*. Glenn Ellyn, Illinois: Child Management Press, 2003

Phillips, A. *Saying 'No'*. London: Faber & Faber Ltd, 1999

Sunderland, M. *The Science of Parenting*. London: Dorling Kindersley, 2006

Webster-Stratton, C. *The Incredible Years: Trouble-shooting Guide for Parents of Children Aged 3–8*. London: Umbrella Press, 1992

Wolf, T. & Franks, S. *Get Out of My Life but First Take Me and Alex into Town*. London: Profile Books, 2002

Difficult Times, Difficult Physical Symptoms

British Medical Association, Professor Jon Ayres. *Understanding Asthma*. Dorset: Family Doctor Publications, 2006

Burningham, S. *Young People under Stress: A Parent's Guide*. London: Virago, 1994

Douglas, L. J. & Richman, N. *My Child Won't Sleep*. Harmondsworth: Penguin, 1984

Ferber, R. *Solve Your Child's Sleep Problems*. London: Dorling Kindersley, 1986

Graham, P. & Hughes, C. *So Young, So Sad, So Listen*. London: Gaskell, 1995

Melville, J. & Subotsky, F. *Does My Child Need Help? A Guide for Worried Parents*. London: Optima, 1992

Difficult Times, Difficult Behavioural Symptoms

Babiker, G. & Arnold, L. *The Language of Injury: Comprehending Self-Mutilation*. Leicester: BPS Books, 1997

Berg, I. & Nursten, J. (eds.). *Unwillingly to School*. London: Gaskell, 1996

British Medical Association, Dr Bob Palmer. *Understanding Eating Disorders*. Dorset: Family Doctor Publications, 2004

Graham P. & Hughes, C. *So Young, So Sad, So Listen*. London: Gaskell, 1995

Health Information Service. 'Sometimes I Think I Can't Go on Any More'. Free booklet (tel. 0800 665544)

Melville, J. & Subotsky, F. *Does My Child Need Help? A Guide for Worried Parents*. London: Optima, 1992

Spandler, H. *Who's Hurting Who: Young People, Self-Harm and Suicide*. Manchester: 42nd Street, 1996

Double Trouble

Baveystock, S. *They Started It: How to Help your Kids Get On*. Harlow: Pearson Education Ltd, 2007

Biggs, V. *Caged in Chaos: A Dyspraxic Guide to Breaking Free*. London: Jessica Kingsley Publishers, 2005

British Medical Association, Dr Jonathan Chick. *Understanding Alcohol and Drinking Problems*. Dorset: Family Doctor Publications, 2006

British Medical Association, Dr D. Jayson. *Understanding Children's*

Behaviour. Dorset: Family Doctor Publications, 2005

British Medical Association, Dr Kwame McKenzie. *Understanding Depression*. Dorset: Family Doctor Publications, 2006

British Medical Association, Professor Colin Terrell & Dr Terri Passenger. *Understanding ADHD, Autism, Dyslexia and Dyspraxia*. Dorset: Family Doctor Publications.

Falkowski, C. *Dangerous Drugs: An Easy-to-Use Reference for Parents and Professionals*. Minnesota: Hazelden, 2000

Forehand, R. L. & Long, N. *Parenting the Strong-Willed Child*. Chicargo: Contemporary Books, 1996.

Greene, R. *The Explosive Child*. New York: HarperCollins, 2001

Hayman, S. *Step-families: Living Successfully with Other People's Children*. London: Vermilion, 2001

LeBey, B. *Remarried with Children*. New York: Bantam, 2005

Lutz, E. *The Complete Idiot's Guide to Step-parenting*. UK: Alpha Books, 1998

Pentecost, D. *Parenting the ADD Child*. London: Jessica Kingsley, 2000

Randolph, E. *Children Who Shock and Surprise: A Guide to Attachment Disorders*. Cotati, California: RFR Publications, 1994

Styron, W. *Darkness Visible*. London: Minerva, 1996

Train, A. *Children Behaving Badly: Could My Child Have a Disorder?* London: Souvenir Press Ltd, 2000

Wolpert, L. *Malignant Sadness: The Anatomy of Depression*. London: Faber & Faber, 1999

Books for Children

Brown, M. & Krasny Brown, L. *Dinosaur's Divorce*. New York: Little Brown, 1988 (for the younger child)

Cadier, F, Daly, M. & Gandini, C. *My Parents are Getting Divorced: How to Keep It Together When Your Mom and Dad are Splitting Up*. New York: Amulet Books, 2004 (for older children)

Cole, B. *Two of Everything*. London: Jonathan Cape, 1997 (children's picture book dealing with marital problems)

Gee, S. *Nobody Asked Me! A Game about Divorce*. Los Angeles: Western Psychological Services, 2003 (a board game about divorce for children aged 8–15)

Levins, S. & Langdo, B. *Was It the Chocolate Pudding? A Story for Little Kids about Divorce*. Washington DC: Magination Press, 2006

Macgregor, C. *Divorce Helpbook for Kids*. California: Impact, 2001

Macgregor, C. *Divorce Helpbook for Teens*. California: Impact, 2004

Macgregor, C. *Jigsaw Puzzle Family: The Stepkids' Guide to Fitting It Together*. California: Impact, 2005

Masurel C. & McDonald, K. *Two Homes*. Massachusetts: Candlewick Press, 2001 (focuses on what is gained instead of what is lost when parents divorce)

Pickhardt, D. & Fisher, J. *The Case of the Scary Divorce: A Jackson Skye Mystery*. Washington DC: Magination Press, 1997 (a ten-year-old boy meets the mysterious Professor Jackson Skye, who enlists his help in solving eight cases, each dealing with a problem the boy himself is experiencing during his parents' divorce)

Powell, J. *What Do We Think about Family Break-up?* London: Hodder Wayland, 2001 (a picture book which looks at the reasons families break up and the resulting changes, and suggests ways in which children can get used to a new kind of family)

Ricci, I. *Mom's House, Dad's House for Kids*. Canada: Simon & Schuster, 1997

Searle, Y. & Streng, I. *The Divorced and the Separated Game*. London: Jessica Kingsley, 1995 (board game to help children come to terms with divorce and separation)

Smith, R. *Divorce and Children: Living in a New Stepfamily*. London: Children's Society, 1998

Stones, R. & Spoor, N. *Children Don't Divorce*. Essex: Happy Cat Books, 1998 (illustrated storybook designed to help children discuss feelings about separation)

Sunderland, M. & Armstrong, N. The Story Books for Troubled Children series is designed to help children who are troubled in their lives and is part of the Helping Children with Feelings series. The stories act as vehicles to encourage children to think about and connect with their feelings. They come as Story and Guide Sets. London: Speechmark, 2002/2003

A Nifflenoo Called Nevermind

A Pea Called Mildred

Helping Children Locked in Rage or Hate

Helping Children Who are Anxious or Obsessional and Willy and the Wobbly House

Helping Children Who Have Hardened Their Hearts or Become Bullies

Helping Children Who Yearn for Someone They Love

Helping Children with Fear

Helping Children with Loss

Helping Children with Low Self-esteem.

How Hattie Hated Kindness

Ruby and the Rubbish Bin

Smasher

Teenager Story – Anxious/Obsessional

Teenager Story – Bottle Up

Teenager Story – Rage or Hate

Teenager Story – Self-esteem

Teenie Weenie in a Too-Big World

The Day the Sea Went Out and Never Came Back

The Frog who Longed for the Moon to Smile

Thomas, P. & Harker, L. *My Family's Changing*. London: Hodder Wayland, 2001

Wilson, J. *The Suitcase Kid*. London: Random House, 1998 (for older children, about how tough it is to live between two homes)

Wyon, L. *Lily's Story*. Nottingham: National Association of Child Contact Centres, 2001 (a picture book that explains how child contact centres can help children of separated parents to keep in contact with their absent parent in a safe and friendly environment)

Wyon, L. & Goodman, A. *Ben's Story: An Introduction to Contact Centres.* Nottingham: National Association of Child Contact Centres, 1999

My Time Chart. Fortnightly planner aimed at children aged 4–10. Helps children to see at a glance which parent they will be spending time with and when during the week. Available from www.resolution.org.uk

Christina McGhee and Stephen Loughead. *Lemons 2 Lemonade: How to Handle Life When Things Go Sour between Mom and Dad.* DVD and workbook available online from www.divorceandchildren.com. For children aged 5–10

When Parents Part. A film made by young people for separating parents and their children. Available online from www.youngvoice.org

Useful websites and telephone numbers

Facing up to Divorce and Separation

Childline
Tel. 0800 1111
www.childline.org.uk
24-hour helpline for children and young people in trouble or danger

Children of Divorce
www.bbc.co.uk/education/archive/divorce
For parents and children who are dealing with divorce

Divorce and Children
www.divorceandchildren.com
Offers helpful information, practical advice and tips for separated and divorced parents on how to help children manage family change

Divorce.co.uk
www.divorce.co.uk
Covers mediation, counselling and information services, looks at personal and emotional questions and has links to further help

Divorce-Online

www.divorce-online.co.uk

Self-help and information service covering all aspects of divorce

Divorce Recovery Workshop

www.drw.org.uk

UK self-help group run by volunteers, offering support, help and understanding to those separated or divorced. Website contains details of workshops and local contacts

Divorce UK

www.divorceuk.com

Advice covering children, money, counselling and property-settlement options. Database of lawyers, case studies and recommended reading list

It's Not Your Fault

www.itsnotyourfault.org

A site for children who are worried about their parents splitting up. Divided into sections for children, teenagers and parents, it helps children to understand a bit more about what is going on and reminds them that it is not their fault

National Association of Citizens Advice Bureaux (NACABx)

www.nacab.org.uk

Information and advice service

National Council for the Divorced and Separated

www.ncds.org.uk

Voluntary group offering support to the divorced, separated or widowed. Gives details of local branches and events

One Plus One

www.oneplusone.org.uk

Monitors contemporary marriages and relationships, focusing on understanding the causes, effects and prevention of relationship breakdown. Provides statistics and a resource library

Relate

Tel. 0845 456 1310

www.relate.org.uk

Counselling, relationship education and training to support couples and family relationships. Offers support to children whose parents are splitting up. The national office can put you in touch with Relate's local centres. Publications available from bookshops, libraries or via website

The Role of Grown-ups

Association for Shared Parenting

www.sharedparenting.org.uk

Promotes need for estranged parents to play an equal part in the upbringing of their children. Has a number of regional branches, and offers help and support to parents, grandparents and other relatives

British Association for Counselling

www.bac.co.uk

Has as part of its mission statement to 'respond to requests for information and advice on matters related to counselling'. Also has a database of local counsellors

British Association of Counselling and Psychotherapy

www.bacp.co.uk

Provides advice on a range of services to help meet the needs of anyone seeking information about counselling and psychotherapy.

Has a database of local counsellors and psychotherapists

CAFCASS
www.cafcass/gov.uk
Information, case studies, advice, contact links and resources for children and young people. DVD and pack 'My Needs, Wishes and Feelings'

Centre for Separated Familes
Tel. 0845 478 6360
www.separatedfamilies.org.uk
Offers practical support to both parents during and after separation, supporting parental responsibilities and the rights of children to continue close relationships with both parents and their wider families

Childcare Link National
www.childcarelink.org.uk
Government site that can point parents in the right direction to find all forms of registered childcare in their local area, plus financial help. Search by postcode

Child Poverty Action Group
www.cpag.org
Information and advice service to help bring relief to child poverty, including information on welfare rights

Children's Society
www.the-childrens-society.org.uk
Deals with all aspects of the problems children face in society, including social exclusion, injustice, ill health, poverty and protection

Community Legal Advice
www.clsdirect.org.uk
Free, confidential and independent legal advice for residents of England and Wales; section on family issues

CompactLaw
www.compactlaw.co.uk
Covers legal matters in England and Wales to do with family and relationships

Couple Counselling Scotland
www.couplecounselling.org
Confidential counselling services, plus details of local centres

Dads UK
Tel. 07092 391489
www.dads-uk.co.uk
National helpline offering support to single fathers

Daycare Trust
www.daycaretrust.org.uk
National childcare charity since 1980, working to promote high-quality, affordable childcare for all. Offers information about childcare and aims to help individuals make the right childcare decisions for their child

Equal Parenting
www.equalparenting.org
UK chapter of the Children's Rights Council. Campaigns for both parents to be treated equally by the law after divorce or separation for the sake of the children

Fathers Direct

www.fathersdirect.com

A charity to support the welfare of children by the positive and active involvement of fathers and male carers in their lives

Fathers 4 Justice (F4J)

www.fathers-4-justice.org

A civil-rights movement (members include men and women) campaigning for a child's right to see both parents and grandparents

Families Need Fathers

www.fnf.org.uk

Help with problems in maintaining a child's relationship with both parents during and after family breakdown. Represents non-residential parents and their children and is primarily concerned with the problems of keeping parents and children in contact after family breakdown. Support, information, statistics and contacts

Family 2000

www.family2000.org.uk

Dedicated to providing help on family issues, whether you are a single parent, married, a grandparent or a step-parent

Family Mediation Scotland

www.familymediationscotland.org.uk

Information about family mediation and local services

Family Rights Group

www.frg.org.uk

Informs parents of their rights when dealing with social services. FRG works to improve the services received by these families

Four or More

www.4ormore.co.uk

Resource for parents of larger families full of practical ideas for what to do and how to have fun

Gingerbread

Tel. 0800 018 5026

www.gingerbread.org.uk

Support, advice and practical help for lone parents and their children via a national network of local self-help groups. Publications and advice line

Grandparents Association

www.grandparents-association.org.uk

National registered charity that gives advice, information and support to grandparents of children affected by a divorce or separation

HomeDad

www.homedad.org.uk

Support group dedicated to helping dads who are staying at home to bring up their children. For full-time and part-time dads and for fathers who are raising children on their own

Home-Start

Tel. 0116 233 9955

www.home-start.org.uk

Volunteers offer friendship, support and practical help in the home to families with at least one child under five years old. Information leaflets and training for volunteers

Kids and Co.

www.childcare-info.co.uk

Information on childcare-related topics and issues

Kids' Clubs Network

www.kidsclubs.com

Information and contact details on out-of-school care clubs

Lone Parents.org

www.loneparents.org

Support for single lone parents who are finding it difficult to cope; online chatroom with others in the same situation

Meet-a-Mum Association

Tel. 0845 120 6162

www.mama.org.uk

Information, advice and contact details of local support groups for single mothers. Local social gatherings and contact for mothers who feel isolated

Mothers apart from their Children (MATCH)

www.match1979.co.uk

Help and support for mothers living apart from their children

Mothers Union

www.themothersunion.org

Information on family concerns from a Christian perspective

Mums' Net

www.mumsnet.com

Product reviews and parenting tips by parents for parents

NACCC (National Association of Child Contact Centres)

www.naccc.org.uk

Information about child contact centres, with 276 member centres around the country – neutral venues where the children of separated families can enjoy contact with one or both parents

National Childbirth Trust

www.nctpregnancyandbabycare.com

Information and support on pregnancy, childbirth and early parenthood

National Council for One-parent Families

Tel. 020 7428 5400

www.ncopf.org.uk

Dedicated to supporting one-parent families in all aspects of life. Free information leaflets; advice on benefits and rights, childcare and holidays

National Family Mediation

Tel. 01392 668090

www.nfm.u-net.com

Helps couples in the process of separation or divorce. Information on mediation and the law and details of local Family Mediation Service Centres

National Newpin (Parent Infant Network)

Tel. 020 7358 5900

www.newpin.org.uk

Runs centres that provide home support, drop-ins, group discussions and training courses for parents with babies and toddlers in the London area

National Society for Children and Family Contact (NSCFC)

www.nscfc.com

Works to prevent children losing contact with one of their parents and to ensure that children keep in touch with the extended family

NHS Direct

www.nhsdirect.nhs.uk

Online healthcare information

One-Parent Families Scotland

www.opfs.org.uk

Information, encouragement and support to lone parents

Parentline Plus

Tel. 0808 800 2222

www.parentlineplus.org.uk

Information resource for any individual in a parenting role. Freephone 24-hour helpline providing general, confidential inform- ation. Useful booklets and publications, and courses for parents

ParentsCentre

www.parents.dfee.gov.uk/centre.cfm

Department for Education and Skills site: information on the National Curriculum, social issues, child development, education and welfare

Parents at Work

www.community.flametree.co.uk

Advice on choosing childcare options

Parents Online

www.parents.org.uk

Advice on education, health and leisure for children during their primary-school years

Precious Little One

www.preciouslittleone.co.uk

Guide to parenting, baby, health and childcare issues

Raising Kids

www.raisingkids.co.uk

Advice on dealing with children of all ages. Covers topics such as healthy eating, homework, pocket money and school reports

Resolution

Tel. 08457 585671

www.resolution.org.uk

Directory of Resolution's 5,000 family lawyers, who are committed to the constructive resolution of family disputes. Pamphlets, fact sheets and directories of local solicitors

Rights of Women

Tel. 020 7251 6577

www.rightsofwomen.org.uk

Provides free, confidential legal advice on a range of issues, including domestic violence, family law, divorce and relationship breakdown

Samaritans

Tel. 08457 909090

www.samaritans.org.uk

Confidential emotional support by phone or email to any person who is suicidal or despairing

Sane

www.sane.org.uk

Support and information for people with mental-health problems

Schoolzone

www.schoolzone.co.uk

Information for students and teachers

Shared Parenting Information Group (SPIG) UK

www.spig.clara.net

Promotes responsible shared parenting after separation and divorce. Offers useful practical items such as a calendar planner and examples of how contact hours can work. News of divorce laws and contact regulations around the world

Single Parent Action Network

www.spanuk.org.uk

SPAN represents one-parent families across the UK. It provides contact details and information for single parents wanting to set up self-help groups

Solo Parents Network

www.soloparentsnetwork.com

Online social club for single parents. Resources, information and help other single parents

UK College of Family Mediators

www.ukcfm.co.uk

Professional body for all family mediators in the UK. Information on family mediation and how to find a family mediator and a list of useful organizations

United Kingdom Council of Psychotherapy

www.ukcp.org.co.uk

Provides information about therapy. Has a directory of accredited, regulated therapists

UK Parents Online

www.ukparents.co.uk

Information about pregnancy, birth, babies and toddlers. Interactive areas in which to meet other parents and share experience and advice

Children: Different Ages and Different Stages

B4 Baby

www.b4baby.com

Information and advice on pregnancy, babies and parenting

Brook

www.brook.org.uk

Information for young people about contraception, sexually trans-mitted infections and pregnancy testing

Child Accident Prevention Trust

www.capt.org.uk

Books and free information on child safety and accident prevention

Connexions

www.connexions.gov.uk

Support for 13–19-year-olds, with information on health, work and education

Open University

Tel. 01908 653231

www.open.ac.uk

The Faculty of Health and Social Care produces home-study packs and videos on babies, children, teenagers and being a parent

Pre-School Learning Alliance

Tel. 020 7833 0991

www.pre-school.org.uk

Advice, support, training publications, magazine

Radio One – Essentials

www.bbc.co.uk/radio1/essentials

Information on sex, drugs, relationships, colleges and universities, travel, work, health and money

Royal College of Psychiatrists

Tel. 020 7235 2351

www.rcpsych.ac.uk/info/young.htm

Produces a series of fact sheets entitled 'Mental Health and Growing Up'. Covers all aspects of child and adult mental-health problems and offers advice for parents

Schoolzone

www.schoolzone.co.uk

Information and help with studies, revision, exam stress and exam dates

The Site

www.thesite.org/relationships/families

Information on family life and friends; helps children deal with parents and divorce, also helpful with other worries and problems

Trust for the Study of Adolescence

Tel. 01273 693311

www.studyofadolescence.org.uk

Tapes for parents, training packs, publications

Well Child

www.wellchild.org.uk

Information on all aspects of child growth, development and health

YoungMinds

Tel. 020 7336 8445

www.youngminds.org.uk

National charity committed to improving the mental health of all children and young people. Telephone helpline, leaflets, seminars and training

Difficult Times, Difficult Physical Symptoms

Allergy UK (British Allergy Foundation)

Tel. 01322 619864

www.allergyuk.org

Encompasses all types of allergies and offers information, newsletter and support network

Asthma UK

Tel. 0207 226 2260

www.asthma.org.uk

Provides a wide range of support for people with asthma and their families. Helpline staffed by specialist asthma nurses. Local support groups

Enuresis Resource and Information Centre (ERIC)

Tel. 0117 960 3060

www.eric.org.uk

Advice on bed-wetting and soiling. Information leaflets and advice; sells bed-wetting protection and alarms

Institute of Family Therapy

Tel. 020 7391 8150

www.instituteoffamilytherapy.org.uk

For young people and families with anxiety, depression and behavioural problems

Kidscape Campaign for Children's Safety
Tel. 020 7730 3300
www.kidscape.org.uk
Anti-bullying and personal-safety information

Mental Health and Growing Up
www.rcpsych.ac.uk
Series of thirty-six fact sheets on a range of common mental-health problems

National Society for the Prevention of Cruelty to Children (NSPCC)
Tel. 0808 800 5000
www.nspcc.org.uk
NSPCC helpline, available to children aged eighteen and under to talk about things that are making them unhappy

Difficult Times, Difficult Behavioural Symptoms

Bullying
www.bullying.co.uk
Advice for parents and children affected by bullying. Information and tips on how to cope, legal advice and email service

ChildLine
Tel. 0800 1111
www.childline.org.uk
Confidential support and advice to children and young people in trouble or in danger

Eating Disorder Association
Tel. 0845 634 7650 (under eighteen); 01603 621414 (over eighteen)
www.edauk.com
Offers information, support and help to anyone affected by eating disorders. Has local self-help groups

Institute of Family Therapy
Tel. 020 7391 9150
www.instituteoffamilytherapy.org.uk
For young people and families with anxiety, depression and behavioural problems

Kidscape
Tel. 020 7730 3300
www.kidscape.org.uk
Protects children from bullying or abuse

National Children's Bureau – Young People and Self-harm Information Resource Website
www.selfharm.org.uk

National Self-Harm Network
www.nshn.co.uk
Website resource list of organizations, publications, support groups, newsletter

National Society for the Prevention of Cruelty to Children (NSPCC)
Tel. 0808 800 5000
www.nspcc.org.uk
NSPCC helpline, available to children aged eighteen and under to talk about things that are making them unhappy

Practical Parenting
www.practicalparent.org.uk
Tips on a wide range of child-behaviour problems

Trashed
www.trashed.co.uk
Information about drugs, their effects and the law

Young Health

www.youth2youth.co.uk

Service run by young people for young people under the age of twenty-three. Advice on pregnancy, suicide, drugs, family and school

Double Trouble

General

Careline

Tel. 0845 122 8622

www.carelineuk.org

Free, confidential crisis-counselling service on any issue

Family Welfare Association

Tel. 0207 254 6251

www.fwa.org.uk

Provides direct services for people with mental-health problems and children and families. Professional referral essential

Mental Health Foundation

Tel. 020 7803 1101

www.mentalhealth.org.uk

Information on all aspects of mental health and emotional issues, including addiction and substance abuse

Traumatic Stress Clinic

Tel. 0207 530 3666

www.traumatic-stress-clinic.org.uk

Offers psychological treatment of children and families following a trauma

Addiction

Addiction Adviser
Tel. 0845 370 0102
www.addictionadvisor.co.uk
Free advice from qualified psychologists, doctors and counsellors

Al-Anon/Alateen
Tel. 020 7403 0888
www.al-anon.alateen.org
Offers help to families and friends of alcoholics or young people whose lives have been affected by someone else's drinking

Alcoholics Anonymous
Tel. 0845 769 7555
www.alcoholics-anonymous
Help for people who think they have a problem with alcohol

Drinkline
Tel. 0800 917 8282
www.netdoctor.co.uk
Help to callers worried about their own drinking and support to the family of people who are drinking

Families Anonymous
Tel no: 0845 1200 660
www.famanon.org.uk
National helpline offering free support to anyone affected by the drug abuse of a family member

FRANK
Tel. 0800 77 6600
www.talktofrank.com
Helpline. Advice and information for young people about drugs.

Free, confidential advice and information about counselling and specialist drug services

Gamanon
Tel. 0870 050 8880
www.gamanon.org.uk
Organization offering meetings for families affected by a gambling problem

Gamblers Anonymous
Tel. 020 7384 3040
www.gamblersanonymous.org.uk
Helpline offering advice for compulsive gamblers and their families

Gambling Therapy
Tel. 01384 241 292
www.gamblingtherapy.org
Free online advice service for those adversely affected by gambling

Gamcare
Tel. 0845 6000 133
www.gamcare.org.uk
Provides support, information and advice to anyone suffering because of a compulsive gambling problem

Narcotics Anonymous
Tel. 0845 373 3366
helpline@ukna.org
www.na.org
Help for people who think they have a problem with drugs

Release

Tel. 0845 450 0215

www.release.org.uk

Services dedicated to meeting the health, welfare and legal needs of drug users and those who live with them. Legal and drugs helpline

Violence

Children are Unbeatable

Tel. 020 7713 0569

www.childrenareunbeatable.org.uk

Provides leaflets on alternatives to smacking

Crossing Bridges

Tel. 0118 959 7333

www.crossingbridges.co.uk

Reading-based centre offering face-to-face advice in the drop-in centre. Website offers helpful children's pages

Everyman Project

Tel. 020 7263 8884

www.everymanproject.co.uk

Offers counselling and support to men who want to change their violent or abusive behaviour

The Hideout

www.thehideout.org.uk

Helps victims of domestic violence

MALE (Men's Advice Line and Enquiries)

Tel. 0808 801 0327

www.mensadviceline.org.uk

Support and advice for male victims of domestic violence, and information for their families and for men who want to change their violent and abusive behaviour

Pathway Project

Tel. 01543 676800

www.pathway-project.co.uk

Organization based in Staffordshire offering a free national 24-hour helpline and refuge accommodation, as well as counselling and support groups, including children's therapeutic play sessions

Refuge

Tel. 0808 2000 247

www.refuge.org.uk

Works in partnership with Women's Aid to provide advice and support to anyone experiencing domestic violence. Provides safe, emergency accommodation throughout the UK. Website offers a useful section with help for children

Southall Black Sisters

Tel. 020 8571 9595

www.southallblacksisters.org.uk

Resource centre based in London providing a service for women who are experiencing violence or abuse. Offers advice, group therapy and counselling, including in Hindi and Urdu

Women's Aid Federation England

Tel. 0808 2000 247

www.womensaid.org.uk

National charity for women and children experiencing physical, sexual or emotional abuse in their homes. Free 24-hour National Domestic Violence Helpline. Online guide: 'The Survivors Handbook'. Children can visit the Hideout website

Women's Domestic Violence Helpline

Tel. 0161 636 7525

www.wdvh.org.uk

Manchester-based organization offering national advice, information and telephone counselling

Adult depression

Association for Post-Natal Illness

Tel. 0207 386 0868

www.apni.org

Offers information and advice to sufferers and their families, and can put people in touch with others who have had similar problems

Beyond the Baby Blues

www.babyblues.freeserve.co.uk

Support and resources for women suffering from post-natal depression

British Association for Counselling and Psychotherapy

Tel. 0870 443 5252

www.bacp.co.uk

Provides a directory listing counsellors and therapists

Depression Alliance

Tel. 0845 123 2320

www.depressionalliance.org

Offers support and understanding to anyone affected by depression and for relatives who want to help. Network of self-help groups

Depression Alliance, Cymru (Wales)

Tel. 029 2069 2891

www.dacymru.ik.com

Provides information and support and has local self-help groups in Wales

Depression Alliance Scotland

Tel. 0131 467 3050

www.dascot.org

Provides information and support and has local self-help groups in Scotland

Fellowship of Depressives Anonymous

Tel. 0870 774 4319

www.depressionanon.co.uk

Self-help groups in England for people who suffer from depression and their carers, offering support

First Steps to Freedom

Tel. 0945 120 2916

www.first-steps.org

Charity offering information and telephone self-help for people with anxiety disorders, with practical advice on how to overcome panic attacks, obsessive-compulsive disorders and withdrawal from tranquillizers

MDF the Bipolar Organization (Manic-depression Fellowship)

Tel. 020 7793 2600

www.mdf.org.uk

Website for young people: www.steady.org.uk

Offers support, via self-help groups, to enable people affected by bipolar disorder / manic depression to take control of their lives

Mental Health Foundation

Tel. 020 7803 1100

www.mentalhealth.org.uk

Charity working with mental-health issues and learning disabilities

MIND (National Association for Mental Health)

Tel. 020 8519 2122

www.mind.org.uk

Works for a better life for anyone experiencing mental distress. Support via local branches, drop-in centres, counselling, advocacy

National Phobics Society (NPS)

Tel. 0890 122 2325

www.phobics-society.org.uk

Provides information and advice to all those affected by anxiety disorders and can refer on to support groups and trained hypnotherapists, cognitive therapists and other complementary therapists

SAD (Seasonal Affective Disorder) Association

Tel. 01903 814942

www.sada.org.uk

Support and information on Seasonal Affective Disorder

Sane

www.sane.org.uk

Support and information for people with mental-health problems

United Kingdom Council for Psychotherapy

www.ukcp.org.co.uk

Provides information and database of trained psychotherapists

New partners

Black UK (Online) Limited

Tel. 0845 193 4431

www.blackukonline.com

An online newspaper for Britain's black community, which encourages dealing with issues about family life, including relationships within stepfamilies. Provides details of helpful organizations

Childline

Tel. 0800 1111

www.childline.org.uk

Helpline for young people in trouble or danger. Fact sheet on the subject of stepfamilies, providing statistics and information on the worries of stepchildren and how Childline can help

Familyonwards.com

www.familyonwards.com

Family site offering support for parents and grandparents of children coping with divorce. Special sections on stepfamilies, divorce and second weddings

Second Wives Club

www.secondwivesclub.com

North American site that aims to provide a haven, a sympathetic forum and support for second wives and stepmothers

Stepfamily Scotland

www.stepfamilyscotland.org.uk

Support and information for all members of stepfamilies and those who work with them. Helpline, information and publications

Learning and developmental disabilities

Advisory Centre for Education

Tel. 0207 354 8318

www.ace-ed.org.uk

Independent national advice centre for parents of children in state schools. Information, advice and training on the law and school issues

Asperger's Syndrome Foundation

www.aspergerfoundation.org.uk

Bi-monthly training seminars for parents and professionals helping those with Asperger's syndrome

Attention Deficit Information Services (ADDISS)

Tel. 020 8906 9068

www.addiss.co.uk

Information, support and training. Refers to local groups in the UK

British Dyslexia Association

Tel. 0118 966 2677

www.bda-dyslexia.org.uk

Advice, local contacts and resources

Contact a Family

Tel. 020 7608 8700

www.cafamily.org.uk

Charity that helps families with children who have any form of disability or special need; provides information about the disabilities, puts families in touch with each other, creating local and national support groups

Council for Disabled Children

Tel. 020 7843 1900

www.ncb.org.uk/cdc

Useful leaflets sent on request.

Parents for Inclusion

www.parentsforinclusion.org

Advice for parents of disabled and special needs children on inclusion into education

Dyscovery Centre (for Dyspraxia)
Tel. 029 2062 8222
www.dyscovery.co.uk
Private assessment centre for neurodevelopmental problems, providing information and training for children and adults living with learning difficulties

The Dyslexia Institute
Tel. 01784 222300
www.dyslexia-inst.org.uk
Provides information, assessment, teaching and training

Dyspraxia Foundation
Tel. 01462 455016
www.dyspraxiafoundation.org.uk
Information and support via UK network to parents and professionals

National Autistic Society
Te. 020 7833 2299
www.nas.org.uk
Valuable information, help and support. Puts you in touch with local families who have children with similar conditions

Websites and resource information provided by Dr Dinah Jayson in association with the British Medical Association

ADHD, specific learning difficulties, dyspraxia
www.add.about.com
www.addconsults.com
www.adders.org
www.addinschool.com
www.additudemag.com

www.add.org

www.addvance.com (for girls and women)

www.adhdnews.com

www.chadd.org

www.dyscovery.co.uk

www.geocities.com/janice13/ADD2.html

www.mindbodysoul.gov.uk

www.sarisolden.com (for girls and women)

Autism/Asperger's syndrome

www.aspergerfoundation.org.uk

www.aspergersyndrome.com

http://info.med.yale.edu/chldstdy/autism

www.mugsy.org

www.rdiconnection.com

www.tonyattwood.com.au

Learning disabilities

www.learningdisabilities.org.uk

Electronic bulletin for children with disabilities/special educational needs

Information for Children

Children's Legal Centre

www.childrenslegalcentre.com

Independent charity offering free and confidential legal advice, negotiation services and mediation for children, young people and anyone with concerns about them. Offers list of resources and publications

Children's Society
www.the-childrens-society.org.uk
Help with problems children face in society, including social exclusion, injustice, ill health, poverty and protection

Childline
Tel. 0800 1111
www.childline.org.uk
Helpline for young people in trouble or danger

It's Not Your Fault
Tel. 0845 7626579
www.itsnotyourfault.org
Offers information and support to young people with divorcing or separating parents

National Youth Advocacy Service (NYAS)
Tel. 0800 616 101
www.nyas.net
Provides specialist help for children and young people up to the age of 25

The Site
www.thesite.org/relationships/families
Information for children who are worried

Further reading

Altman, N., Briggs, R., Frankel, J. Gensler, D. & Pantone, P. *Relational Child Psychotherapy*. New York: Other Press, 2002

American Psychiatric Association. *Diagnostic and Statistical Manual of Mental Disorders: DSM-1V* (4th edition). Washington: American Psychiatric Association, 1994

Axline, V.M. *Dibs in Search of Self*. Harmondsworth: Penguin Books, 1964/1990

Bee, H. *The Developing Child*. New York: Grove Press, 1985

Berg, I.K. *Family-based Services: A Solution-focused Approach*. New York: Norton, 1994

T.J. Berndt & G.W. Ladd (eds). *Peer Relationships in Child Development*. Chichester: Wiley, 1989

Bion, W. *Learning from Experience*. London: Karnac, 1988

Bowlby, J. *The Psychoanalytic Study of the Child*. vol. XV: 9. London: Hogarth Press, 1960

Bowlby, J. *Attachment and Loss*, vol. 1: *Attachment*. New York: Basic Books, 1969/82

Bowlby, J. *The Making and Breaking of Affectional Bonds*. London: Tavistock Publications, 1979

Bowlby, J. *A Secure Base: Clinical Applications of Attachment*. London & New York: Routledge, 1988

Casement, P. *On Learning from the Patient*. London: Routledge, 1991

Children Act 1989. Chapter 41. London: HMSO 1994

Clarkson, P. *Gestalt Counselling in Action*. London: Sage, 1989

Dais, M. and Wallbridge, D. *Boundary and Space: An Introduction to the Work of D. W. Winnicott*. London/New York: Karnac/Brunner Mazel, 1981

DeGrandpre, R. *Ritalin Nation*. New York: Norton, 1999

Donaldson, M. *Children's Minds*. New York: Norton, 1978

Durrant, M. *Creative Strategies for School Problems*. New York: Norton, 1995

Erikson, E.H. *Childhood and Society*. London: Triad/Granada, 1977 (original work published 1950)

Erikson's Stages of Psychosocial Development. http://allpsych.com/psychology101/moral_development.html

Fordham, M. *Children as Individuals*. London: Free Association Press, 1996

Freud, A. *The Ego and the Mechanisms of Defence*. London: Hogarth, 1936

Freud, S. 'The Ego and the Id' in vol. 11 of the Penguin Freud Library, A. Richards & J. Strachey, (eds), J. Strachey (trans.). Harmondsworth: Penguin, 1979

Freud. S. 'Inhibitions, Symptoms and Anxiety' in vol. 10 of the Penguin Freud Library, A. Richards & J. Strachey (eds), J. Strachey (trans.). Harmondsworth: Penguin, 1979

Freud's Stages of Psychosexual Development. http://allpsych.com/psychology101/moral_development.html

Friedman, M., Glasser, M., Laufer, E., Laufer, M. & Whol, M. 'Attempted Suicide and Self-Mutilation in Adolescence'. *International Journal of Psychoanalysis*, 53: 179–83, 1972

Fulghum, R. *All I Really Need to Know I Learned in Kindergarten*. London: Grafton, 1989

Fuller, P. *Art and Psychoanalysis*. London: Writers and Readers Publishing Co-operative, 1980

Geldard, K. & Geldard, D. *Counselling Children: A Practical Introduction*. London: Sage Publications, 1997

George, E., Iveson, C. & Ratner, H. *Problem to Solution: Brief Therapy with Individuals and Families*. London: BT Press, 1990

Gerhardt, S. *Why Love Matters: How Affection Shapes a Baby's Brain*. Hove & New York: Brunner-Routledge, 2004

Gil, E. *Play in Family Therapy*. New York: The Guilford Press, 1994

Goldenberg, I. & Goldenberg, H. *Family therapy: An Overview*. (4th edition) California: Brooks/Cole Publishing Company, 1996

D. Goldman (ed.) *In One's Bones: The Clinical Genius of Winnicott*. Northvale, New Jersey: Jason Aronson, 1993

Goleman, D. *Emotional Intelligence*. London: Bloomsbury, 1996

Gorell Barnes, G. *Family Therapy in Changing Times*. Basingstoke: Macmillan Press Ltd, 1998

Gottman, J. *What Predicts Divorce: The Relationship between Marital Process and Marital Outcomes*. Hillsdale, New Jersey: Lawrence Erlbaum, 1993

P. Graham (ed.). *Cognitive Behaviour Therapy for Children and Families*. Cambridge: Cambridge University Press, 2005

Herman, N. *Why Psychotherapy?* London: Free Association Books, 1987

Home Office. Domestic Violence Factsheet Issue 2, November. Croydon: Home Office Research and Statistics Department, 1995

Hughes, D.A. *Facilitating Developmental Attachments*. North Bergen, New Jersey & London: Jason Aronson, 1997

Hughes, D.A. *Attachment-Focused Family Therapy*. New York & London: W.W. Norton & Company, 2007

Jeffers, S. *Feel the Fear and Do It Anyway*. London: Arrow, 1987

Jung, C.G. *Psychological Reflections*. London: Routledge, 1928/1998

Jung, C.G. *Memories, Dreams, Reflections*. Fontana Press: London, 1961/1995

Jung, C.G. *The Development of Personality*, vol. 17. London: Routledge, 1981 (first published in England in 1954)

Kalff, D.M. *Sandplay*. Boston: Sigo Press, 1980

Karen, R. *Becoming Attached: First Relationships and How They Shape Our Capacity to Love*. Oxford & New York: OUP, 1994

Klein, M. *Love, Guilt and Reparation, and Other Works 1921–1945*. London: Hogarth Press, 1981

Klein, M. *Envy and Gratitude, and Other Works 1946–1963*. London: Virago, 1988

Knights, B. *The Listening Reader: Fiction and Poetry for Counsellors and Psychotherapists*. London: Jessica Kingsley, 1995

Kohlberg, Lawrence. *Essays on Moral Development*, vols 1 & 2. San Francisco: Harper and Row, 1981

Kohlberg's Stages of Moral Development. http://allpsych.com/psychology101/moral_development.html

Kovacs, M. 'Rating Scales to Assess Depression in School-aged children'. *Acta Paedopsychiatrica*, 46, 305–15, 1981

Lethem, J. *Moved to Tears, Moved to Action: Brief Therapy with Women and Children*. London: BT Press, 1994

Lewis, D.O., Mallouh, C. & Webb, V. 'Child Abuse, Delinquency and Criminality'. D. Cicchetti & V. Carlson (eds). *Child Maltreatment, Theory and Research on the Causes and Consequences of Child Abuse and Neglect*. Cambridge: Cambridge University Press, 1989

Lobascher, M.E. 'Psychological Assessment: Cultural, Social, Educational Implications'. *Paediatric Neurology*, 2008

Maslow, A.H. *Toward a Psychology of Being* (2nd edition). New York: Viking Penguin, 1971

McNiff, S. *Art as Medicine*. London: Piatkus, 1994

Metcalf, L. *Parenting Towards Solutions: How Parents Can Use Skills They Already Have to Raise Responsible, Loving Kids*. New Jersey: Simon & Schuster, 1997

Miller, A. *The Drama of being a Child: And the Search for the True Self*. London: Virago, 1987

Miller, A. *For Your Own Good: The Roots of Violence in Child-Rearing*. London: Virago, 1987

Miller, A. *Thou Shalt Not be Aware: Society's Betrayal of the Child*. London: Pluto, 1991

Miller, L. *Understanding Your Baby*. London: Tavistock Clinic, Rosendale, 1992

Mills, J.C. & Crowley, R.J. *Therapeutic Metaphors for Children and the Child Within*. New York: Brumer/Maze, 1986

Mirrlees-Black, C. 'Estimating the Extent of Domestic Violence: Findings from the 1992 British Crime Survey'. Research Bulletin (37)

Moore, T. *Care of the Soul*. New York: HarperPerennial, 1994

Moore, T. *Dark Nights of the Soul*. USA: Gotham Books, 2005

Murphy, J. & Barry, D. *Brief Intervention for School Problems: Collaborating for Practical Solutions*. New York: Guilford Press, 1997

Murray, L. 'Effects of Postnatal Depression on Infant Development: Direct Studies of Early Mother–Infant Reactions', in R. Kumar & I.F. Brockington (eds), *Motherhood and Mental Illness 2: Causes and Consequences*. London: Sheldon Press & Boston: Little Brown & Company, 1988

NSPCC: *Experiments in Living: The Fatherless Family*. London: Civitas, 1988

NSPCC: *Response to the Social Exclusion Task Force Families At-Risk Review*. NSPCC, 2007

Oaklander, V. *Windows to Our Children*. New York: The Gestalt Journal Press, 1978

Panskepp, J. *Affective Neuroscience: The Foundations of Human and Animal Emotions*. Oxford: Oxford University Press, 1998

Peele, S. *Visions of Addiction: Major Contemporary Perspectives on Addiction and Alcoholism*. New York: Free Press, 1987

Piaget, J. *Play, Dreams and Imitations in Childhood*. New York: Norton, 1951

Rhodes, J. & Ajmal, Y. *Solution-focused Thinking in Schools*. London: BT Press, 1995

Rogers, C. *On Becoming a Person*. Boston: Houghton Mifflin, 1961

Rothenberg, M. *Children with Emerald Eyes: Histories of Extraordinary Boys and Girls*. New York: E.P. Dutton, 1987

Saint Benedict. *Saint Benedict's Rule*. Herefordshire: Ampleforth Abbey Press, fourth century/1997

Schore, A. 'The Effects of Early Relational Trauma on Right-Brain Development, Affect Regulation, and Infant Mental Health.' *Infant Mental Health Journal*, vol. 22: 214, 2001

Schwartz, A. & Schwartz, R.M. *Depression – Theories and Treatments: Psychological, Biological and Social Perspectives*. New York: Columbia University Press, 1993

Scott Peck, M. *The Road Less Travelled*. New York: Simon & Schuster, 1978

Segal, J. *Melanie Klein*. London: Sage Publications, 1992

Selekman, M. *Pathways to Change: Brief Therapy Solutions with Difficult Adolescents*. New York: Guilford Press, 1993

Selekman, M. *Solution-focused Therapy with Children*. New York: Guilford Press, 1997

Sours, J. 'The Anorexia Nervosa Syndrome'. *International Journal of Psychoanalysis* 55, 1974

Steiner, D. *Understanding Your 1-Year-Old*. London: Tavistock Clinic, Rosendale, 1992

Stern, D.N. *The Interpersonal World of the Infant*, New York: Basic Books, 1985

Stern, D.N. *Diary of a Baby: What Your Child Sees, Feels and Experiences*. New York: Basic Books, 1990

Stimmel, B. *Alcoholism, Drug Addiction and the Road to Recovery: Life on the Edge*. New York: Haworth Medical Press, 2002

Sunderland, M. *Using Story-telling as a Therapeutic Tool with Children*. Oxfordshire: Speechmark Publishing, 2000

Tustin, F. *The Protective Shell in Children and Adults* (2nd edition) London: Karnac, 1990

Walsh, B.W. & Rosen, P.M. *Self-Mutilation: Theory, Research and Treatment*. New York/London: Guilford, 1988

Weininger, O. *Children's Phantasies: The Shaping of Relationships.* London: Karnac Books, 1989

Weininger, O. *View from the Cradle: Children's Emotions in Everyday Life.* London: Karnac Books, 1993

Whitmore, D. *Psychosynthesis Counselling in Action.* London: Sage Publications, 1991

Wickes, F.G. *The Inner World of Childhood: A Study of Analytical Psychology* (3rd edition). Boston, Massachusetts: Sigo Press, 1988 (original work published 1927)

Wilson, N. *With the Best of Intentions.* Australia: Noel Wilson, 1991

Winnicott, D.W. *Collected Papers: Through Paediatrics to Psycho-Analysis.* London: Tavistock & New York: Basic Books, 1958

Winnicott, D.W. *The Family and Individual Development.* London: Tavistock, 1960

Winnicott, D.W. 'The Mother–Infant Experience of Mutuality', in *Parenthood: Its Psychology and Psychopathology.* Anthony and Benedec (eds). Boston: Little Brown, 1970

Winnicott, D.W. *Home is Where We Start From.* London: Penguin & New York: Norton, 1986

Winnicott, D.W. *Playing and Reality.* London: Tavistock, 1971

Winnicott, D.W. *Babies and Their Mothers.* London: Free Association Books, 1988

Winnicott, D.W. *Thinking about Children,* Ray Shepherd et al. (eds). London: Karnac Books, 1996

Worden, J.W. *Children and Grief, When a Parent Dies.* New York: Guilford Press, 1996

Zinker, J. *Creative Process in Therapy.* New York: Vintage Books, 1978

Index

cortisol 80, 238
counselling/counsellors 57–63, 64, 127, 233, 235
   choosing 58, 59
cutting (self-harm) 204–11, 213, 217

dating
   men 40–41
   women 30–31
   see also affairs; new partners
demonizing partners 37–8, 86, 116–17, 124, 273–5
depression
   adult 38, 86, 87, 88, 89, 121, 219, 236–9, 257, 327–8
   childhood 58, 62, 126, 131, 132, 162, 166–7, 169–70, 255, see also sadness
   post-natal 199, 200
   signs in adults 236–7
   signs in children 166–7
developmental disabilities, children with 63, 246–7, 249–53, 255–7, 258
   'general developmental delay' 247
   information on 330–33
   specific developmental disabilities 249–50, 255–7
   see also dyslexia; dyspraxia
disabled children 247–9
discipline see boundaries and rules, setting
divorce laws 28–9, 39

doctors/GPs 22, 24–5, 28, 57, 61–2, 74
   and counselling sessions 58
   referrals to therapists 61, 62, 126–7, 256
dormant feelings (in children) 116, 130, 213, 218
'dragon children' 180–95, 215–16
drinking see alcohol abuse
drug abuse/addiction
   adult 51, 120, 121, 219, 221–4, 225–30, 232
   children 120, 123, 126, 213, 217
   information on 321, 322, 323–5
dyscalculia, children with 249
dyslexia, children with 56, 249–50, 253–5
   information on 331, 332
dyspraxia, children with 56, 249–253
   information on 332
   and soiling 147, 148

early-morning waking 157, 160, 166
eating disorders 58, 87, 123, 126, 192–3, 213, 320
eating habits 23
   see also eating disorders
eczema 131, 150–51, 169, 286–7
educational psychologists 63, 195, 255–6
emotions, adult: and children 279, 281

nightmares/night terrors 93, 157, 169

night-time roaming 93, 94

tummy pains 57, 106–7, 131, 132–6, 140–41, 168, 286

punishments and rewards, use of 97–8, 177, 179, 194, 198, 203, 278

Oaklander, Violet: *Windows to Our Children* 57

obsessive compulsive disorders 58, 250

overcompensation 82, 185

over-helpful children 110–11
    see also 'too good' children

over-protective mothers 80–83

overweight children 192

quarrelling *see* fighting; violence

questions, answering children's 265–7, 268, 282–3
    see also information, giving children

peace-keeping (by children) 211, 212–13

perfectionism (in children) 213–14

period pains 136–40

pinching 91, 96

police, the 28, 71–3, 75, 181, 235

power, exaggerated sense of (in children) 99–102, 278–9
    see also 'dragon children'

pregnant women 80–81

pre-school children 85–90

presents, giving 36, 276

psychosomatic illnesses 57, 61–2, 131–2, 166
    headaches 57, 131, 132, 141–5, 168–9
    legs not working 107–8
    period pains 136–40

recovery time (after break-ups) 51–2

refuges for battered women 235

refusal to go to school *see under* school

refusal to see a parent 117–18, 119, 120–23

relatives *see* friends and relatives; grandparents

relaxation techniques 160

remarriage *see* new partners

Resolution 63, 315

responsibilities, taking on (children) 78–9, 110–13
    see also 'too good' children

responsibility for marriage breakup, feelings of 79, 99

rewards and punishments, use of 97–8, 177, 179, 194, 198, 202, 203, 278